Jan Ort

The Roma as Agents of the "G*psy Question"

Belonging, Mobility
and the Resettlement Policy
in Socialist Czechoslovakia

CHARLES UNIVERSITY
KAROLINUM PRESS 2024

KAROLINUM PRESS is a publishing department of Charles University
Ovocný trh 560/5, 116 36 Prague 1, Czech Republic
www.karolinum.cz

© Faculty of Arts, Charles University, 2024
Translation © Phil Jones, 2024
Cover photograph © Courtesy of State Archive Košice
Copyediting by Martin Janeček
Set and printed in the Czech Republic by Karolinum Press
Layout by Jan Šerých
First edition

A catalogue record for this book is available from the National Library
of the Czech Republic.

Research for this book was financed by Grant no. 19-26638X, "Genocide,
Postwar Migration and Social Mobility: Entangled Experiences of Roma
and Jews", funded by the Czech Science Foundation, carried out at Faculty
of Arts, Charles University, 2024.

ISBN 978-80-246-6052-3
ISBN 978-80-246-6053-0 (pdf)
ISBN 978-80-246-6054-7 (epub)

https://doi.org/10.14712/9788024660530

The original manuscript was reviewed by Celia Donert (University
of Cambridge), and Elena Marushiakova (University of St Andrews
& Institute of Ethnology and Social Anthropology SAS, Bratislava).

Contents

Acknowledgments

This book is published with the support of the Grant Academy of the Czech Republic as part of the project entitled Genocide, Post-war Migration, and Social Mobility: The Entangled Experiences of Roma and Jews. It is based on a thesis that in the original Czech version was entitled *Romové jako aktéři cikánské otázky. Náležení, mobilita a přesidlovací politika v Československu 60. let,* which was defended at the Faculty of Arts, Charles University, Prague.

The research itself could not have been conducted without the willingness of its participants, especially the Romani interviewees. I am hugely grateful for my meetings with Elena Cinová, Peter Kudráč and the sisters Monika H and Marcela S. I would like to thank all of these for their willingness to read my final text (or parts of it). I would also like to thank the staff of all of the archives and libraries referred to.

I owe a debt of gratitude to Helena Sadílková, who undertook the role of my supervisor with great commitment and was more than happy to discuss the various stages of my research and offer me her honest opinion of the text as it was being written. Much of what I formulate and emphasise in the book is the outcome of numerous discussions with her. I would also like to thank all of my colleagues at the Seminar of Romani Studies at the Faculty of Arts, Charles University, who have inspired me since my undergraduate studies with their sensitivity to research and writing about the Roma and their rigour when enquiring into the lived experience of the Roma and their actorial perspective.

Equally, the insights of people from other disciplines, especially history and social anthropology, have been crucial. Here I would like to thank Yasar Abu Ghosh, Pavel Baloun, Martin Fotta, Jan Grill and Matěj

Spurný for their insightful comments. I would also like to thank my colleagues from the project team, namely Renata Berkyová, Lázsló Csosz, Kateřina Čapková, Markéta Hajská and Michaela Lônčíková. The feedback provided by both reviewers, Celia Donert and Elena Marushiaková, was extremely helpful. I would also like to thank Chris Hann, Cătălina Tesăr, Alexander Mušinka and Lucie Segľová for their support at various points during work on the dissertation. The cooperation provided during the initial phase of research by Helena Sadílková and Romana Hudousková was invaluable.

Many thanks to Phil Jones for translating the text into English, and to Martin Janeček from Karolinum Press House for editing the book.

I would like to thank my own and my wife's parents for the support and care (for me and other actors affected) during periods of intense work on the book.

And to Petra, Jonáš and Matyáš I offer my heartfelt thanks for their endless patience and energy.

This emphasis culminated in the mid-1960s with the adoption of the government resolution referred to in the introduction, the purpose of which was the organised resettlement (*přesídlení*) and dispersal (*rozptyl*) of the Roma in Czechoslovak society at that time. The Romani settlement in Kapišová was top of the list drawn up by the district authorities for immediate eradication, and its inhabitants were to be relocated en masse to Czechia. The Roma who were already living in Czechia at that time agreed to sell their dwellings to the municipality for the purpose of demolition. Similarly, several other families found their own housing and employment in Czechia following an appeal by the Slovak authorities. The remaining families signed up for an "organised transfer" (*organizovaný přesun*) to twinned villages in the district of Přerov, and this took place the following year. These included the family of Michal K, whose words opened this introduction.

The Romani settlement in Kapišová, which originally housed more than 200 people, was to be irrevocably erased from the village map. However, things did not go as planned. The family of Michal K and his brother Ján K had an experience common to many other displaced families when they were allocated housing in their resettlement destination that was woefully inadequate to their needs. Michal K's daughter recalls how both families turned on their heels and left overnight to return to their home village. They managed to make it back home shortly before non-Romani villagers turned up in order to carry off materials from the homes in the settlement, as one of them recalled in an interview with me. Both families, Michal's and Ján's, had enjoyed relatively higher socio-economic status in the village, with Ján even holding the position of sole Romani councillor. Perhaps this is why the presence of the returning families was accepted, even welcomed, according to Michal's daughter. In this way, both families maintained the continuity of the Romani settlement in the village.

0.1.1 Agency, continuity, discontinuity

The ambivalence of social position within the Slovak countryside, the ongoing experience of migration and dislocation, and the confrontation with policies targeting G*psies are the fulcrum points around which the story of the Roma of Kapišová illustrates well the broader reality and historical background of the Roma in post-war Czechoslovakia. On the other hand, this same story shows how necessary it is to take into account locally and historically contingent contexts and, as a result, prefigures the diversity of experience and agency of the Roma.

In addition, however, the study highlights the need for a more subtle differentiation of the positions of "non-Romani" actors, including individual state bodies. It thus sketches the contours of a broader field of manoeuvre, in which the practice of the central policy targeting G*psies is negotiated within networks of actors and relations, of which the Roma are an integral part. The story of the Kapišová Roma thus allows for a reframing of policies towards G*psies that can be seen not only as the history of efforts to control and manage the lives of socially non-conforming populations, but, through the example of specific practices, can also be understood through the continuity of Romani strategies of sociability. Although registered as "nomads" (*kočovníci*) and therefore targeted for legal resettlement, the Roma of Kapišová continued to migrate for work, sometimes with the blessing of several non-Romani agents such as employers and authorities in Czechia. At the same time, they maintained the continuity of belonging and presence of the Roma in a village in Slovakia, even though, classified as G*psies, they should have been resettled and their settlement definitively removed. Here again, they managed this with the acquiescence of non-Romani agents, in this case their neighbours and the local authority.

In summary, the introductory story adumbrates well the space within which this book is situated, in which the sharp dichotomy is blurred between the state on the one hand, and the Roma as the "eternal outsiders" and victims of its coercive and socially engineering policies on the other. A space in which the position of individual actors is not given in advance, but forms the subject of negotiation, a negotiation that includes the by no means automatically assumed application of a dominantly defined classification of the populace. At the same time, the study foreshadows the way in which I will trace these relations and processes, i.e. by means of a microhistorical approach that emphasises aspects of localism and temporality and combines different types of historical sources, especially archival materials and oral-history interviews.

0.2 The Roma in Czechoslovakia and Policies towards G*psies

In the 1970s, the British sociologist Will Guy offered several reasons as to why Czechoslovakia was important in respect of the study of Romani history. One reason was the fact that there had been two large-scale, systematic attempts to assimilate the Roma in this country. The first took place in the second half of the 18th century under the reign of the Habsburg monarchs Maria Theresa and Joseph II. The second was under the communist regime through a policy that Guy dates back to 1958 (Guy 1998 [1975], 16–17), which culminated in an organised resettlement programme in the wake of a government resolution of October 1965. In order to understand the context of the genesis and realisation of the communist assimilation policy in general, and the resettlement programme in particular, it is worth recalling another aspect that attracted Guy's attention to the history of the Roma in Czechoslovakia, namely, the divergent development of the situation of the Roma in Czechia and Slovakia. Guy reminds the reader that developments in Czechia were more similar to the situation of the Roma in the countries of western Europe, which was characterised by harsh anti-Roma measures leading to yet more mobility. In Slovakia, which had previously been part of the Kingdom of Hungary, the Roma became an integral part of the local socio-economic systems while contributing to their transformation.[3] Likewise, their situation during the Second World War was also different. In the Slovak Republic (1939–1945), the Roma faced various forms of persecution (at the end of the 1930s there were around 80,000 living there in total), which resulted in considerable loss of life. However, in general, they avoided the fate of the Roma in the Protectorate of Bohemia and Moravia, where many perished in concentration camps and only a few hundred survived the war (Nečas 1999; for a more detailed comparison of the fate of the Roma in both regions, see Sadílková 2020).

The post-war Romani population in Czechia was overwhelmingly made up of immigrants from Slovakia, whose migration must be seen as part of broader population movements after the Second World War. Like other inhabitants of mainly rural areas of Slovakia, the Roma arrived as a workforce in emerging industrial towns and cities, often as

---

3   There is, understandably, a degree of generalisation taking place, something that Guy himself admits. The situation of the Roma may have differed significantly within the two regions under discussion. As regards the situation prior to the Second World War, in Czechia we can basically distinguish between the situation of (semi-)itinerant "Bohemian" Roma and "Moravian" Roma, who were settled in specific villages and also displayed a high level of integration in locally formed socio-economic structures (see, for example, Horváthová 2005). In Slovakia, on the other hand, we might distinguish between the situation of the settled "Slovak" Roma and the (semi-)itinerant "Vlax" Roma (also referred to as *Lovara*) with their different migratory trajectories and, to some extent, different language and cultural system (see, for example, Hajská 2024, 15–24).

a result of organised recruitment drives. However, they were also part of the repopulation of the Bohemian borderlands, from which nearly three million Germans had been forcibly removed after the war (see, for example, Gerlach 2010). As the situation in Kapišová illustrates well, when tracing the post-war movement of the Roma (see Ort 2022b), one must not overlook the asymmetrical social belonging in which, despite a considerable degree of integration into local socio-economic systems, they found themselves because of a strong association with the racialised category of G*psyness. For many of them, the Second World War had underscored the experience of paternalism and racism and the fatal disruption of relations with their immediate non-Romani neighbours (see Sadílková 2020). And so for many of the Roma, post-war migration also meant an escape from these historically entrenched, highly power-inequitable relational structures. At the same time, the large-scale migratory movement of the Roma that began in the very first post-war years gave rise not only to new populations of Romani immigrants and individual communities in specific locations, but also to transnational networks between Slovakia and Czechia that ensured the movement of people, goods and various forms of capital for decades to come, in many cases right up to the present day.

It was in this context that the post-war policy towards the Roma – or rather towards citizens who were categorised as G*psies and later as "citizens of G*psy origin" (*občané c*kánského původu*) – was formed. The existing socio-economic marginalisation of the Roma, which was noticeable especially in the segregated settlements of mainly eastern Slovakia, but also visible in towns and cities in Czechia, where newly arrived Romani families often lived in substandard conditions, was interpreted by the central authorities as a sign of their allegedly entrenched "cultural backwardness" (*kulturní zaostalost*). In this respect, the prevailing view of the Roma represented a kind of continuity even after the communist coup d'état in 1948. However, in the official approach to the Roma, which had been taking shape in communist Czechoslovakia since the early 1950s, this backwardness was blamed mainly on the previous bourgeois and Nazi regimes and their anti-Roma policies. In this respect, the policy towards the Roma was accompanied by a belief that, with the appropriate care, they would emerge from their "cultural backwardness" to become fully-fledged members of the society of communist Czechoslovakia. Looked at from the other side, as far as the newly established communist regime was concerned, the figure of the "G*psy labourer" (*c*kánský dělník*) became one of the key performance indicators of the formation of the new socialist society and its legitimacy (see Donert 2017, Spurný 2011).

In the 1950s, in an effort to "re-educate" (*převychovat*) the G*psies, the central authorities combined various approaches, including the forced removal of children from the "unhealthy environment of G*psy families" (*nezdravé prostředí c*kánských rodin*). They also considered the possibility of enshrining in law the cultural rights of the Roma in line with the Stalinist approach to national minorities and through the ideological training of representatives of the Roma, who themselves were formulating their own ideas regarding the societal position of the Roma as a group (Donert 2008). However, as far as the local authorities and non-Romani population were concerned, anti-Roma feelings persisted, and these gave rise to growing demands for the adoption of specific restrictive measures. It was voices from the provinces that provided an important context for the approval of Act 74/1958 on the Permanent Settlement of Nomadic Persons, which basically proceeded to criminalise the Roma and was thus intended to consolidate the legitimacy of the communist dictatorship as it passed through its first significant crisis (Spurný 2011, 282–285). The definitive move towards a policy of assimilation and thus a refusal to grant specific cultural rights to the Roma was formulated in the same year in a government resolution on Work amongst the G*psy Population. The resolution defined G*psies as a social group that was to be freed from their "backward way of life" (*zaostalý způsob života*), primarily through full inclusion in the labour force (Jurová 2008, 688). It was to this formulation of the communist regime's approach to the Roma that Guy made reference when he spoke of the second systematic attempt to assimilate the Roma in Czechoslovakia.

0.2.1 Resettlement policy

There were three main goals in the policy drawn up in 1958, the fulfilment of which was intended to lead to the complete assimilation of the Roma in the society of that time. The first was their full inclusion in the labour force. The second, backed up by Act 74/1958, placed restrictions on two-way migration between Slovakia and Czechia. And the third was the "liquidation of G*psy concentrations" (*likvidace c*kánských koncentrací*), especially the eastern Slovak "G*psy settlements" (*c*kánské osady*; Guy 1977, 177–181). Over the course of the following years, however, these objectives were not met. Guy identifies the main reason as being the sluggish approach taken by the Municipal National Committees (MNVs), which were largely responsible for implementation of the policy. This is evident in internal documents from the central authorities, which referred to a reluctance on the part of the local authorities to overcome entrenched anti-Roma prejudices that were proving an obstacle, especially when dealing with the housing situation (Jurová 2008). Guy adds, however, that there was also an economic dimension. The responsibility of Municipal National Committees was not backed by the provision of adequate funding, the result being that local authorities had to raise their own funds in order to enact the measures referred to above. In addition, it was becoming apparent that in eastern Slovakia itself, where the housing and employment situation was most acute, there were not enough job opportunities for the Roma living there. Guy concludes that inasmuch as there was any success, it was in the sphere of employment, though adds that this was paradoxically thanks to ongoing migration, which, despite centralised efforts to limit it, was tolerated by the authorities in Slovakia and employers in Czechia (Guy 1977, 309–318).

Guy also notes that ongoing evaluations of the ineffectiveness of the assimilation policy did not conclude that it should be rejected or revamped, but on the contrary intensified and its underlying principles maintained. It was against this backdrop that demands for the creation of a new and more effective administrative structure increased. The Slovak authorities in particular began to stress the need for an organised transfer (*přesun*) of a larger number of Roma from its eastern regions to Czechia, and voices were heard pushing for the introduction of quotas applying to G*psies in individual towns and districts (ibid., 315). These tendencies culminated in the adoption of Government Resolution No. 502, approved on 13 October 1965. While continuing to pursue the overall goal of the "permanent employment of adolescent and adult G*psy citizens and raising their standard of living and cultural standards", the Resolution's drafters sought to overcome earlier problems in its implementation. The resolution created an interdepartmental Government Committee on G*psy Population Issues, an independent coordinating and advisory body that took over the role that had formerly been performed by the Ministry of Education and Culture (ibid., 253). In this new administrative structure a similar committee was also set up under the Slovak National Council, along with special commissions answering to the National Committees at the level of regions, districts and towns. The new structure was allocated special funding from the state budget to cover the implementation of specific measures.

As in the case of the 1958 Act, strictly speaking this resolution cannot be seen as a centrally drafted totalitarian top-down policy, but, at least to some extent, as a response to pressures applied by regional actors (see Lucassen 2008). For a long time, the Roma in Czechoslovakia were most concentrated in eastern Slovakia, a region also characterised by a high number of socio-economically marginalised and racially segregated settlements. As far as the local (but also central) authorities were concerned, these settlements represented a significant security and hygiene risk (Donert 2017, 113–116). Going back to the early 1960s, if not earlier, the Regional National Committee (KNV) had argued that the predicament of the east Slovak Roma could not be resolved on a purely regional basis (see, for example, Haišman 1999). And so inasmuch as the government resolution instructed the newly appointed Government Committee to draw up a timetable for the "liquidation of G*psy concentrations" (Jurová 2008, 1003–1006), this was to some extent a response to these demands from the Regional National Committee and, later, from the Communist Party in Slovakia (Donert 2017, 159). Demands for more systematic and top-down instruments of control over the lives of the Roma continued to be voiced even in those regions in Czechia that were the frequent destinations of post-war Romani migrants from Slovakia (see Chapter Four).

At its first meeting on 18 December 1965, the Government Committee approved the document "Principles for the organisation of the dispersal and transfer of the G*psy population for the purpose of liquidating undesirable G*psy concentrations in accordance with Party and government resolutions", in which it instructed the state authorities to "draw up a timetable for the long-term liquidation of G*psy streets and neighbourhoods in Czechia and G*psy settlements in Slovakia" (Jurová 2008, 1031).[4] Two basic tasks were to be borne in mind when drawing up the timetable:

I. the creation of a plan for the dispersal of the G*psy population within the borders of regions and districts

II. the creation of a plan for the transfer of part of the G*psy population from Slovakia to Czechia

---

4   Priority was to be given to the "liquidation of G*psy settlements" in areas popular with tourists (the region of the High Tatras in Slovakia, as well as the Romani settlement in Velká Ida near Košice "in the interest of the health of the workers of the East Slovak Ironworks" (Jurová 2008, 1031).

To these was added a third point, which unpicked the assumptions behind the concepts of "dispersal" and "transfer". It stated that dispersal and transfer were to be organised "on the basis of voluntary consent" and with the prior "provision of accommodation and employment" for the resettled families and individuals. At the same time, it was necessary to keep "precise records of the families concerned and to provide them with further care in their new living conditions so that the process of their re-education can be further monitored." In light of their previous experience with anti-Roma prejudice in society, the National Committees were instructed to create "the conditions for the necessity of understanding the dispersal and transfer among the rest of the population [i.e. non-Roma: author's note]", for which purpose a media campaign was to be created (see Chapter Two). For the purpose of the transfer between Slovakia and Czechia, partnered regions were designated, which were then to stipulate the districts from which families could be sent from Slovakia to Czechia. The "organised" character of resettlement was contrasted with "undesirable unrestrained migration" (*nežádoucí živelná migrace*), which is how the ongoing two-way movement of the Roma between Slovakia and Czechia was perceived. The authorities were to stamp down on the latter type of migration, and in such cases the Roma "were to be returned to their original place of residence".

Although the removal of Romani settlements and the resettlement of their inhabitants was to have been carried out as early as 1966 (and in fact was already being carried out to some extent even prior to the 1965 resolution coming into force), the relevant timetable was not drawn up by the appointed Government Committee until 1967–1970. According to this plan, a total of 380 families were originally to be relocated in Czechia and 5,984 families in Slovakia (the timetable was gradually modified, in part in response to its failed implementation). A total of 2,177 families were then to be relocated from Slovakia to Czechia. Another 8,500 families were to be relocated after 1970 (Guy 1977, 274–276; see also Pavelčíková 2004, 91–92). The implementation of these measures was to be based on the newly introduced classification of the G*psy population into three groups depending on the degree to which they were deemed to be assimilated into the dominant society. The first category was to include almost assimilated G*psies with only the last remnants of an "undesirable way of life" (*nežádoucí způsob života*), while the third comprised what were defined as pathological cases with no prospect of "re-education" (*převýchova*). In the middle was the second category, i.e. individuals and families determined to break free of the "unhealthy environment" (*nezdravé prostředí*) of "G*psy concentrations" (see Chapter Two especially). Although the latter were to be the primary targets of resettlement policy, restrictions on freedom of movement were to apply to all G*psies regardless of their categorisation.

0.3 Reflections on the Resettlement Policy and Practice

It was the restrictions on freedom of movement that were at the heart of criticisms of the government resolution. As well as politically engaged Roma, ordinary folk affected by the new rules pointed to its discriminatory nature. However, as I show in Chapter Four, the criticism from the Roma in most cases did not target the underlying logic of the resolution, but rather its failure in practice. Thus Milena Hübschmannová, a qualified Indologist with a long-standing, fierce interest in Romani culture in the broadest sense of the word, can be considered the most strident public critic of the basic precepts of the assimilation policy at that time. For example, in a 1968 essay on the social position of the Roma intended for a non-specialist readership (Hübschmannová 1968), she pointed to the unconstitutionality of restrictions on freedom of movement. In 1967, she published a report in the revue *Literární noviny* in which she used the example of a particular family to highlight the desperate plight of the Roma in the eastern Slovak settlement of Veľká Ida caused by the terms of the resolution (Hübschmannová 1967). She drew attention to the discriminatory basis of the government resolution in a more scholarly text published in *Sociologický časopis* in 1970 as part of a wider critique of the official concept of the "G*psy question" (*c*kánská otázka*; Hübschmannová 1970). In the same year, a criticism of the unconstitutional character of the government resolution appeared in the Memorandum of the Union of Gypsies-Roma (the formulation of which Hübschmannová was in part responsible for; Memorandum SCR 1970), and the same criticism appeared in the section of Charter 77 devoted to the situation of the Roma in Czechoslovakia (Prečan 1990). The assimilation policy also received bad press abroad. Its development was summarised by the Czech lawyer and exiled writer Otto Ulč (1969), and of particular interest is the large dissertation written by Guy, based on field research carried out in eastern Slovakia in the early 1970s (Guy 1977). This is a key study that, for its detailed presentation of the genesis and practice of assimilationist policy towards the Roma in post-war Czechoslovakia, remains unsurpassed. I draw on it in various ways during the course of this book.

0.3.1 Post-revolutionary reflections in Czech and Slovak historiography

After the Velvet Revolution of 1989, the resettlement policy in particular, and the assimilationist policy of communist Czechoslovakia in general, was the target of open hostility, above all in respect of its alleged fatal impact on the lives of Romani people living here. This broader-based criticism viewed the policy pursued by the communist regime towards the Roma as highly paternalistic and disrespectful of the interests of the Roma themselves. However, the highly evaluative language used is not backed by an adequate analysis of the impact of the policy. The Romani interests are present implicitly rather than explicitly and are to some extent replaced by a generally formulated interest in preserving Romani culture, understood here as a kind of coherent value system. In his text on the genesis of institutional interest in the Romani population in post-war Czechoslovakia, for example, Haišman has the following to say regarding the resettlement programme:

> Beginning somewhere in the deliberations of deluded or uneducated party experimenters in eastern Slovakia, reshaped by the party secretariats, including those at the top, Czechoslovakia, with its government programme of "measures aimed at resolving the issues of the G*psy population", entered a phase of **undisguised criminal ethnocide**, which in the normal world (and in relation to other ethnicities) would be condemned by international forums, including the UN. (Haišman 1999, 182, emphasis J. O.)

In his text, Haišman relies almost exclusively on a published collection of archival documents compiled by historian Anna Jurová – herself the author of one of the most important post-revolutionary works on the post-war history of the Roma in the region under examination – focusing on the "development of the Romani issue in Slovakia after 1945" (Jurová 1993). Jurová also examines the creation and implementation of the resettlement programme, though even she does not address the opinions and experiences of the Roma themselves. Moreover, she adopts certain stereotypical ideas of the distinct "psyche" (*psychika*) and "social habits" (*společenské návyky*) of the Roma, with the result that in many instances she fails to maintain a critical distance from the official discourse she is critiquing. Such problems can be encountered in the work of historian Nina Pavelčíková, who charts the development of the post-war situation in Czechia in a similar way. She, too, relies exclusively on archival materials presenting the perspective of the authorities, and in a separate chapter on the "general characteristics of the Romani ethnic group" she is guilty of the orientalisation and exoticisation of the group thus described, rather than providing greater insight into the experiences and agential positions of the Roma in society at that time. Following this logic, she concludes in another text that the outcome of the government resolution was "merely another fateful intervention into the traditional way of life of the settled Romani communities, breaking up family and kinship relations" (Pavelčíková 2010, 84).

Nevertheless, the fact is that for a long time the two works referred to above were the only comprehensive publications for Czech and Slovak readers that summarised the post-war policies towards the Roma, offered an overview of the official documents, and thus became an important starting point for further interrogation of the problem.

In the post-revolutionary period, an evaluation of the resettlement policy was returned to by two of its contemporary actors, or rather participants in the debate surrounding it at the time: the ethnographer Eva Davidová, and the specialist in Romani studies Milena Hübschmannová. At the time the government resolution took effect, both women were in contact with specific Romani families affected by the central policy. However, even they restricted their post-revolutionary texts to general appraisals without any in-depth analysis or case studies. In her text for the anthology *Černobílý život* (Life in Black and White), for instance, Davidová asserts that the programme "was not only ill-conceived but completely misguided, since the so-called voluntary nature of the dispersal meant in practice that Romani families were obliged to move to a selected district regardless of their family ties and other circumstances of family life in their original home" (Davidová 2000, 74). As I will discuss below, Davidová published a monograph in 1965 in which she endorsed the assimilation policy of the time and spoke approvingly of the concept of "resolving the G*psy question" (*řešení c*kánské otázky*). However, although as an employee of the East Slovak Regional National Committee she participated in the accompanying media campaign (see Chapter Two), she was quick to condemn the actual outcomes of the programme in a letter to the Central Committee of the Communist Party of Czechoslovakia (ÚV KSČ), citing as an example the situation of the

Roma in an Eastern Slovak municipality she knew well (Sadílková et al. 2018, 150–155).

In contrast, Hübschmannová adopts a basically consistent position that draws on her work from the late 1960s even in the texts she wrote after 1989. In one of the latter, she wrote the following regarding the resettlement programme: "It was clear that the decree was unworkable. But how many human destinies had to be drastically affected before it was shown to be so!" (Hübschmannová 2000a, 138). She addresses the specific effects of the resolution in another text that focuses on the oral folklore of the Roma in Slovakia. In addition to the "spontaneous" migration of the Roma from Slovakia to Czechia, she cites "violent dispersal" (*násilný rozptyl*) as effecting a change to the rhythm of life of Romani families and entire Romani communities and thus causing the wholesale disruption of their "traditional" (*tradiční*) socio-cultural systems (Hübschmanová 1993, 1999a,b). In these later texts, Hübschmanová refers to the 1965 resolution in fairly general terms. Her work from the late 1960s thus offers a more detailed insight into the impact of the resolution in practice on the lives of specific families.

Generally speaking, while Pavelčíková and Jurová resort to an exoticising discourse featuring a supposedly distinct Roma "mentality" in their efforts to capture at least in part the agential perspective of the Roma, Hübschmannová and Davidová, for all the differences in their positions and approaches, tend to view Romani culture as a coherent socio-economic and value system embedded in a particular place (in this case the settlements and environment of the east Slovak countryside, see Chapter Three) and connected with a "traditional" way of life. Together with the post-war migration to cities in Czechia, it was the social engineering assimilationist programme that, by this logic, led to the fatal disruption of such systems.

Even taking these studies into account, however, the truth is that the prevailing focus in studies of the resettlement policy written after the Velvet Revolution on the perspective of the state authorities has foregrounded the question of why these assimilation policies in communist Czechoslovakia failed. Davidová had already expressed her concern regarding the success of the entire programme in the letter referred to above to the Central Committee of the Communist Party in 1966. She pointed to the lack of readiness for the planned "dispersal", especially with regard to the living conditions in the planned resettlement destinations; the anti-Roma prejudices of the non-Romani population, which were seemingly to be discouraged by means of the distribution of the Roma among the non-Romani population; and a lack of information amongst the Roma themselves. Davidová warned that these factors placed the entire project at risk, and inadvertently revealed her belief in the soundness of the basic policy by writing that "the trust lost [...] will be difficult to regain and restore afterwards" (Sadílková et al. 2018, 150–155).

The entire programme did indeed collapse soon after, as is clear from the failure to meet the resettlement schedule on the one hand, and the ongoing "undesirable migration" on the other (Guy 1977, 333–338). The newly appointed Government Committee was abolished in November 1968, and the government resolution itself expired in 1970 in Czechia and in 1972 in the Slovak regions of the new federation.[5] At the same time, the authors of later studies (see Jurová 1993, Pavelčíková 2004) identified reasons similar to those that Davidová had warned of for this perceived failure. Above all this involved the lack of preparedness of the entire resettlement programme, the successful implementation of which depended on communication between the specified partner districts. While it seems that the Slovaks were more than willing to get rid of "their" Roma by sending them to Czechia without any prior confirmation of suitable living conditions, many districts in Czechia resisted the arrival of what they called "foreign G*psies" (*cizí C*káni*; Guy 1977, 286–297). In this respect, the much vaunted "voluntary" nature of participation in the plan was also thrown into doubt, since the Roma were to be, if not directly coerced, then at least coaxed into participating (Pavelčíková 2004, 93). As the attitudes of the authorities indicate, the implementation of the "dispersal" programme was to encounter the anti-Roma prejudices of both authorities and local residents who were against the distribution of the Roma in society. Under these conditions, what the resettlement programme actually meant in practice was merely the further production of mobility (Guy 1977, 278–286). This then added to the "undesirable migration" already underway, which the authorities were powerless to prevent even though it was supposed to be prohibited (ibid., 304).

0.3.2 Localised studies

In addition to their attempts at a comprehensive overview of the development of policies toward Romani people, some authors produced

---

5   In 1969 Czechoslovakia adopted a new constitution establishing two autonomous republics, with the Czech Socialist Republic and the Slovak Socialist Republic being equal and sovereign parts of the Czechoslovak Federation.

localised studies of their implementation (Pavelčíková 1999; Růžičková 2012; Slačka 2015). These allow for a more subtle differentiation of the positions of individual actors and the tracking of certain historical continuities and discontinuities.

It was especially Sadílková, who, in both her unpublished dissertation and other texts too (e.g. Sadílková 2017, 2018, 2020; Sadílková et al. 2018, 2024), calls for the de-victimisation of the Roma in the narrative of their post-war history in Czechoslovakia. In her own localised study, she suggests how to work with the specific policies of the communist regime from the other side, i.e. as policies that in practice entered in unexpected ways into agential economic strategies and the broader social strategies of the Roma themselves.[6] Though she does not address the resettlement policy in detail, on the basis of her research in a specific location she suggests that centralised efforts to demolish the settlements may have been met with interest on the part of those Roma keen to move out. Sadílková's perspective is not entirely new. It was similarly formulated by Stewart (1997) in his ethnography of the Roma in socialist Hungary, and specifically in respect of the resettlement policy by the sociologist Guy (1977, 329–330), whose emphasis Sadílková picks up on. Sadílková throws light on this neglected area and develops it at a time when debates on the history of the Roma under socialism were still dominated by a strongly evaluative narrative in Czechia, Slovakia and further afield. She does so both as part of a growing international trend to portray the Roma not as historical victims but as agents in their own right (see the *Prague Forum for Romani Histories*; also, for instance, Roman et al. 2021; Marushiakova and Popov 2021, 2022), and also within the context of earlier revisionist approaches to and discussions around totalitarianism, and within the context of considerations of the formation of the legitimacy of the communist regime (see, for example, Pullmann 2009, 2011, 2012; also Rabinach 2006).

The most detailed examination of the genesis and implementation of the Czechoslovak communist regime's policy towards the Romani population, including the concept of resettlement, is contained in the thesis[7] by the sociologist Will Guy. This text is valuable for several rea-

---

6   Dobruská similarly integrates the implementation of the resettlement programme into migration trajectories and transnational social networks (Dobruská 2018; Ort and Dobruská 2023).

7   This is an unpublished dissertation, the conclusions of which Guy summarised in other texts (see Guy 1998, 2001).

sons. First of all, in addition to a substantial historical section that relies primarily on archival sources, it also draws on ethnographic research in which Guy was accompanied by Davidová in the early 1970s. The result is an extensive work that confronts the state assimilationist policies with the situation of the Roma in specific locations in eastern Slovakia and – thanks to the ongoing migration – in Czechia, basically at the same time the policies in question were being enacted or shortly afterwards. The localised studies enabled Guy to distinguish more finely the positions of the individual actors, which, in addition to tracking the interests of the Roma, led him to put a name to the diverse and often contradictory approaches taken by the state's central and regional authorities. This then gives rise to a basic thesis, elaborated in more detail, according to which opposition to the central assimilation policy came not so much from the Roma themselves, but from the local authorities upon which the successful implementation of the policy primarily relied. Guy's work is unique in that, through his foreign affiliation (he wrote his thesis while affiliated with Bristol University), he was able to indulge in a comprehensive and open critique of the communist regime in Czechoslovakia. However, although he urges us to take into account the experiences of the Roma themselves (see also Sadílková 2016, 281), in his case, too, the main focus is on the perspective of the state authorities and, as the title suggests, their attempt to assimilate the G*psy population.

When tracing the failure of the concept of resettlement, Guy refers to the same factors as the work referred to above, and confirms that the success of the entire programme relied on the District and Municipal National Committees, whose interests, however, conflicted with central policy. Guy notes at this point that inasmuch as the assimilation policy outlined in the 1958 resolution failed due to the lack of enthusiasm displayed by the National Committees, which were unwilling to bear the costs of the central policy and persisted in their anti-Roma attitudes, the introduction of a new administrative structure and the allocation of special resources over and above the existing budgetary provision failed to overcome these problems. Though the special commissions established at individual regional levels were independent of other bodies of the National Committees, Guy points out that their members were local non-Romani residents and they often reproduced anti-Roma prejudices (Guy 1977, 328–329). The centrally appointed Government Committee on G*psy Population Issues, which was composed of representatives of individual ministries and whose counterpart also operated at the Slovak National Council, was run as an advisory and coordinating body that itself had no tools with which to overcome the persistent anti-Roma prejudices at regional levels and to enforce implementation of the resettlement programme (ibid., 318–330). Moreover, the Government Committee had no independent control mechanisms and could only monitor implementation of the set timetable on the basis of reports from the National Committees themselves. The latter, meanwhile, very soon came to realise how ineffectual the entire administrative structure was, and after an initial enthusiasm soon became lax in their reporting (ibid., 318–325).

Although Guy identifies ingrained anti-Roma prejudice and the comprehensive racialisation of the Roma as the main cause of the failure of resettlement in particular and assimilation policies more generally, his analysis is valuable in that he contextualises the implementation of these policies within the broader political and economic changes taking place in the latter half of the 1960s. Thus, according to Guy, the internal contradiction of the policy under scrutiny was that while the Czechoslovak economy, after the deep economic crisis of the first half of the 1960s and the collapse of the Third Five-Year Plan, followed a path of overall decentralisation, the assimilation policy towards the Roma was again reliant on greater centralisation under the government resolution of 1965. This situation did not only involve the dysfunctionality of the new administration, but a total loss of control over the planning process. Guy analyses this paradox of the planned resettlement schedule on the level of housing and employment, summarising it as follows:

> During the mid-1960s the prospects of success for the G*psy policy of assimilation by dispersal were already deteriorating as a direct result of contemporary economic developments. The balance of new house-building was altering in favour of the more expensive privately-owned co-operative flats, whilst central controls over employers were progressively removed allowing, on the one hand, some firms to refuse G*psy workers and apprentices they did not want, but, on the other, the new co-op production units to recruit G*psies as casual labourers to travel the country in mobile gangs. (ibid., 320)

The last phenomenon mentioned by Guy was in direct contradiction with the official logic of assimilation, which was supposed to be achieved through the permanence of housing and employment. In addition, there was the ongoing "unplanned" migration, which exceeded the number of families to be resettled by a factor of three and, together with the dismal implementation of the timetable, demonstrated the ineffectiveness of the entire concept. Guy concludes that despite the complete removal of some of the eastern Slovak settlements, overall there was no improvement to the dismal living conditions in these dwellings, nor was the total number of residents reduced, since the organised relocation and migration did not even match their natural reproduction rate (Guy 1977, 341–342).

0.3.3 The resettlement policy in the new narrative of Romani history

In 2017, the historian Celia Donert published a monograph entitled *The Rights of the Roma: The Struggle for Citizenship in Postwar Czechoslovakia*. This is an important contribution to the reframing of the narrative of Romani history in Czechoslovakia and thus the approach to Romani history in general. On a broader scale, its input is twofold. On the one hand, Donert seeks to de-victimise the Roma by conceiving of their history as the story of their own struggle to be accorded a dignified place in society. Accordingly, she rejects the history of the Roma as a parallel historical line and views it as an integral part of Czechoslovak – and by extension European and world – history. The passage in which she addresses resettlement policy (2017, 159–168), however, suggests that her conception of Romani agency has its limits (on this, see the discussion at the beginning of Chapter One). Although Donert cites several written complaints made by the Roma in relation to implementation of the programme, here, too, she sticks primarily to the perspective of the state and the ensuing evaluation of the "success" of the policy under examination. Thus, even her contribution is valuable for its broader contextualisation and newly highlighted points, though she does not grant this as much space as Guy.

Donert argues that policy toward Romani people shifted during the 1960s away from its earlier emphasis on employment. Coinciding with a more general evolution in the nature of the state's concern for its citizens, the Roma increasingly came to be seen not just as workers, but as citizens and objects of care (ibid., 143). This meant a shift in emphasis to the "way of life" and a holistic concern for the Romani family. From a growing gender perspective it was sexualised Romani women who represented the main obstacle to the social assimilation of the Roma. This was a reflection not only of the popular securitisation discourse of the time regarding the threat of a "population explosion" (*populační exploze*) associated with this group (the Great Replacement of its time: see Chapter Two), but as Donert sees it this also foreshadows the policy of forced sterilisation that just a few years later would impact mainly Romani women (see Sadílková 2019). Viewed from this angle, the central concept of "resolving the G*psy question" ensuing from the 1965 resolution was also an attempt at the systematic management of the quality of life of the Romani population and the elimination of their "backward lifestyle". In addition to summarising the known factors of its failure, in which she references Guy, Donert emphasises the logical contradiction at its heart. She points out that in focusing on quality of life it was the way of life of G*psies that was naturally understood in terms of "social inadaptability" and "parasitism" in official discourse. The Roma, who according to the official logic had attained a degree of assimilation, were no longer viewed as G*psies, and so the endeavour to eliminate the "backward way of life of the G*psies" naturally led to its reproduction as a social problem regardless of the degree to which specific aspects of central policy had been implemented (see Chapter Two).

0.4 Roma as an Integral Part of Society

It is clear from this brief overview of the literature that the overriding focus on the perspective of the state leaves very little room for the perspective and experience of the Roma themselves and consequently provides very limited opportunities to trace the nature of their agency. It is precisely these two basic objectives that I pursue in this book. I examine how the centralised policy of the Czechoslovak socialist state toward what it called G*psies played out in practice, since up till now no one has described its impact on the lives of the Roma themselves. I am not interested in overturning the evaluative significance that has been assigned to the assimilation policy as a whole in Romani studies and within broader reflections on socialist policies in respect of the Roma. Instead, I wish to examine the nature of Romani agency in relation to the practice of state policies targeting them (either implicitly or explicitly), that is to say, the relationship between the Roma and the state and the position of the Roma in the society of socialist Czechoslovakia as well as other countries. In reconstructing the "diversity of Romani experience" (Guy 1998 , 14–15) and attempting to answer these questions, I have run up against an ongoing ambivalence. In many places my work points to a strong sense of social belonging and participation amongst the Roma, while at the same time evidencing their historically entrenched exclusion and the racial discrimination and segregation they faced. It follows the agential strategies of the Roma themselves, but operates in the space of the coercive policies of the state and its individual authorities. It points to both the diversity but also the often contradictory attitudes, interests and actions of individual actors, both on the part of the state and amongst the Roma themselves. At the same time, it subverts the clear dichotomy between the state on the one hand and the Roma on the other. However, I would like to point to important emphases that both ensue from what I write in the four main chapters and also intersect more broadly with the overall understanding of the position of the Roma in non-Roma societies. Firstly, I do not view the Roma as a priori alien in the sense of being an externally positioned group seeking social integration, but as an integral part of society, however much they may be excluded under particular circumstances (see also Ort 2022b). Such a reversal of perspective on the one hand removes the Roma from the essentialised position of "eternal outsiders" (ibid.), while making it possible to confirm the anchoring of Romani history – or perhaps that should be "Romani histories" (see *Prague Forum for Romani Histories*) – within broader historical processes. According to this logic, I do not think of the Roma as a clearly defined population group, since I understand the implementation of the state's policies towards G*psies and their effects on specific people as the subject of an ambiguous negotiation between the individual actors involved.

0.4.1 Regional and sub-ethnic outline of research interest

As well as indicating how the situation in Czechia and Slovakia was different, the localised studies contained in the individual chapters (see Chapter Two and Three) reveal the significant diversity not only of Roma/non-Roma relationships in individual municipalities, but also of the positionalities and strategies of sociability of individuals and families. Instead of reiterating an infinite diversity, I would now like to explain the regional scope of selected studies and thus of the entire book, and point out the specific elements and limits it entails. In doing so, I anticipate in part the discussion surrounding the representativeness of microhistorical studies that I will elaborate on in Chapter One.

I chose as the starting point of my research the situation in the district of Humenné in eastern Slovakia in its expanded form after the re-structuring of the districts in the early 1960s, when it included what are now the border regions of Snina and Medzilaborce. My choice was guided by the fact that the District National Committees were intended to be responsible for the successful implementation of the resettlement programme, and the district archives contained a large part of its documentation. However, the discovery of several unique sources prompted me to look at two other locations, both in what was then the district of Bardejov (now the district of Svidník). This involves the introductory study of the village of Kapišová and the final study of the nearby village of Šemetkovce (see Chapter Four). Although the inclusion of Bardejov allows for a partial comparison and highlights some differences as to how the resettlement policy was applied at the district level, overall these are regions with very similar characteristics. The two neighbouring border regions formed the northern part of the easternmost point of Slovakia and thus belonged to a long-standing economically marginalised area characterised by linguistic, ethnic and religious diversity, as well as by high rates of local population emigration over the long term. This is also an area that was viewed in orientalising and racialising terms as backward and the subject of internal colonising policies during the creation and consolidation of the society of the interwar Czechoslovakia (Holubec 2014; Baloun 2022). Similarly, in the 1960s, eastern Slovakia found itself at the centre of interest of state policy towards the Roma due to the high concentration of Romani settlements associated with a "backward way of life", whose inhabitants were selected for relocation and dispersal throughout Czechoslovakia. The choice of this region as the starting point for monitoring the practice of the resettlement programme is in this respect logical, though it was not the only candidate. My research project and, indeed, this book, would have looked quite different if I had focused on a region in Czechia. I have attempted to deal in part with this asymmetry in Chapter Four, where I follow the stories of resettled/migrating Romani families within the context of corresponding regions in Czechia. Even so, I was in the end guided by the logic of the ties these families had to their place of origin in Slovakia.

At the same time, I feel it incumbent upon me to acknowledge the essentially exclusive focus of this book on those Roma who were long settled in specific locations in Slovakia and in most cases only arrived in Czechia after the Second World War. The demarcation of this population group, which in percentage terms dominated the Romani population in post-war Czechoslovakia, might appear somewhat artificial, since it includes a relatively wide range of ways of socialising in non-Romani society. However, it makes sense in relation to other, numerically under-represented groups of Roma (e.g. the original Bohemian and Moravian Roma and the Sinti, a large number of whom perished in concentration camps during the Second World War, or the Vlax Roma), due to the deeper internal differentiation wrought by a different historical experience as well as by language (see, for example, Elšík 2003). Although this aspect of my work is important, since the population group thus defined was the one most impacted by the policy under consideration, the omission of the experience of those Roma with different sub-ethnic self-identification and historical experience cannot be viewed as self-evident and must not be overlooked. In the context of this book, for instance, the question arises as to why resettlement policies did not affect concentrations of Vlax Roma in Czechia and Slovakia, which to an extent arose as a consequence of the 1958 Act on the Permanent Settlement of Nomadic Persons (see Hajská 2020, 2024).

0.4.2 Terminology

On the whole I use the umbrella term "resettlement policy" to refer to the programme enshrined in Government Resolution No. 502/1965. This simplifies matters considerably, since it does not cover all aspects of this policy, which also specified more complex tasks in the sphere of housing, employment, education, public enlightenment and sociological research. On the other hand, the term encapsulates the core of the resolution, which will form the focus of this book, namely, resettlement as a key tool for re-education, social inclusion and "resolving the G*psy question". In the literature this policy is often spoken of as a "policy of dispersal" (*rozptylová politika*)or "dispersion campaign" (*kampaň rozptylu*). I have chosen to emphasise "resettlement" as an umbrella term encompassing various types of controlled population movement, be this dispersal within individual districts or the transfer from Slovakia to Czechia. I retain the term "dispersal" in order to represent the enforced logic of designated population movement, according to which the "concentration of G*psy populations" was to be avoided (see Chapter Four). In connection with the attempt to eliminate existing "G*psy concentrations", I use the official term "liquidation" (*likvidace*) given my focus on eastern Slovakia, above all in relation to what were known as "G*psy settlements" (see Chapter Three).

I use the term "G*psy Commission" or sometimes just "Commission" to refer to the interdepartmental bodies established at the level of regions, districts, cities and larger municipalities under the central Government Committee on G*psy Population Issues (with its counterpart at the Slovak National Council). This is an unofficial term used by several parties, and at the same time an umbrella term for the names of commissions that varied from document to document ("Commission for the Resolution of G*psy Questions", "Commission for the Resolution of Questions Pertaining to Citizens of G*psy Origin", "Commission for the Resolution of Questions Pertaining to G*psy Populations/the G*psy Population", etc., including their Slovak variants).

I use the term "Roma" as a category of ethnic self-identification with regard for the word *Roma* (pl.) in the Romani language. I do so knowing that not all of the people I refer to in this way were speakers of Romani at the time the government resolution was enacted, and that many of them in certain contexts thought of themselves as G*psies, while others distanced themselves from such a designation. In the textual references to "G*psies", I use an asterisk, a practice common in the anthropological and historical literature on the Roma. Although I consider it important to distinguish analytically between the terms "Roma" and "G*psies", given the often negative and offensive connotations of the latter term, I do not want to reproduce it in full. I will write the term with a capital "G". However much G*psies were defined primarily as a social group in the official policies of the time, the category was never fully free of associations with ethno-racial characteristics.

Nevertheless, as regards language I was still faced with a dilemma: how to remain faithful to the terms used at the time while not allowing the text to become tainted with the often dehumanising language used in relation to the Roma, especially given that my primary concern is to capture the perspectives and experiences of these people. Similarly, how not to overwhelm the text with references to G*psies, the "solution to the G*psy question", the "dispersal of the G*psies", and the "liquidation of G*psy concentrations", while nonetheless conveying the flavour of the language used during the period under examination that chronicles attitudes towards the Roma, and not slipping into ahistoricism? Moreover, one should not forget that the dominant discourse was inscribed in the language of the texts (complaints, requests, etc.) of the Roma themselves, a feature I analyse as representing both the instrumentalisation and sharing of this discourse. The use of quotation marks is only a partial solution, and the reader (especially the Romani reader) may sometimes feel overwhelmed in certain passages by the dominant language of the time. This is another reason I have tried to be sparing with such language. For example, in many places I write about the policy towards the Roma, thus defusing the tension between the official category of G*psy and the term denoting ethnic self-identification. However, I do this not when I am analysing discourse but simply making reference to a policy aimed a certain group of the population, with full awareness of the fact that, despite the ambivalence of the official category of G*psyness, it was the Roma being targeted by policies aimed at G*psies. On the other hand, I deliberately use contemporary terms when analysing the discourses surrounding them, whether this involved G*psies (see Chapter Two above all), or the "liquidation of G*psy concentrations" (see Chapter Three), or "dispersal" (see Chapter Four). The boundaries of such designations are not entirely clear, and in many cases I approach the choice of terms somewhat intuitively. Though it is impossible to resolve the dilemma outlined above completely, I believe that it needs to be addressed not only in relation to the readability and historical empirical precision of the text of this book, but also to broader considerations regarding the writing of Romani histories.

I refer to the places discussed by their real names. When writing of people I sometimes use their full names and sometimes their Christian name followed by surname initial. I use full names in the case of people who were public figures and whose position as full actors in the period debates and equal partners in the sociological analysis of specific situations I seek to acknowledge. A typical example of this would be Koloman Gunár from Brekov, who himself wrote a book about the Roma in his village. In contrast, as regards most of the individual actors I opt for the partially anonymised format for the sake of personal data protection and the sensitivity of some of the information being discussed. The same applies to the interviews conducted with many of the contemporary witnesses, with whom I agreed on said practice.

0.4.3 Structure of the book

Prior to the empirically based chapters, there is a chapter devoted to my own theoretical and methodological background. Here I situate resettlement policies within a discussion of the work of James C. Scott, both his conception of state power in the application of state engineering policies (Scott 1998), and his understanding of resistance as a mode of response to these policies by marginalised populations (e.g. Scott 1985). I shall follow these contributions to the related anthropological discussion, which seek to make a finer distinction between different actors and to break down the sharp boundaries between state and society and between domination and marginalisation. Here I shall draw on the mode of anthropological thinking "from the margins" (Tsing 1994), developed for the anthropology of the state (Das and Poole 2004). In attempting to articulate a more complex relationship between marginalised populations and a dominant state, I will draw on the work of Holly High, who has studied the resettlement of poor farmers in Laos (High 2005, 2008). High emphasises that it is impossible to ignore the expectations and aspirations that the farmers themselves projected onto the state resettlement policies. And when the implementation of resettlement in practice often led to the deepening of their pauperisation and precarisation, the farmers did not blame the policy itself but rather the dysfunctional state as a whole. At the same time, referencing the anthropologist Leo Howe (1998) I shall show that not even the relationship between domination and marginalisation is fixed, and that there is a constant struggle going on between people as to who will be on the side of the dominant and who will bear the stigma of marginalisation. Such a distribution of positions also affects who is actually impacted by state policies. In the first chapter I argue that while policy toward the G*psies was targeted on a relatively unambiguously defined group of people, it cannot be narrowly thought of in relation to the Roma alone, but rather as a policy that entered into local socio-economic systems that oversaw the specific form in which it was materialised and had the potential to transform it. Connecting anthropological issues to the historical themes of this book then led me quite naturally to already existing historical approaches that are acknowledged to have been inspired by anthropology, be this the concept of microhistory or the "history of everyday life" (*Alltagsgeschichte*). Among other things, I open up a discussion on the representativeness of studies that purposefully reduce the scale of research and track the everyday actions of "ordinary" actor-individuals. I am at this point lending my voice to those who argue that historians thus oriented, similarly to anthropologists, do not study "villages" as such, but investigate broader social phenomenon as they are played out "in villages" (Geertz 1973, 22). However, reflections upon the methods of archival research and oral history eventually led me to consider the "villages" themselves, above all with regard to the expectations and interests of the research participants, i.e. the people I interviewed.

In Chapter Two, I look at the negotiations involved in deciding to whom the centrally formulated policy was to apply. I ask the key question as to who actually is a "G*psy" (*C*kán*), by tracing both the different ways in which this category was defined, and the negotiation of its association with specific people during implementation of the resettlement policy. A new categorisation ensued from Government Resolution No. 502/1965. The G*psies were now divided into three groups depending on the degree of social assimilation versus the extent of their "backwardness". The policy of resettlement was to apply to those of category II, who, though living in the "unhealthy" environment of "G*psy concentrations", would, it was assumed, extricate themselves from such a background if offered assistance. However, the understanding of G*psyness as a kind of social deviation coexisted alongside other social discourses according to which G*psies were identified and judged on the basis of ethno-racial characteristics. As a result, while some of the Roma were denied the opportunity to participate in the resettlement programme because they did not meet the official criteria of G*psyness, the freedom of movement of any and all Romani people could be restricted on the basis of ethno-racial criteria. In presenting the discourses surrounding the concept of G*psyness at that time, I am primarily interested in the backdrop against which it was negotiated in everyday relations. I shall focus on the village of Brekov, where the local Roma managed to achieve a high degree of acceptance in local relations and the validity of the category of "problematic" and "backward G*psies" was reserved for Roma beyond the boundaries of their home village. Within the framework of the resettlement policy, however, the label G*psies stuck to a single family in the village. This family then disrupted the overall image of the integration of the local Roma and, as socially non-conforming, eventually became part of the official resettlement to Czechia. Based on this example, I argue that G*psyness as a category potentially applicable to the Roma based on racial criteria also played an important role in structuring relations between the Roma themselves.

In Chapter Three I will focus on one of the key pillars of the resettlement policy, namely, the effort to "liquidate undesirable G*psy concentrations", above all the (east) Slovak settlements. In addition to specific features of the implementation of liquidation, I will seek to shed light on its broader premises, i.e. the way in which individual agents related to settlements as distinct social, cultural and physical spaces. In this respect, the official discourse regarding the settlements that spoke of them as a threat to security and sanitation was underpinned by a predominant expert discourse in which they were defined as the habitats of a "culturally backward way of life". In turn, critical voices that viewed the assimilation policy as causing the disruption of the socio-cultural systems of the Roma had a tendency to view the settlements as the natural environment for the realisation of a distinctive Romani culture. Other authors, when tracing the territorialisation of the Roma in settlements, emphasise the crucial role of the local authorities and non-Romani villagers as guardians of non-Romani territorial hegemony. Focusing on the agency of the Roma themselves, I shall attempt to reconcile these opposing views by showing that all of these aspects played a role in how the settlements were understood by their inhabitants. In many documented cases, the inhabitants shared a view of the settlement as being not a place characterised by materially inadequate living conditions, but also as the site of cultural "backwardness" and socio-economic stagnation. In this respect, the Roma's economic and social strategies to some extent met with centralised efforts to eradicate such places. Inasmuch as the implementation of central policy was negotiated within the context of broader, locally anchored, socio-economic relations, this did not mean simply the disruption of socio-cultural ties among the Roma themselves (as discussed by critics of the policy), but also the potential to disrupt racially motivated segregation. I argue, however, that this aspect of resettlement policy was more an opportunity for individual families situated in a certain way rather than an opportunity for an overall reframing of local relations. Using the example of the Podskalka settlement near Humenné, I show that despite the long existing spatial mobility outside the settlement, usually into Humenné itself, the Roma were not always in full agreement with the official discourse, but regarded the settlement as a distinct social and cultural space with ambitions for administrative autonomy. This was not a space separated from the surrounding world, but a place within and by means of which the Roma were able to realise broader social participation (e.g. through their own school, football team, fire brigade, associations and activities).

The emphasis on the removal of settlements was naturally bound up with the relocation of their inhabitants in accordance with the logic of dispersal. I focus on this aspect in Chapter Four, in which I look at the resettlement of the Roma from Slovakia to Czechia, which took place against the backdrop not only of the post-war migration of Roma between the two regions of what was then Czechoslovakia, but also the longer-term effort to control the movement of G*psies as "nomads" (*kočovníci*) and "fluctuants" (*fluktuanti*). In this chapter, I seek to undermine a fixed understanding of migrating/resettled Roma in terms of their uprooting from established socio-economic and cultural ties, which was inherent not only in the critique of assimilationist policies, but in the overall view of the post-war movement of the Romani population and the transformation of its socio-economic ties. I will show that, unlike the non-Romani population, who saw the planned relocation as a threat to non-Romani territorial hegemony, the Roma themselves saw it as an opportunity for social inclusion. In this respect, they criticised the dysfunctionality of centralised policy and the anti-Roma attitudes of specific authorities, or pointed to the discriminatory nature of restrictions on freedom of movement. However, I note here the ineffectiveness of the enforced control of movement itself, since most Roma maintained the continuity of their own migratory trajectories even against the backdrop of the implementation of the policy under consideration, and the "organised movement" to designated places affected only individuals from the whole of the Humenné district. When tracing the prevailing experience of migration, I will show that the official emphasis on "dispersal" may have met with the specific migratory strategies of individual Romani families. These families, however, in their efforts to achieve a certain spatial and socio-economic autonomy, relied on maintaining earlier ties, not only with other families in Czechia, but, in a certain "transnational" social field, with those living in Slovakia. Finally, in order to capture more comprehensively the actual process of resettlement, I will focus on the situation of families resettled from Šemetkovce in Slovakia to Jičín in Czechia. Unique material in the form of interviews conducted by Hübschmannová with various actors of the resettlement programme carried out in the late 1970s, allows me to differentiate more subtly the agential positions and experiences of the Roma themselves and to highlight the hitherto neglected gender perspective. The discussion of the situation in regions of Czechia is at least a partial counterbalance to the primary focus of this book on the region of eastern Slovakia. At the same time, it will allow me to show that, however much resettlement and migration offered many of the Roma an opportunity to escape the historically entrenched racial hierarchies of the eastern Slovak countryside, in Czechia, too, the category of G*psyness may have clung to them, along with its local and historically conditioned meaning and the policies ensuing therefrom.

1. CHAPTER ONE
Romani Agency, Anthropology and History

One of the key texts for anyone wishing to understand resettlement policies is James C. Scott's *Seeing Like a State* (1998). Scott examines the phenomenon of resettlement within the broader context of the social engineering practiced by the modern state and its attempts to control its inhabitants. He argues that such policies are doomed to fail because they ignore *metis*, i.e. local and specific knowledge and understanding. Scott's contribution to this debate is useful for a broader contextualisation of communist policies towards the Roma, policies that seek to force "legibility" on their subjects in order to control and surveil them. From this perspective it was both the opaque "G*psy concentrations" and the two-way migratory movement of the Roma between Czechia and Slovakia that posed a threat to the sovereignty of state power.

Scott's analysis of these power mechanisms has been criticised for portraying the state as a relatively homogenous actor and over-simplifying its policies as straightforward top-down processes (see, for example, Higgs 2004). This critique was followed up by Lucassen, who looked at the dynamics of negotiating policies towards persons labelled G*psies in terms of the relationship between the central and local authorities (Lucassen 2008). This perspective is highly relevant as regards policies towards the Roma in post-war Czechoslovakia, where, as I suggested in the introduction, they may have represented a response to pressure from the regions, and where the interests of the central and regional authorities may often have been in conflict (see Guy 1977, 318–330). Lucassen, who traces the different historical development of "anti-G*psy" policies in England and Germany, concludes his text by raising further questions regarding Scott's understanding of state power, which now relate to the social position of the Roma themselves. Since Scott cites a weak civil society as one of the conditions allowing for the implementation of social engineering policies, Lucassen wants to know whose interests said civil society would defend. He points to the forced sterilisation policies in Sweden and Switzerland, i.e. two "fully developed democracies" (ibid., 440). In doing so he highlights the unequal position of the Roma and other marginalised/racialised groups in European and other societies. This emphasis is also relevant to the situation I am looking at. According to Scott's analysis, the entire population of the former Eastern bloc countries would fit the description of being dominated by state power. However, this then no longer provides a tool for understanding the specific position of the Roma, who as G*psies were excluded from these societies in various situations under diverse circumstances. The shift in emphasis to the position of marginalised populations resonates with the writings of those authors who reproach Scott for his single-minded focus on top-down processes and his neglect of bottom-up reactions (e.g. Tilly 1999).

It should be pointed out that Scott has in fact examined these bottom-up reactions at length elsewhere (see especially Scott 1985, 1990). However, according to the subsequent debates, his concept of resistance threw up similar problems, homogenising the actions of marginalised actors within an overly static and sharp definition of the relationship between domination and marginalisation. It is on the debate surrounding the conceptualisation and means of tracing the complex agency of marginalised populations that I will focus in this introductory chapter. I will seek answers in various anthropological approaches, the application of which to historical research I will discuss in the second part of the chapter.

It is clear that these questions are highly relevant when looking at the post-war history of the Roma in Czechoslovakia. In response to the prevailing focus on the principles of the exercise of state power over the Romani population, it was Sadílková who pointed out that pursuing this perspective contributes to the victimisation of the Roma and an understanding of their history as primarily one of "oppression" (Sadílková 2020). Donert went in a similar direction, reframing the narrative of the Roma in Czechoslovak territory with an emphasis on their active social participation (2017). Despite the importance of her book (see the Introduction), it also raises questions regarding how to grasp the Romani agency thus highlighted. Indeed, in Donert's concept it refers mainly to the political and social participation of socio-economically better off Roma. As a result, she has received somewhat intemperate criticism from the authors of the provocative book *Historicizing Roma in Central Europe* (2020, see also Shmidt 2022). Both Schmidt and Jaworsky accuse Donert (along with many other writers) of reproducing the dominant logic of agency and thereby confirming existing racist structures. I agree that the Romani agency as described by Donert is limited. However, the criticism aimed at her by Shmidt and Jaworsky has obvious flaws. Firstly, both on a general level and in relation to Donert in particular, one cannot help but feel that the arguments of the writers being criticised are often cherry-picked and presented in a simplistic and selective manner. Secondly, throughout the book the Roma (yet again) feature almost exclusively as passive objects of academic research (see also Slačálek 2023). Such a position is defensible to a certain extent, since the central interest is in those who produce knowledge about the Roma. However, within the context of efforts to "decolonise thinking", it is all too apparent how Shmidt and Jaworsky's theoretically oriented work fails to provide an alternative understanding of Romani agency and capture their experience. Moreover, the sporadic examples of alternative approaches indicate that the two authors also have a somewhat schematic understanding of the position of the Roma in a society of non-Romani dominance. This is apparent in a footnote relating to the resettlement policy of the 1960s that I discuss in this book. In it, the authors point out that Donert's concept of agency does not include the actions of those Roma who resisted the resettlement policy. Here, on the one hand, Shmidt and Jaworsky omit those parts of Donert's book in which she offers a partial insight into the implementation of the centralised measures of the communist regime and analyses the requests and complaints of the Roma addressed to the central authorities; while on the other, like Scott, they present an alternative view of Romani agency in equally limiting terms of resistance.

As important as I think it is to embrace the decolonisation of thought and to reflect upon whiteness in the current production of knowledge about the Roma, I believe that such a position should not forsake empirical honesty and anchorage. The editors of *Gypsy Economy*, a collection of anthropological studies of Romani modes of sociability in a world of non-Romani dominance, offered a similar emphasis. In the introduction to the anthology, Micol Brazzabeni, Ivone Manuela Cunha and Martin Fotta expressed their belief that "an adequate political response to the problems that Roma and G*ypsy populations face should not result in treating people as passive victims by denying them their creativity and capacity for struggle on their own terms", while also advocating ethnography as the most appropriate tool for studying the complexity of such responses (Brazzabeni et al. 2015, 9). It is the ethnographic approach that allows for a finer distinction of the nature of agency in complex networks of actors and socio-economic relations.

1.1 Ways of Studying Agency

1.1.1 Margins as a starting point for analysis

When pursuing this position, the approach "from the margins" developed by the anthropologist Anna Tsing (1994) is particularly useful. Tsing stresses that the margins as she sees them represent neither geographic locations nor sites of deviant departures from social norms. Instead, she argues, they indicate "analytic placement that makes evident both the constraining, oppressive quality of cultural exclusion and the creative potential of rearticulating, enlivening, and rearranging the very social categories that peripheralize a group's existence" (Tsing 1994, 279). Tsing argues that the shift of anthropological interest from the study of remote places to Western societies has, paradoxically, contributed to a false dichotomy between complex global cultural processes and local static cultures, and that "explorations of 'cultural imperialism' and 'globalisation' continue to downplay the creative agency of non-European-origin peoples" (ibid., 283). Within this dichotomy, the author argues, "some places appear to generate the global, while other places seem stuck in the local" (ibid., 282). Tsing herself perceives at least a dual meaning in the study of "remote" places. On the one hand, she argues that such spaces must be released from a static conception of culture and studied as part of broader cultural, political and economic processes in the light of new anthropological approaches. On the other, such a study allows us to verify and revise Western anthropological frameworks and thus contributes to a more comprehensive understanding of broader socio-cultural processes.

As regards the context I am examining here, the development of the concept of "from the margins" can be seen as a call to observe the experiences and attitudes of the Roma as a peripheralised population, without accepting the currently dominant idea of their social deviation as G*psies. Tsing also reminds us of the dimension of gender, building on feminist theorists who have applied an intersectional approach from the margins to the position of black women (bell hooks 1984, Crenshaw

1991). It is by taking this dimension into account that I will not restrict my study of Romani agency to the socio-political participation of higher status Roma, but will track a wider range of their positionalities, including the stories of those Romani families who were ultimately peripheralised within locally defined Romani communities (see the situation in Brekov, Chapter Two) or, more specifically, the experience of Romani women (see the situation of families in Jičín, Chapter Four).

In order to illuminate what marginal spaces can be observed in the case of the practice of the state policy of the communist regime, it is useful to move towards the concept of margins as introduced by Veena Das and Deborah Poole for the anthropology of the state (2004). In the introduction to *Anthropology in the Margins of the State*, the authors delineate the spheres of interest of such an approach: firstly, the marginalised population within the framework of specific states; secondly, the spaces of illegibility and the blurring of state power; and finally, bodies as domains of the exercise of state power, categories of social pathology, and the determination of who belongs to the society of the state and who no longer does. In their introduction, the editors blur the rigid boundary between the state and society, tracing the sites where state power intersects with other types of authorities. Where Scott points to the modern state's efforts to achieve the legibility of its inhabitants (1998), Das and Poole invert this perspective and uncover the margins as spaces in which the state and its policies become illegible to its inhabitants. They trace the Janus-faced nature of the state, which is identified by specific inhabitants as having caused their own marginalisation on the one hand, while on the other being the locus onto which various desires and expectations are projected. Like other writers (see above), in the end Das and Poole, too, stress that these people are not passive victims and identify the margins as spaces of creativity in the everyday, whose ethnographic observation is the most appropriate tool for exploring the nature of state power.

This approach is extremely useful when following Romani agency within the framework of the implementation of state policies. Here I show that different types of authorities overlapped within the environment of rural eastern Slovakia. This was so in the case of the non-Romani population, who on the one hand occupied superordinate positions within a strongly racialised hierarchy of socio-economic relations, while at the same time holding positions in the local and district authorities tasked with the implementation of state policy. In many cases, however, it was individual Roma – often those with relatively higher social and economic capital within specific Romani communities – who held important positions in the relevant authorities and co-determined who would be affected by particular policies and how, and who would benefit from them (see, for example, the housing development in Podskalka, Chapter Three). As I will detail more closely in the work of the anthropologist High (see below), the idea of the Janus-faced nature of the state, from whose policies the Roma hoped to improve their own status, is also useful in this respect. Here, too, the margins do not only allow us to capture the experience of marginalised populations, but also to understand the broader functioning of society and the application of the categories of normality and social deviance (see Sokolová 2008), which I analyse here by means of the category of G*psyness (see Chapter Two especially). In this respect, this book bears witness to how the situation of people who were already living in marginalised regions (both eastern Slovakia itself, but also the border regions of Czechia) and who were further marginalised and excluded as G*psies, came to the attention of the central authorities of the communist regime, whose policies towards the Roma contributed to the consolidation of its own legitimacy (Spurný 2011).

1.1.2 Dominance and resistance

Criticism of Scott for his neglect of the capacity of marginalised populations to respond to manifestations of state dominance is largely unwarranted, as it was Scott who had previously worked with forms of agency of poor farmers in southeast Asia, specifically their "everyday forms of resistance" (1985, 1990), and later "the art of not being governed" (2010). Scott, too, drew on longstanding ethnographic research when pointing out that the forms of resistance he was following were otherwise difficult to pin down and, unlike overt acts of resistance such as uprisings, are not depicted as important in "histories of resistance" (see especially Scott 1985). Scott's focus on small everyday forms of resistance, which are hidden both from those who wish to suppress them and from the social scientists who wish to study them, is reminiscent of Shmidt and Jaworsky's criticism of Donert, who, they claim, focused on large-scale manifestations of agency that left behind a visible trace, while neglecting the smaller forms of agency of socio-economically disadvantaged Romani villagers.

However, Scott's concept of resistance has been called too simple by several authors, including Das and Poole, who felt it was not up to the task of pinning down the complexity of agency in the marginal spaces they studied (2004). The anthropologist Lila Abu-Lughod, who warns of the danger of romanticisation, seeks a more sensitive approach to resistant praxis (1990). Inspired by Foucault (1978, 1982), she analyses resistance not as an act that stands outside of power structures, but one which is an intrinsic part of them. She sees ethnographic observation of resistance as a way of diagnosing complex power relations. Using the example of Bedouin women, Abu-Lughod shows that within such intersectionally understood structures, partial practices of resistance can operate in contradictory ways. At the same time she shows that resistance to certain forms of power can reproduce and reaffirm other forms of oppression. This more subtle situating of resistance within complex structures of power relations allows for a shift in emphasis from the resistance of ordinary Romani villagers to the resistance of local authorities and non-Romani populations who held out against the disruption of the territorialisation of the Roma and their absorption into "non-Romani" developments in particular locations. It was approaches such as these that Guy then identified as one of the key factors in the failure of the communist regime's assimilation policies in general and resettlement policies in particular. Abu-Lughod's emphasis thus allows for a more complex understanding of the practice of these policies, which, though they might target primarily the Roma as G*psies, ultimately enter into broader, locally anchored socio-economic relations in specific ways. In these relations, the resistance of some may reproduce the racial oppression of others. At the same time, this emphasis supports the claim that resistance as a concept is very limited when it comes to capturing diverse forms of agency. Inasmuch as Abu-Lughod says that resistance is usually accompanied by an attachment to other forms of power, the question remains as to how to analyse these attachments.

The domination–resistance dichotomy postulated by Scott for understanding relations between the state and society is interrogated by anthropologist High (2008) in her research. In a discussion about the internal resettlement projects in Laos, and in line with the emphases referred to above, High primarily follows the expectations, aspirations and life strategies of the resettled villagers themselves. Even though she shows that the expectations of the villagers were unrealistic and that many of them might end up suffering even greater poverty as a consequence, their aspirations and initial willingness to participate in state-defined policies cannot be ignored. In the end, she writes, the disappointed resettled villagers did not take issue with the resettlement programme itself, but the way it was being implemented, the blame for which they attributed to dysfunctional state institutions. In contrast, High argues that resettlement programmes were to some extent in line with an understanding of spatial mobility as tightly bound up with social mobility (see Grill 2012). In contrast to the limiting opposition of resistance to state domination, High offers the concept of "experimental consent", in which villagers, while acquiescing to state policies, continuously reinterpreted them in the light of newly emerging conditions and the continuity of their own socio-economic strategies.

In a similar fashion, I show that in criticising the resettlement policy, Romani people themselves have often not targeted its fundamental objectives, but rather its dysfunctionality (see Chapter Four). The concept of "experimental consent" also resonates with the approaches taken by other authors, who in ethnographically informed approaches articulated the relationship of the Roma to the Czechoslovak state during the communist period. Drawing on his own field research, anthropologist Jan Grill offered historical insight into the development of the economic strategies of the Roma in a specific village, concluding that the local Roma were able to selectively exploit several aspects of socialist policies towards the G*psies without succumbing to the pressure for cultural assimilation (2015a,b; see also Sadílková 2017).

In their polemic with High, a collective of authors engaged in the debate on resettlement policies in Laos has pointed out that, by drawing on Scott's distinction between "public" and "hidden transcripts" (1985, 1990), the attachment to state policies can be read precisely as a product of asymmetric power structures in which the socio-economically less advantaged cannot afford to express overt, i.e. public, criticism (Braid et al. 2009). When High responded that it is not possible to position oneself simply as the arbiter of social reality who determines what utterances express the "authentic" opinions of their speakers and which are the product of existing power inequities (2009), she was following up on a more detailed critique formulated with Scott's thesis in mind by the linguist and anthropologist Susan Gal (1995). In a review essay on Scott's book (1990), Gal rejects the postulated distinction in which public displays of power on the part of subordinate actors represent the suppression of a kind of authentic self. Drawing on her own socio-linguistic research in a bilingual community in Hungary, she points out that a single person can express different, often self-contradictory, views, including those that demonstrate resistance to official languages and ideologies. Gal concludes that "these contrasting stances cannot be classified as posed versus genuine", but that they are "evidence of the coexistence of deeply felt yet contested discourses" (ibid., 413; see also Gal 1993). What Gal and High are driving at is the perception of two different faces of the state described above, in which both emotions, or perhaps frames of mind, have equal quality and validity (see Das and Poole 2004).

1.1.3 Negotiating marginalisation

In addition to a simplistic conception of resistance and its romanticisation (Gal 1995, 420), Gal accuses Scott of flattening the "great range of power relations evident in the diverse social formations of the historical and ethnographic record into a single opposition between dominant and subordinate" (ibid., 414–415). Gal argues that the assumption that the dominant and subordinate are always "clearly definable, unified, and separable groups, unambiguously opposed to each other" is highly problematic (ibid., 417). Citing Caroline Humphrey, she identifies state socialism in particular as a typical example of "nested hierarchies", in which individual inhabitants can undergo both the experience of dominance and the experience of subordination (ibid., 416; see Humphrey 1994). The anthropologist Leo Howe (1998) has described the dichotomy between domination and marginalisation postulated by Scott as excessively static. Scott, he argues, fixes poor farmers too much in their marginalised position by not including in his analysis the constant struggle over who will escape from the subordinate position and join the side of domination. Howe bases this emphasis on his own ethnographic research among the unemployed residents of Belfast, Northern Ireland, who aspired to the status of the deserving unemployed, while casting dominantly understood notions of "scrounger" and "beggarman" into a differently defined faction of the unemployed.

Through Howe's view of the position of the marginalised, which is no longer automatic but acquires a specific situational-relational character, it is possible to further undermine the homogenisation of the position and experience of the Roma in non-Romani societies. At the same time, such an approach resonates with how some authors have already described the negotiation of the social position of the Roma, specifically in the Central European region. In these cases, however, it was not the category of (un)deserving unemployed that participated in the formation of an understanding of dominance and marginalisation, but the heavily racialised category of G*psyness, with the diverse social attributes historically linked to it and associated with it in broader societal discourse.

The anthropologist Yasar Abu Ghosh, writing of a small town in the south of the Czech Republic, described how some of the Roma living there were successful in their strategy of "escaping G*psyness" by casting this category onto a differently defined faction of the local Romani population (Abu Ghosh 2008). A similar dynamic has been described by the anthropologists Cecilia Kovai and Kata Horváth in a village in Hungary, where some of the local Roma sought to "silence G*psyness" in their everyday interactions with the non-Romani world, while accusing other local Roma of displaying it in exaggerated fashion (Kovai 2012, Horváth 2012). What is important in respect of this book is that such a principle of Roma relating to their non-Romani surroundings and to the formation of internal relations between the Roma themselves has also been described for the rural areas of eastern Slovakia. In this case, I draw mainly on my own long-term field research in a small village in north-eastern Slovakia, where G*psyness was not only a question of ethnic stereotypes, but was inscribed within the structure of local relations. Association with this category meant partial exclusion from the local community and so, as in the Hungarian village in question, it was through a strategy of concealing the characteristics of G*psyness that the local Roma sought to affirm their local belonging and thus reinforce their own social status (Ort 2021, 2022b; see also Grill 2015b; Hrustič 2015a,b). As difficult as it is to reconstruct such relations historically, I will show that a similar logic applied to the internal differentiation of the Roma was in operation in the municipalities where I observed the outcome of the resettlement policies (see especially Chapter Two).

As Horváth and Kovai point out, it was the content of socialist policies that played a part in creating this logic of relations. The socialist state understood G*psyness as a category of cultural backwardness and social deviation, and held out to the Roma themselves the false promise that if they consistently "silenced their G*psyness", they would be fully included alongside their non-Romani neighbours (Horváth 2012). Similarly, Sokolová pointed out that within the context of socialist Czechoslovakia, the person "who counted as a 'G*psy' in the eyes of the state had very little to do with supposedly 'real' ethnicity, since it was more a case of being situated within officially sanctioned categories of the proper and improper, the normal and deviant, and integrated and non-integrated" (Sokolová 2008, 43). The illusion of the promise held out of full belonging to non-Romani society to which Kovai and Horváth refer rested on a historically anchored racial discourse that persisted in society and that cast the Roma in an inferior position regardless of their socio-economic status and dominantly understood degree of inclusion in socialist society. While the central authorities spoke of an ethnically and racially neutral policy and associated the category of G*psyness with cultural backwardness and social deviance, racial assumptions about G*psies continued to enter into the way that central policies were formulated on the one hand, while playing their part in who was ultimately labelled a G*psy in the way they were implemented on the other.

In a similar fashion, the ambiguous delineation of the target group of such policies provided relatively generous room for manoeuvre for individual actors at the local level. The negotiation of the category of G*psyness among the Roma themselves, and its reflection on the part of the local authorities, is of particular interest to the present study because it may have co-determined in individual cases not only who would be affected and in what way, but also, perhaps, who would be in a position to benefit and who would not. For this reason, too, it would be highly misleading to look at resettlement policies in particular, but also at policies directed towards the G*psy population in general, exclusively in relation to a separate narrative of "Romani history", or, from the other side, "policies toward the Roma". In order to capture the dynamic of the negotiation of the positions of individual actors and their relations (i.e. the relations of dominance and marginalisation), it is far more accurate and useful to think of resettlement policy as a central measure that was the outcome of certain historically contingent (and even regionally embedded) processes, a measure that did not necessarily affect only the Roma in its implementation, but entered into locally negotiated relations in a specific way, where its more ambiguous practice (i.e. the more ambiguous delineation of the target group) was decided, and where it had the potential for the comprehensive transformation of entire local socio-economic systems.

1.1.4 The social position and identity of the Roma in Central Europe

In his classic ethnography of the Roma in socialist Hungary, the anthropologist Michael Stewart shows that the Roma in the village he studied benefited from socialist policies as employees of the local factory. They also "laundered" the money earned through *gadje* work by means of the economic practice of "Romani" work (*Romani butji*), which was part of the symbolic formation of Romani cultural identity face-to-face with a dominant non-Romani world (Stewart 1997). However, this mode of existence in the non-Romani world that Stewart described for the cultural conservative group of "Lovara" (i.e. Vlax Roma) cannot be smoothly transferred to the majority Romani population in eastern Slovakia, where the cultural boundaries between the Roma and their non-Romani neighbours were not nearly as sharp, and where the Roma emphasised their own belonging to the region and participation in the local way of life (see Ort 2022b).[8]

In order to support a position from which it is not necessary to understand the attachment to the dominant orders exclusively as their camouflaged subversion, I will discuss the understanding of identity and the social position of the Roma in central Europe in more detail. As I have argued elsewhere (Ort 2022a), in this respect the work of the Romani studies scholars Elena Marushiakova and Vesselin Popov is fundamental. These authors view Romani identity in general through the concepts of *community* and *society*, as two interrelated dimensions of social position. In addition to attributing a distinct ethnic identity to the Roma, Marushiakova and Popov argue that the Roma in central and eastern Europe have formed an "integral part of the relevant civic nations with their related national identities" (2020, 42). This dual nature of Romani identity has been examined in greater detail by the Greek anthropologist Aspasia Theodosiou with regard to the role of the category of place in the (self-)identification of the Roma (2004). Theodosiou argues that the category of place is usually overlooked in ethnographic texts on Romani sociability, on the one hand because of an assumed Romani nomadism, and on the other with an emphasis on the locally independent "imagined communities" (Anderson 1983). When anthropologists moved away from explaining distinctive Romani culture through a different place of origin and shifted the emphasis to everyday interaction with the non-Romani world (see Stewart 2013), Theodosiou claims they paradoxically turned *place* into a mere backdrop for these interactions and an "invisible category of analysis" (2004). Drawing on her research on the Greek-Albanian border, Theodosiou shows that place played a key role

---

8   In this respect, the differences cannot be understood regionally, but rather in terms of the internal cultural differentiation of the Roma themselves. As I have already mentioned, a very similar dynamic of relations to that I observed among the Roma in eastern Slovakia has been described for the Hungarian community by Horváth and Kovai (Horváth 2012; Kovai 2012). Apropos the controversy surrounding the different conception of "G*psy labour" among the Roma in Hungary, see Horváth (2005). Regarding the Vlax Roma in eastern Slovakia and their economic strategies, see Hajská (2015, 2017, 2024).

in the self-identification of the local Roma, who were at the same time understood to be an integral part thereof. Theodosiou regards the village being studied as a "doubly occupied place" (Stewart 1996), of which the relationship between the Roma and non-Roma (or *Yifty* and "Greeks") was an inherent part and in which difference was not something that came necessarily from *outside*, but which also grows *within* (Theodosiou 2004, 38). Theodosiou acknowledges that the position of the Roma was asymmetrical in this respect given their association with the exclusionary category of G*psyness discussed above. And so according to her, the Roma were perceived as "local, but not indigenous" (ibid.). I have already developed in detail this complex view of Romani identity, in which the Roma are understood as a natural part of the local socio-economic systems (see also Olivera 2012), in respect of the situation of the Roma in a small village in northeastern Slovakia (Ort 2022b), but I shall work with it in this book. I believe that it is this approach, which takes into account the various forms and levels of the social belonging of the Roma, that allows us to leave behind ideas of the Roma as a clearly circumscribed marginalised group of social outsiders.

An understanding of Romani identity as firmly anchored in local systems seems all the more relevant here since this book focuses on the period of socialism. According to Marushiakova and Popov, it is precisely this period of socio-economic development that is a key factor in the degree to which the Roma are integrated into the societies of central and eastern Europe (Marushiakova and Popov 2020). As I showed in my research in eastern Slovakia, it was the Roma themselves who tended to view the period of socialism as the high point of their own social participation and upward social mobility: the arrival of capitalism, on the contrary, was associated with a decline in their socio-economic status (for similar recollections see Kramářová et al. 2005; Sidiropolu Janků 2015). However, I am not trying to create an impression of total compliance with socialist policies on the part of the Roma or ignore specific areas of resistance and subversion. Instead, I wish to move beyond the binary oppositions referred to above and open up a wider field within which dynamic forms of Romani agency can be traced that can also, perhaps, be understood as "experimental consent" as described by High (2008, but also 2005), into which the Roma projected their hopes and expectations, and whose policies they attempted to incorporate into their own economic strategies and broader strategies of sociability. At the same time, just as High did not resort to defending resettlement programmes in Laos, so it is not my aim to offer a reassessment of the Czechoslovak

state's resettlement policy, which is regarded by the dominant historical narrative as one of the symbols of the communist regime's violence
against the Roma. In fact, my aim is not to evaluate this policy at all,
but, on the contrary, to disentangle it from the necessity of evaluative
positions that are usually attached to the study of socialist policy towards
the Roma in general, as recently remarked upon by Marushiakova
and Popov (2020).

1.1.5 Anthropology, history and studies of agency

The authors mentioned so far are united by the fact that all were anchored to some extent in the discipline of anthropology, and some of them
have cited ethnographic research as a key to grasping the complexity of
the relations under consideration and the agential creativity of specific
people (see Abu-Lughod 1990; Brazzabeni et al. 2015; Das and Poole
2004). In the case of historical research, it is easy to draw on precisely
those historical trends inspired by anthropology. It is no coincidence
that representatives of these very tendencies have placed individuals as
important historical agents at the core of their interest. This "return of
the actor to history" (Horský 2014) represented a response to developments in historical research since the early twentieth century that were
moving away from the "great man theory of history" (van Dülmen 2000)
in favour of tracking social structures that implied collective actors defined by shared socio-economic status. The problem with such an approach, which established itself under the title "history of mentalities",
resided in the homogenisation of the actors thus defined and the false
autonomy of the collective mentalities under consideration (Burke 1997).
In the newly conceived emphasis on the individual, a balanced view of
the relationship between actor and structure was to ensue simultaneously
in the wake of the anthropological and sociological discussion in which
this false opposition had been reconciled, most notably by Anthony Giddens (1979) and Pierre Bourdieu (e.g. 1977, 1990). For these authors,
while the individual's agency was to some extent conditioned by structure, it was each individual actor who co-created such a structure and,
moreover, possessed the capacity to reshape it.

One of the important authors who moved away from determining collective mentalities and emphasised diversity of experience, attitude and
action among individual actors was the Italian historian Carlo Ginzburg,
who back in the mid-1960s had already applied such an approach to the

study of Italian popular culture (1983 [1965]). He went still further in his classic text *The Cheese and the Worms*, in which he reconstructed the thought world of the heretical miller in 16th-century Italy (1980 [1976]). Ginzburg's microhistorical approach (see below) was taken up by representatives of the German school of historical anthropology, as exemplified in the classic text by Hans Medick (1987) entitled "'Missionaries in the Rowboat'? Ethnological Ways of Knowing as a Challenge to Social History". Medick reiterates that in light of the prevailing preoccupation with structure, attention needs to be turned to the actions of specific actors and the role of culture needs to be taken into account, not as an isolated autonomous entity, but in its dynamic relational form. It is here that Medick sees the advantage of historians being inspired by the discipline of anthropology, which, he argues, cultivates a sensitivity to peripheral themes and to alterity in general. A focus on the position of individuals from marginalised social groups has, according to Medick, been noticeably absent from histories of European modernisation and industrialisation. However, he also points out that it is not possible to slip into understanding these individuals as victims, but as actors in their own right, cultivating their own creative forms of resistance. This emphasis can also be found in the approach that has in German scholarship become known as *Alltagsgeschichte* or the history of everyday life. Its adherents originally focused on the period of the German Third Reich. They shifted their attention away from the Nazi leaders to ordinary people, whose everyday actions they saw as key to understanding the acquisition and exercise of Nazi power (Lüdtke 1995). They, too, focused on the lives of those who have "remained largely anonymous in history" (ibid., 4). However, they did not look at their actions and experiences in isolation, but regarded them as being inseparable from the context of their emergence and impact (ibid.).

Methodologically, these historiographic trends converge in the microhistorical approach, which can be characterised to some extent by a reduction in the scale of enquiry in order to discover otherwise hidden aspects of social relations. And so the primary object of research in the microhistorical approach may be the individual (as in the case of Ginzburg's miller Minocchio), family or, typically, the village. Returning to the initial discussion of research into Romani agency in socialist Czechoslovakia, it is not surprising that the historical studies thus defined (i.e. of specific villages or families), have led to the depiction of complex forms of Romani agency, even though their authors do not necessarily openly subscribe to microhistory or do not reflect upon its approach more closely (see Grill 2015a,b; Hajská 2020, 2022, 2024; Sadílková 2017, 2020). At the same time, however, the microhistorical approach suggests that the objects of study so defined cannot be seen as fixed, but understood as changing over time and space within the context of broader social and cultural developments (Levi 2001).

Advocates of microhistory and the history of the everyday have faced questions concerning the explanatory value of such scaled-down studies. Is not a focus on the everyday a romanticising view of history, an approach that clings to detail and is unable to contribute to an understanding of overarching historical processes (see Lüdtke 1995)? As regards my book, which also relies primarily on studies of specific Romani families and locations, the answer to such questions can be summarised as follows (see also Levi 2001): it is by means of a microhistorical approach and engagement with the discipline of anthropology that it becomes possible to trace various forms of Romani agency that are otherwise either homogenised or completely overlooked. In this respect, the emphasis on Romani agency is not merely a discursive game aimed at combating the stereotypical image of the Roma as historical victims or passive recipients of state policies. Just as Medick argues that if we fail to include the experience of members of marginalised groups, the image of industrialisation and modernisation is incomplete (see above), so it can be argued that without including the experience and agency of the Roma as a distinct and highly marginalised minority, the image of the functioning of socialist society as a whole remains incomplete. At the same time, as Giovanni Levi argues in his advocacy of microhistory (2001), the reduction of scale in the microhistorical approach does not imply a clear delineation of an isolated research area, but rather the establishment of a starting point of analysis from which to trace specific social phenomena, which is itself an inseparable part of the broader socio-economic and political contexts. In this respect, proponents of the microhistorical approach agree with the American anthropologist Clifford Geertz and his assertion that "anthropologists do not study villages, they study *in* villages" (Geertz 1973, 22; italics original). Thus, by focusing on the *village* (individual, family, etc.), according to Levi the microhistorical approach does not ignore the complexity of the networks of actors and relations of which the "village" is a part. On the contrary, the reduction of scale makes it possible to trace the contradictoriness of these relations and to capture better the possibilities and limits of the autonomous actions of individuals (Levi 2001).

1.1.6 The question of representativeness

When High turned her attention from the oppressive nature of resettlement policies in Laos to the social mobility strategies of poor villagers (High 2008), her critics pointed out that she chose overly specific examples that did not reflect the experience of the majority of those resettled (Braid et al. 2009). I confess that I faced a similar dilemma during the course of my research. As much as I knew that a comprehensive assessment of resettlement policy was not the aim of my research, I nevertheless felt it necessary to focus on those villages where resettlement policy had impacted significantly the local socio-economic relationships and lives of the Roma themselves. The effort to find a village where the implementation of resettlement policy represented a significant turning point in the life of the Romani community as a whole eventually led me outside the Humenné district, whose regional boundaries had originally circumscribed my research interest. I found myself in the village of Kapišová (in the district of Svidník, formerly Bardejov), regarding which I had heard from people in the region during my previous research in the Svidník district that as part of resettlement policy the local Roma had been loaded onto a bus with their musical instruments and taken to Czechia, and that as they were leaving, a bulldozer arrived and razed their shacks to the ground. As my research continued, it became clear that the situation in Kapišová was far more complicated and by no means fitted the description of a one-off mass transfer of the entire local Romani community to Czechia (see the Introduction). Although I eventually came into possession of relatively unique archive materials relating to the complete resettlement of the Roma from village of Šemetkovce (coincidentally neighbouring Kapišová, see Chapter Four), my experience bore out the claims made by Levi for the microhistorical approach in respect of representativeness. According to Levi, there are no "typical examples" and it is difficult to generalise, because the general is always made up exclusively of uniqueness and the very distinction between the general and the particular is therefore baseless (Levi 2001). Hence, the concept of the "normal exception" is used in microhistorical writing (see, for example, Magnússon 2020, 27–29). Moreover, as I have already argued, the microhistorical approach, by its very nature, deliberately targets marginal cases, and it is from this perspective that dominant narratives are examined and revised. High made a similar argument in her response to critics, reminding them that no case study is sufficiently typical, and that her study served not to create a representative picture of resettlement policies, but to highlight new perspectives from which to read the implementation thereof (High 2009).

I confess to adopting such an approach in this book, since I am not interested in a comprehensive assessment of the impact of the events under examination on the lives of the Roma in socialist Czechoslovakia. On the other hand, the implementation of the resettlement programme has up till now been subject only to limited examination in specialist literature. Although I have shown that an understanding of it is strongly anchored within the interpretative framework of the oppressive nature of the communist regime and the Roma as its victims, I hesitate to proceed directly to an examination of the dominant narrative without a broader, more descriptive, mapping of the specific practice. At this juncture I would like to return to a point I made in the introduction to this chapter regarding the book by Shmidt and Jaworsky. It is certainly beneficial to open up new approaches and to critically examine existing narratives within the context of the study of Romani history. However, the problem with the history of the Roma in the territory under examination and elsewhere is that there are still very few historical studies that have focused on the experiences and life trajectories of the Roma themselves, and many of the more theoretical studies lack a similar empirical grounding. I believe that this is one of the important dilemmas that faces anyone writing about Romani history: on the one hand, how to write about Romani history and not slip into a positivist "filling in the blank spaces" without any ambition to answer more general questions; and, on the other, how not to give up on a more descriptive approach to Romani history (as the history of heterogeneous Romani experiences), interest in which has long been neglected in the broader societal and more specifically academic environment.

Although I believe that the idea that one could comprehensively map a selected social phenomenon (in this case the implementation of the resettlement programme in socialist Czechoslovakia) is delusional, in the following chapters I will not focus on the life trajectories and strategies of the Roma from one particular municipality, but on the situation pertaining in several locations in eastern Slovakia, especially in the former districts of Humenné and Bardejov. Following the movement of individual families from these villages, I will then focus on different places in Czechia. Spreading my interest amongst multiple individuals, families, municipalities, districts, and both regions of what was at that time a single state will, on the one hand, allow me to present a more flexible picture of the disparate elements of the implementation of the policy under examination, and, on the other, will allow me to highlight the heterogeneity of the Romani experience already alluded to several times in this chapter.

1.2 Methods

A common feature of microhistory is the paradoxical situation whereby researchers are often directed to official written records that depict the actions and ways of existence of those marginalised individuals and population groups under consideration as forms of social deviance (e.g. Magnússon 2020). A good example of this is the classic work *The Cheese and the Worms*, already referred to, in which Ginzburg reconstructs the thought world of a heretical Italian miller on the basis of Inquisition records. Returning to the start of this chapter, a similar paradox is to be found in one of Scott's important arguments regarding social engineering policies. Scott shows that one of the characteristics of the functioning of the modern state is the attempt to exert control over not only its own population, but also the physical space of its own territory. It was this that gave rise, for example, to the allocation of surnames, the numbering of buildings, the parcelling of land, the settlement of inhabitants, the regular and transparent urban architecture, and so on. Scott argues convincingly that such efforts to render population and territory legible are not merely descriptive, but actively participate in the process of their homogenisation, thereby undermining diversity as a fundamental building block of the functioning not only of society, but also of the entire environment to which it is attached (Scott 1998). The key point here, however, is that such descriptions did not only render the population legible to state officials, but can be retrospectively utilised by historians, who are able to draw on them in the form of written sources stored in state institutions. In the context of Romani studies, Adéle Sutre points to a similar paradox, albeit from a different perspective, in her microhistorical study of an extended Romani family that exhibited extreme transnational (and transcontinental) mobility in the early 20th century (2014). Sutre argues that the wealth of materials she was able to draw on when charting the movements of said family was derived from the "specific regime of visibility" that made the family stand out, whether this was due to mobility and the controls placed on it, or the family's eccentric style of dress. Hübschmannová makes a similar argument in relation to wider research interest in the Roma, concluding that unless the Roma stood out and met the dominant requirements of normality, they were not considered Roma for research purposes (Hübschmannová 1995).

The Roma in post-war Czechoslovakia were also becoming more visible thanks to significant migratory activity that kept the authorities busy on both the central and local levels. The archive materials recording efforts to control a socially non-conforming population contain at least two pitfalls. Firstly, they capture only a relatively narrow segment of Romani life in post-war Czechoslovakia. And secondly, they view the Roma from outside, and can therefore only to a limited extent convey their agency. On the other hand, some of the archival material was generated by the Roma themselves, and I work with many of these texts in this book. At the same time I try to achieve a critically and ethnographically informed reading of these materials (see Tauber and Trevisan 2019) by combining them with other types of sources, mainly oral history interviews.

1.2.1 Oral history

The oral history method began to establish a place for itself in response to the limitations of written archival materials in the early 1970s at the latest, when it gradually chiselled away at the hitherto undisputed status of written sources in historical research (see, for example, Portelli 1991, Prins 2001). As in the case of microhistory, oral history as a method focuses on marginalised groups of the population that tend to be filtered out of the grand historical narratives, while also emphasising the diversity of individual experiences and attitudes. At the same time, proponents of oral history have questioned the supposed objectivity of written sources and pointed to the necessity of taking into account the context within which they were created and of reflecting more deeply on the actual situation of research in archives (e.g. Dirks 2002). This is in response to ongoing and sometimes harsh accusations regarding the unreliability and lack of scientific rigour and subjectivity of oral sources on the part of "classical" historians (e.g. Prins 2001). The aim of this subsection is not so much to defend oral history as compared to dominant written sources. This topic has been addressed by others (e.g. Portelli 1991, Prins 2001). Moreover, within the Czech context, oral history has a relatively strong tradition and enjoys a relatively high degree of institutionalisation (see, for example, Mücke 2013, Vaněk 2019, 2022, Vaněk and Mücke 2016). However, I will select certain points from the discussion referred to and relate them to my own research – in which I relied on oral and written sources simultaneously – and more generally to the study of the post-war history of the Roma in Czechoslovakia and elsewhere.

Here, I draw heavily on Sadílková, who in her dissertation mapped out in detail the historiographic approaches to the post-war migration of the Roma from Slovakia to Czechia, and who also drew on a combination of written and oral sources in a detailed case study with a similar thematic focus (2016). Sadílková shows that both approaches had until that time almost always been used separately when studying the history of the Roma in Czechoslovakia. The pitfalls of using written sources, which spoke more about how the Roma were perceived by the various authorities than about their own lives and perspectives, have been most strongly articulated by Hübschmannová (1995). As Sadílková (2016) points out, in Hübschmannová's case, oral history emerged as part of her own ethnographic research, the method she drew on when analysing the position of the Roma in the dominant society of pre-war Slovakia (see, for example, Hübschmannová 1998, 2000b) and, along with her students, the fate of the Roma during the Second World War in the same territory (especially Hübschmannová 2005). As regards the post-war period, however, an emphasis on written materials, and thus the state perspective, has long predominated, both in texts aiming to map the history of the Roma (especially Jurová 1993, Pavelčíková 2004), and in work with broader thematic ambitions (Spurný 2011, 2016, also see Sadílková 2013). However, authors who have attempted to grasp the narrative of Romani history in a new way have also drawn almost exclusively on archive materials, be this Věra Sokolová, who mapped the continuities and discontinuities of the discourse on the G*psies in socialist Czechoslovakia (Sokolová 2008), or Donert with her emphasis on the role of the Roma in negotiating centralised policies targeting minorities (Donert 2017, though she includes interviews with several contemporary actors in her sources as an aside). In contrast, as Sadílková discusses in detail, an oral history approach to the post-war history of the Roma in Czechoslovakia featured strongly in the student dissertations of the department of Romani Studies founded by Hübschmannová at the Faculty of Arts of Charles University in Prague. However, these papers either completely omit, or make only marginal use of, written archive materials (see Sadílková 2016, 90–101).[9] The post-war period is touched upon in two other publications

---

9   Sadílková refers to works by Cichý (2003), Houdek (2008), Šebová (2006) and Růžičková (2012). Meanwhile, work by Mižigár (2016) and Hlaváčová (2016) was defended under Sadílková's supervision. The authors of all of these texts aim to write a regionally defined

based exclusively on oral history interviews (Kramářová et al. 2005, Sidiropolu Janků 2015). In this regard, Sadílková warns of the need to link these two approaches (though see Serinek et al. 2016), and calls for a dialogue with the discipline of anthropology I have already discussed here (for the Czechoslovak context see, for example, Hajská 2020, 2022, 2024; Ort 2022b; Sadílková 2016, 2017, 2020; Sadílková and Závodská 2021). I should point out that, though this is a relatively recent trend in the historiography of the Roma in Czechoslovakia, it is not new within the context of the wider debate on the use of oral sources. For instance, one of the pioneers of the oral history method, the Belgian historian and anthropologist Jan Vansina, emphasised as early as 1985 that oral history was not merely a supplementary method in cases where archival materials were insufficient, but that "[oral sources] correct and complete other sources, just as much as other perspectives correct it" (Vansina 1985, 199; as cited in Prins 2001, 122). Moreover, as Portelli has pointed out, the very distinction between oral and written sources is partly misleading, since written sources very often have oral origins, and oral sources are processed into written form by researchers, whether in transcripts of recorded interviews, field notes, or in published texts (Portelli 1991).

1.2.2.Research into the practice of the resettlement policy

Dirks's call for anthropological reflection upon the position of the researcher inclines me to examine the circumstances of my own research. This will also allow me to elaborate more precisely on some aspects of the combination of the two types of sources. My research began while I was studying for my master's degree in Romani studies, when Helena Sadílková, Romana Hudousková and I were mapping a post-war history of the Roma focusing on the situation on Prague. My colleagues and I opted for biographical interviews with several period witnesses (all but one of whom were women), whose narratives were then placed within a broader historical context (Hudousková et al. [unpublished]). During the

---

history of Romani families, with an emphasis on their arrival in Czechia from Slovakia after the Second World War. At the same time, it should be noted that their work with archive materials varies considerably, with some authors neglecting them and others reporting low success rates when searching for relevant materials in local archives. Some of the authors work with archival materials but without any ambition to conduct a deeper dialogue with oral sources.

course of finalising the project, I had already spent some time in eastern Slovakia, where I conducted my ethnographic research (see Ort 2022b). We decided to take advantage of this and pursue additional research in those villages from which the families of those interviewed came to Prague after the war. And so in the spring of 2015, I visited Ľubiša and Dlhé nad Cirochou, two villages in the district of Humenné, where I recorded interviews with both Romani and non-Romani residents and perused the local municipal chronicle. In addition, I visited the district archive in Humenné, which was my first experience visiting an institutional archive. As I slogged through the archives, finding only fragments of the minutes taken during meetings of the Municipal National Committees (MNV) or school reports, the director of the Archive came to ask if I would be interested in boxes containing materials pertaining to the "liquidation of G*psy shacks" (*likvidácia c*gánskych chatrčí*) in the fonds of the District National Committee (ONV) in Humenné. There was a total of three boxes containing detailed documentation of the purchase and demolition of individual dwellings, including how new housing was provided, either within the region or by relocating the families concerned to Czechia. Though it initially looked like I would spend barely a day in the archive, subsequent to this find I returned for a full week in order to photograph the materials in their entirety. The documents had not yet been properly organised and indexed and were provided to me on the personal initiative of the archive director. When I requested the same materials six years later in order to verify the content of some poorly photographed pages, I was denied access by another member of the staff on the grounds that the materials were still being processed. Although the temporal contingency of collected data is usually associated with the oral history method (see Portelli 1991), my experience has taught me that archival research also has an important temporal dimension, not to speak of the haphazard and unpredictable ways in which written sources are or are not archived and preserved (Dirks 2002). This was by no means an isolated experience during the course of my research. When I attempted to track down archival materials relating to the functioning of the G*psy Commission at the District National Committee (ONV) in Přerov, where according to the official schedule, Roma from the village of Kapišová (see Introduction) were to be resettled, I was informed by a member of staff that the materials in question had been completely destroyed in the floods of 1997. However, the overriding problem of the temporal contingency of the data obtained became apparent when I attempted to record interviews with contemporary witnesses more systematically.

In my original research project, I set out to record interviews with both the Roma and their then non-Romani neighbours in the villages in question. Ideally, I wanted to record the narratives of state officials or local councillors, who had been important actors in the implementation of the centrally formulated policy. I soon discovered that there were very few witnesses who would have been of a more advanced age in the mid-1960s and might therefore have taken an active role in shaping individual or family life strategies. Those who might have held office in state institutions were untraceable. This is one of the reasons why I had to rely more heavily than I had originally planned on archival research or on interviews with witnesses who were often still children during the period under study or who had only a passing knowledge of family histories from the period in question.

On the other hand, I saw with my own eyes that the Roma also created many written sources (Marushiakova and Popov 2021; Sadílková et al. 2018, 2024). These sources, which included various types of requests and applications, represent an important insight into the life trajectories and attitudes of individual Roma and Romani families, even though they remain within the confines of official communications and thus represent only a certain segment of Romani agency. Both in terms of expanding the source base and understanding the relationship of the Roma to their own past and ethnic identity, it was hugely enriching for me to meet local Roma who themselves were actively and systematically seeking to enshrine the history of the Roma within their own community. This was how I came into contact with Koloman Gunár, who has written a study of the history of the Roma in village of Brekov based on interviews with contemporary witnesses (see Chapter Two). His daughter, Elena Cinová, continued his work with more ethnographic interviews (Cinová et al. 2024). She also collaborated closely with Peter Kudráč, who mapped the history of the Roma in the Podskalka settlement near the town of Humenné (see Chapter Three). Kudráč also recorded interviews with contemporary witnesses, and in addition had previously collected several archival documents from local Roma, especially photographs, using which he and Cinová created a public exhibition at the cultural centre in Podskalka.

1.2.3 Oral history and collaborative research

Brekov and Podskalka were two of the locations where the implementation of the resettlement programme and migration to Czechia in general involved only some Romani families and where a significant number of Roma were still living when I was conducting my research (Podskal-ka remained an exclusively Romani housing estate administered by the Humenné municipal authorities). However, there were no longer any Roma living in some of the other villages, precisely as a consequence of their relocation to Czechia. In these cases I focused on archival research for the Slovak segment of my work, recording several interviews with non-Romani witnesses from the villages in question. I then supplemen-ted this work with research in the relevant districts and municipalities in Czechia, where, in addition to visiting archives, I tried to track down surviving witnesses of the resettlement policy. Among other things, I tracked down Romani witnesses from Papín, a village in Slovakia, from which the entire Romani population decamped at the end of the 1960s (see Chapter Four). In autumn 2021 I recorded the stories of two sisters, Monika H (born 1971) and Marcela S (born 1977),[10] whose father grew up in Papín, as well as an interview with Pavlína B (1948),[11] who well remembered leaving her native Papín.

Before meeting these three women, I had been attempting to recon-struct the story of the Roma of Papín by searching in regional archives in Slovakia, which personally I found to be quite exciting detective work. I interviewed an elderly non-Romani villager Ján Ž (born 1946) in Papín itself,[12] who provided me with valuable information and insights into local relations. However, his narrative irritated me with its overly pater-nalistic, at times even dehumanising retrospective view of the Roma of Papín, along with occasional racist remarks regarding Romani people in general. Despite being aware of the importance of oral history, having previously immersed myself in archival materials, I was more than ever struck by how the interviews with the Romani women opened up a whole new perspective, not only with regard to this particular case study, but in relation to my research as a whole. The interviews were replete with ambiguities and internal contradictions, and in some places the accounts given were at odds with what I had learned from other sources. Above all, however, my witnesses managed to convey to me the "freshness and

---

10 Interviews with Romani women Monika H (b. 1971) and Marcela S (b. 1977), recorded by the author in September 2021 and February 2022 in Horní Podluží in Czech (recordings in possession of the author).
11 Interview with Romani woman Pavlína B (b. 1948), recorded by the author in September 2021 in Březno in Romani and Czech (recording in possession of the author).
12 Interview with non-Romani man Ján Ž (b. 1946), recorded by the author in July 2021 in Papín in Slovak (recording in possession of the author).

richness of detail" of everyday life (Prins 2001, 139) as it related to life in Slovakia and later in Czechia. The strong contrast with my previous reading of archive materials concerning the village reinforced feelings I experienced during interviews with other Romani (and non-Romani) people both before and after, namely, that the radical dimension of oral history resides in the historian's involvement in the whole story and their participation in the actual production of data (Portelli 1991). I was acutely aware of this during interviews in which Romani witnesses agreed to go on record in Romani.[13]

Papín is a good starting point for illustrating how I worked with different types of sources. Even during my interview with a non-Romani villager, and during later interviews with female witnesses from amongst the original Roma of Papín, I already had relatively detailed archival materials at my disposal relating, inter alia, to the history of the relocation of the Romani settlement within the territory of the village itself, as well as the later resettlement of its inhabitants to Czechia. To begin with I did not interrupt their narratives except to pose questions. Gradually I revealed information I had previously acquired, both in order to stimulate further recollections, as well as to initiate a discussion regarding certain contradictions opening up between archival sources and their own memories. For example, Ján Ž, a non-Romani villager born in 1946, had no idea that up until Second World War, Romani people had lived in the very heart of the built-up parts of Papín, before being evicted about two kilometres from the village – to what Ján himself had always considered the natural location of the Romani settlement – under the terms of a 1941 decree (see Jurová 2002, 27). And according to archival materials, in the 1950s and early 1960s, there was still communication taking place between the ONV in Humenné, which was pressing for the relocation of the Roma back to the village, and the MNV in Papín, which steadfastly resisted such a move (see Chapter Three). In my opinion this example illustrates some of the specific features and benefits of oral history, rather than its limits. This interview, during which Ján Ž was able to provide a fairly detailed description of specific Roma who

---

13 This was an option I offered to everyone, though many were no longer active speakers of Romani or did not feel comfortable. It is via this oft overlooked linguistic level that I nail my colours to the mast of the Prague school of Romani studies, since it was the founder, Hübschmannová, who placed a fundamental emphasis on a knowledge of Romani in her research among the Roma and who, in her oral history interviews, monitored a certain linguistic level, i.e. how specific historical events and processes were understood and named by the Roma themselves (see, for example, Hübschmannová 1993, 1995, 1999a).

lived in Papín, suggests that the notion of a Romani presence in the village before the Second World War had essentially disappeared from local memory altogether.

Remaining in Papín, two differing descriptions of the Romani settlement at that time serve as an example of the need to take into account the context of the sources studied and the differing perspectives of witness accounts. Ján Ž described the settlement as follows:

> The Roma used to live here, in little huts nailed together, as they live everywhere [in eastern Slovakia]. They lived between Nižná Jablonka and Papín. That's a village about five kilometres away. About halfway along there's an inlet by the river that runs through, and that's where they used to live, in those huts. But how many of them, I can't say. Twenty maybe, but there were just six or seven of those huts. But as I say, they were just little huts nailed together.[14]

His austere description of the settlement, with its "little huts nailed together", contrasts strongly with the colourful recollections and descriptions of his contemporary Pavlína B:

> There was a beautiful river. I'm forever telling them [her children] that I'd love to see that river, seriously. Young boys, fifteen, sixteen, seventeen, used to go swimming there. There was a kind of waterfall, fish used to jump out of the water and they went swimming there. The girls, for instance, used to go in dresses, they had these flimsy dresses, and the boys had red boxer shorts [laughs], so they went swimming. They used to have campfires in the summer, I remember that as though it were yesterday. It was like a meadow, there were shacks in rows on both sides.[15]

In the second part of the interview, I showed Pavlína B a photograph of a dilapidated building from the Papín settlement taken from the ONV archive in Humenné. It turned out to be the house in which Pavlína B grew up, which in turn encouraged her to reminisce further.

> They [the Slovaks] treated my mum very differently. And we had a really nice house. She [mum] kept chickens, geese and sheep. I often wondered why she had sheep, and then it occurred to me that a guy, a Slovak, used to come and

---

14   Interview with Ján Ž (b. 1946), *op. cit.*
15   Interview with Pavlína B (b. 1948), *op. cit.*

shear the sheep and pay my mum money. [...] We had a large garden at the back. On the other side we had a garden too, we had cherry trees and by the well my mother grew vegetables, carrots and parsley. It was always Mehur [a non-Romani villager?] who came scrumping. But my mum said "I'll give you some" and then we used to visit him for stories.[16]

The difference between these two accounts, which is not only a matter of how the settlement is described but also the wealth of detail offered and the narrator's involvement, is largely due to the fact that while Pavlína B grew up in the settlement as a Romani woman, Ján Ž approached it as an outsider who had grown up in the village itself. However, the context in which both statements were made cannot be discounted. While Ján Ž drew on a stereotypical image of Romani life in the settlements of eastern Slovakia ("little huts nailed together, as they live everywhere"), Pavlína B made no effort to conceal the nostalgia she felt for her childhood in the settlement (and in Slovakia more generally), and repeatedly expressed a desire to pay the place a visit (see Sadílková 2016, 153–160). Her recollections were enhanced by a photograph of the very house she had grown up in, a good example of how some archival materials can prompt further recollections in interviews with contemporary witnesses.

If an emphasis is to be laid on the context of the sources under consideration, then an important framework for the oral history interviews is the way the Roma relate to the period of communism, an era remembered with fondness by those I spoke to. Having examined this dimension within the context of the relationship between the Roma and the state (see above), here I would like to focus on its relevance to the oral history method. These positive memories of the communist period are interesting in this respect, especially when set against the long dominant historical narrative in which the communist regime is associated above all with the dire effects of the assimilation policy on Romani identity and socio-cultural structures. Sadílková (2016, e.g. 99) has previously drawn attention to this contradiction. This might be a good point to introduce at least two further aspects relating to broader discussions pertaining to the utilisation of oral history. Oral history sometimes faces similar criticisms to the entire microhistorical approach, namely, that in its focus on detail and the lived experience of the individual it is unable to contribute to an understanding of broader historical processes (see

---

16   Ibid.

Prins 2001). Interviews with Romani witnesses show that without oral history the image evoked of such processes can be very incomplete or one-sided. As Sadílková points out, oral history can be used not only as a source for "mapping the local history of a certain (minority) group and capturing their view of their own past, but as a possible source for the local (re)contextualisation of dominant historical interpretative narratives" (Sadílková 2016, 99). In this respect, the oral history method corresponds well to the "from the margins" approach already discussed.

The second aspect to be looked at concerns how such testimony should be approached. In the discussion referred to above regarding the resettlement of villagers in Laos, critics of High pointed out that, just because the villagers said that they were ok with the state policy did not mean it was true: they may have been saying it within the context of research and in light of the asymmetrical power relationship between the state and its poor citizens (see above). In the case of oral history, this kind of discussion then raises questions regarding the selectivity of human memory and its tendency to idealise the past. Is it then appropriate to read similar accounts by the Roma relating to the communist period as idealised nostalgia?[17] Like the anthropologist Berdahl, who analysed (n)ostalgic recollections of the communist period in East Germany (Berdahl 1999), I believe that such accounts must not be trivialised (see also High's response; 2009), but must be taken seriously as reflections of lived experience. This is experience of both the period of time being recalled and the period during which it is recalled. Indeed, in the interviews I conducted, the Roma themselves often contrast life under communism with the deterioration of their socio-economic position and the decline in social security in the post-revolutionary period (see Ort 2022b). A good example from the studies discussed below would be the situation of the Roma in the Podskalka settlement near Humenné (see Chapter Three). One witness, Elemír T (born 1940), told me how, thanks to the resettlement policy, he, like many other Roma, was able to acquire a much coveted apartment in the town of Humenné.[18] However, after the Velvet Revolution, the apartments were gradually privatised and many Roma, including Elemír T, were evicted for rent default and forced to

---

17 Matěj Spurný poses a similar question in the introduction to his book. However, he does not elaborate on the oral history method, which he uses sparingly, and not at all in the chapter on the Roma (Spurný 2011; see also Sadílková 2013).
18 Interview with Romani man Elemír T (b. 1940), recorded by the author in May 2019 in Podskalka in Romani (recording in the possession of the author).

move back to the settlement. Again, my aim here is not to offer an evaluation of communist policy towards the Roma, but merely to point out certain important dimensions to the understanding of oral history narratives and their context.

1.3 The Ethical Dimension of Research

I have argued, with reference to Portelli, that the radicalism of oral history resides in the way it draws the researcher into the process of shaping the data. However, this is not a purely methodological question, but also an ethical one. In oral history interviews, the researcher enters into a particular situation in which the relationship between interviewer and interviewee is "replaced by the conviction that two people, each bringing a different kind of knowledge to the interview, share equally in a process of discovery" (Yow 1995, 53). Both interested parties enter into such a relationship with different hopes and expectations, which do not end when the interview comes to a close (Halbmayr 2009). In the case of interviews with Romani witnesses, which is my main concern here, the personal investment of the narrators was often evident as they set about tracking the history of their families or locally defined Romani communities. I felt this intensely during meetings in Slovakia with Koloman Gunár, and later with his daughter Elena Cinová, as well as with Peter Kudráč, all of whom had already been working on similar local histories themselves. Upon meeting up, we shared the materials we had collected thus far and compared our findings. For instance, I received from them recordings and transcripts of interviews with people who were no longer alive at the time of my research or did not feel up to another interview. However, I felt a similar personal involvement in many of my interviews with contemporary witnesses in Czechia who had lost ties to their native villages in Slovakia. The sisters Monika H and Marcela S, who themselves had previously been involved in tracking down the obscure history of their family, were very keen to meet. Our first interview lasted all of five hours, during which time, after their introductory words, we perused archive materials and attempted to identify the names of the Roma originally from Papín and the relationships that pertained between them. During our meeting, the sisters would call other living relatives to ask about some of the names and to clear up the nature of relationships and events. They then brainstormed a list of suitable people with whom I could conduct more interviews. Perhaps even more powerful was an experience I had during my interview with Pavlína B, who was born in Papín but had not seen Slovakia since the late 1960s. I got in touch with her via her granddaughter, who attended regular reunions of Romani high school students where she happened to mention that her family came originally from Papín. She quickly arranged a meeting with her grandmother and passed on requests from the family that I bring the materials I had tracked down thus far. When Pavlína B discovered that I had already gathered a lot of information and that I had indeed several times visited her native village in Slovakia, during the course of our conversation she often switched to the role of interviewer in an effort to find out how things were in Papín. Slightly confused by the entire situation, she even on occasion turned some of my questions regarding life in the village on me, perhaps under the impression that I was more qualified to answer them. Above all, she repeatedly expressed a wish to revisit her native village.

There are at least two things I find important about the atmosphere of such encounters. One is the interest of the Roma, already mentioned, in their own locally embedded history. This challenges both the popular stereotype of the Roma as living purely in the present, as well as ethnographically anchored anthropological concepts according to which Romani identity is formed above all in day-to-day relationships without reference to shared history or specific place (see Gay Y Blasco 1999, 2001; Stewart 1997). Above all, however, these encounters led me to rethink the entire focus of this book. The interest displayed by certain Roma in charting the history of their families and the places they came from led me to reassess the claim made by Geertz. My feeling is that in this book I am not merely observing certain phenomena "in villages", but, together with the participants and partners in my research, I am studying the "villages" themselves (cf. Geertz 1973, 22). Such a conclusion is a partial response to the dilemma I mentioned above between a more interpretive observation of social phenomena and a more descriptive mapping of the still little known history of the Romani people as a history of their experiences, agency, life trajectories and places. My hope is that I have managed both.

2. CHAPTER TWO
Who Counts as a G*psy?

The archive fonds of the Financial Department of the Humenné District National Committee (ONV) pertaining to the removal of the shacks in Romani settlements, the discovery of which sparked my interest in the resettlement policy, consists of nearly one hundred and fifty files, each containing documentation on one house and the family that lived in it. This usually includes a valuation of the property and information regarding the family's occupation and living conditions in their new residence, be this in Slovakia or Czechia. The municipality of Brekov, which is located just a few kilometres from the county seat of Humenné, is dealt with in just one file held on the clearance of Regina D's house.[19] The story of Regina's family as told in this chapter will help in answering the question of who ultimately was affected by the resettlement policy, which in the official language targeted "G*psies" (*C*káni*).

In Brekov I recorded an interview with local Rom Koloman Gunár (born 1948), in which I asked him about the practice of the resettlement programme in the district. He replied that the Roma in Brekov had not been affected. According to him, the circumstances surrounding the case of Regina D were exceptional:

> One family left the village. They had a brick house. The lady raised all the children herself. Her husband was in gaol for shooting a man. They had a fight in the pub and he had an illegal gun at home. He returned home, got the

---

19 ŠOkA Humenné, f. Finanční odbor ONV Humenné, kart. 15, sp. 47, "D. Regina, Brekov" [unprocessed].

gun and shot him. And he was sent to prison. She raised all the children and when he [her husband] was supposed to return home, the other citizens didn't want him here, the majority didn't want him continuing to live here. So they decided to take advantage of the opportunity of the state buying the shack. It was a normal building, but the state demolished it. They [Regina D's family] received twenty thousand and moved to Ostrava [Silesia]. He didn't live for long, maybe four or five years at most. But she couldn't come back here with the children and they had nowhere else to go. A bulldozer had razed it to the ground. That's right, just the one family.[20]

According to this version of events, the resettlement policy was deployed to get rid of a family that the other inhabitants of the village did not want living there because of an event that had taken place around fifteen years previously. Such an interpretation certainly makes sense and illustrates that practice of the central policy was linked to a locally specific and historically shaped hierarchy of relations. I argue here that this case was not simply about an ongoing sanction applied by the village community against a single member (and his family). I show that the resettlement of this family can also be understood within the context of the dominant discourse of that time of G*psies and how this category was negotiated in locally defined communities. In this respect, the resettlement programme was reminiscent of the way in which relations were defined between "respectable/civilised" Roma and those who were deemed criminalised "culturally backward freeloaders" who were unable to conform to social rules. The family under consideration may have represented the embodiment of this dominantly understood category, not only because the father of the family was branded a murderer, but also because he had moved to the village from a different village and was thus seen as "foreign" in a traditionally virilocal environment. The resettlement of this family can thus be seen not only in terms of the attitudes of the "majority", to quote Gunár, but also against the backdrop of the way the local Roma self-identified, in the process actively maintaining the category of locally established (i.e. "respectable") Roma.

Tracing the ways in which relations between the residents of Brekov were shaped can help address the broader question of the elusive

20 Interview with Koloman Gunár (b. 1948), recorded by the author in May 2019 in Brekov in Slovak (recording in the possession of the author).

definition of the target group of the centrally approved policy, as well as its practice. However, before I get into a more detailed description of the historical development of the position of the Roma in the village community of Brekov, I will spend the first part of this chapter analysing the discourse that existed at that time around G*psies, both on the official ideological and demotic level. As authors have pointed out before me, the concept of G*psyness was located on an unclear boundary between the categories of social deviation and cultural backwardness on the one hand, and race on the other (see Donert 2017, Sokolová 2008). My aim is to analyse the ambivalent logic of G*psyness within a local context and thus to highlight not only the ways in which the state categorised its citizens and drew the boundary between normality and deviance, but above all how this logic might have been reflected in the structuring of relations in specific places, relations between the Romani and non-Romani inhabitants and between the Roma themselves.

2.1 Discourse of G*psyness

2.1.1 Official categorisation

In order to implement Resolution No. 502/1965, a new categorisation of G*psies was introduced by the Government Committee based on a person's "adaptability" [přizpůsobivost] within dominant society. The first group was to consist of those who displayed a high degree of social assimilation. This meant that, in addition to regular employment, they already lived outside the "G*psy environment", which was said to reproduce an undesirable way of life. The second group comprised those who, though still part of the "concentrations", displayed an interest in leaving this "unhealthy" environment. The third group was made up of "extremely backward G*psies" who, it was claimed, displayed the most socio-pathological traits and a resistance to "re-education" and social change. Those belonging to the first group were to be offered minimal assistance in eliminating the last traces of their "G*psy way of life". Instead, the resettlement programme was to focus on the second category. Conversely, repressive and coercive measures were to be used against the third, "incorrigible" group. This included children being removed from their families and placed in state care, a measure that was framed as "protecting" them from a socio-pathological environment (see Jurová 2008, 1003–1031).

It is clear that, inasmuch as the communist regime's objective was the integration of Roma into dominant society, its ensuing policies were doomed to fail given that its classification system continued to reproduce the category of the (socio-pathological) G*psy (see Donert 2017, 163–168). It is significant that the classification system referred to above originally included four categories, the first of which (the zero category) included fully assimilated G*psies. However, following a meeting of the Government Committee, this category was quickly abolished since it was seen as irrelevant to the policy of assimilation (see Jurová 2008, 1003–1031, also Guy 1977, 260–264).

The historian Donert shows that, unlike the earlier division of G*psies into settled, semi-settled and nomadic enshrined in the government resolution on Work amongst the G*psy Population of 1958 (see Jurová 2008, 688), the newly introduced classification was to act as a benchmark for the state administration (Donert 2017, 157). It should not be forgotten that this system was to determine who would and would not be included in the resettlement programme. However, as much as the Government Committee assumed that a person's designated "lifestyle" provided relatively objective criteria for the purpose of classification, there remained considerable room for manoeuvre as regards the actions to be taken by the local authorities, where ethnic and racial characteristics continued to play a key role (ibid., 157–158).

Evidence of the ambiguity surrounding the concept of G*psyness is to be found in archival materials from the G*psy Commission fonds of the East Slovak Regional National Committee (KNV) in Košice. This was the body that dealt, inter alia, with the case of Mr V from the district of Košice, who wished to buy a detached house in Pardubice (eastern Bohemia) and move his fourteen-member family into it. In the complaint he submitted, he claimed that the G*psy Commission of the Pardubice ONV (Czechia) "did not want to give its consent to the purchase of the house on the grounds that for this district the transfer of G*psy families from Trebišov [Slovakia] was planned". After hearing the complaint, the chairman of the Commission in Pardubice declared that approval would be granted for the purchase of the house on condition that the acceptance of this family would be "included as part of the transfer" from Trebišov. This demand was rejected by Juraj Špiner, commissioner of the Košice KNV, on the grounds that it was not possible to restrict the transfer of families from Trebišov, and that the person named was a "fully civilised resident and therefore cannot even be registered as a G*psy problem". Špiner also argued that "such G*psies as he

[Mr V] and his children are not covered by the directives issued by the Government Committee".[21]

In this and other cases, Špiner used the term "civilised" in order to *support* the efforts of certain Roma to obtain accommodation in Czechia, even though this was outside the framework of the official plan. However, in other cases the exact same justification, i.e. that a person was "excessively civilised", was cited when *rejecting* their application. Mrs L, for instance, had her application to purchase a property rejected by Špiner, who explained his decision as follows: "I do not consider this to be a G*psy problem, since she [Mrs L] is a fully civilised person and is availing herself shrewdly of her origins."[22] Similarly, two Roma who tried to sell off their newly built detached houses with gardens located in a Romani settlement met with failure. On the one hand, the authorities acknowledged the difficulties surrounding the sale ensuing from the fact that a "white person" would not wish to purchase a house "among G*psies", while a "G*psy citizen" would not have sufficient funds to buy the property. On the other, the Commission of the KNV refused to include these buildings in the "liquidation of G*psy settlements" because the houses in question were worth more than 50,000 crowns and could not be classified as "shacks".[23]

The ambiguity surrounding the concept of G*psyness here resides in the fact that, though specific inhabitants were clearly identified or self-identified as G*psies on the basis of certain criteria (in this case mainly ethnic or racial), other criteria (social and economic) cast doubt on this classification. The KNV, which dealt with the relevant applications and complaints, could, on the one hand, have supported the socio-economic strategies of these individuals, given that they had been removed from the resettlement programme and were thus no longer subject to restrictions on the free movement of the Roma. On the other hand, according to a similar logic, certain individuals were prevented from benefiting in any way from the policy as framed. Some of the cases I have cited are also referenced by Donert, who illustrates the contradictions and tensions referred to by quoting a "tautological" (Donert 2017, 163) statement

---

21 ŠAKE Košice, f. Komisia Vsl. KNV pre cigánske obyvatelstvo, kart. 20, sp. 012/67, "Ján V.", 10 March 1967.
22 ŠAKE Košice, f. Komisia Vsl. KNV pre cigánske obyvatelstvo, kart. 20, sp. 61/68, "L. Irena, vyjádrenie k sťažnosti", 8 March 1968.
23 ŠAKE Košice, f. Komisia Vsl. KNV pre cigánske obyvatelstvo, kart. 20, sp. 88/68, "Žiadosti o vykúpenie rodinných domov", 27 September 1968.

pertaining to the case of Mr V: "We would just like to point out that if all G*psies were like him, we would have to deal with the problem of other people and not that of the G*psies."[24]

These cases, however, illustrate another important fact. The ambiguity of the definition of G*psyness left room for the promotion of the interests of individual actors: not only the Roma themselves, but also the local authorities. What this meant was that, on the one hand, the authorities in Czechia were doing their best to prevent the arrival of Roma from Slovakia; and on the other, the authorities in Slovakia (in this case the KNV) were doing their best to send local Roma to Czechia, even though this might not be in strict accordance with the official timetable. Similarly, Guy pointed out that the classification of the Roma into official categories in Slovakia may have resulted more from the efforts of the local authorities to include "their" Roma in the planned programme timetable and thus to ensure their resettlement, than on any proper assessment of their way of life (Guy 1977, 475–476).

However, in this chapter I do not want to restrict myself to defining the category of G*psyness as it appears in the communications of individual authorities of the socialist state and the ways in which citizens were officially classified. I will attempt to unpack the ways in which the category of G*psyness participated in the structuring of historically shaped and locally contingent socio-economic relations, both as a category that historically relegated the Roma to an inferior position in a heavily racialised socio-economic hierarchy, but also as a category of official policy that emphasised the dimension of social adaptability. First, I will illustrate in greater detail the way the category of G*psyness was understood at that time. This is because I do not wish to take for granted the ambivalence between the categories of social deviance and ethnicity/race, just as I do not want to merely point out the contradiction between the officially declared equality of all citizens and the racist practice of specific measures of the socialist state, as convincingly corroborated by Sokolová (2008). I believe that tracing the contours of the way that G*psyness was understood in the period under consideration will allow me to emphasise that, however much notions of the G*psies exhibited an apparent continuity in Czechoslovakia, as well as more broadly in European (Western) culture (see Sokolová 2008, especially 103–131),

---

24 ŠAKE Košice, f. Komisia Vsl. KNV pre cigánske obyvatelstvo, kart. 20, sp. 012/67, "Ján V.", 10 March 1967.

they were contingent upon the political and social context of that time. With this in mind I hope to disrupt the homogenisation of the character of the communist regime and the ways in which social (non-)belonging were shaped.

2.1.2 Racism as an obstacle to re-education

When Sokolová analyses the official discourse surrounding the G*psies during the 1950s and 1960s, she focuses on three authors: the historian Zdeňka Jamnická-Šmerglová and her book *Dějiny našich cikánů* (The History of Our Gypsies; 1955); Jaroslav Sus and his *Cikánská otázka v ČSSR* (The Gypsy Question in the Czechoslovak Socialist Republic;1961); and *Cikáni včera, dnes a zítra* (The Gypsies Yesterday, Today and Tomorrow) by Karel Nováček (1968). Sokolová argues that while all three authors spoke of the "backwardness of the G*psies" as being something that needed to be addressed through social assimilation, there were differences in the way they perceived the distinctive features of G*psy culture or way of life (Sokolová 2008, 121–131). In Sokolová's view, Jamnická-Šmerglová's description of the distinctive character of the G*psies contains traces of colonial and racialising thinking enshrined in the key question posed by her book: "Will they become human?" (Jamnická-Šmerglová 1955, 5). The related metaphor of "children" (*děti*) then gives rise to a method of assimilation being advocated that involved patient (re-)education and activities in the sphere of public enlightenment. Sokolová notes that differences observed in "mentality" (*mentalita*) and "sensitivity" (*citlivost*) were translated by later authors into "social characteristics". "The rhetoric of cultural difference was gradually transformed into a social pathology that legitimised the demand for the articulation of stricter assimilationist programmes," she concludes (Sokolová 2008, 126–127).

Sokolová is thinking in particular of the contributions of Sus and Nováček, which she places side by side in terms of approach. The shift of these authors from the earlier arguments of Jamnická-Šmerglová can also be seen in their definitive rejection of the idea that the Roma possess distinct cultural rights and a turn towards a more repressive assimilationist policy at the end of the 1950s. In this respect both books can be seen as a retrospective legitimisation of this shift in central policy (see, for example, Donert 2008, Spurný 2011). I will focus on the second author, Nováček, who published his book in 1968 and thus comments directly on the resettlement programme (even though the publication is based on his doctoral thesis, which he defended in 1964, i.e. a year before the central approval of the resettlement policy; see Donert 2017, 169).

Nováček contends that the difference, i.e. the "backwardness", of the G*psies must be seen as the outcome of their long-term isolation, a "distinctive development accompanied by constant oppression and persecution" (1968, 5). However, according to him, these developments had led not only to a "backward way of life", but also to the maintenance of distinctive anthropological (i.e. physical) features and an idiosyncratic "G*psy psychology" (*c*kánská psychologie*; ibid., 35–36). At the same time, when referring to the historical persecution of the G*psies, Nováček indirectly answers Jamnická-Šmerglová's question when he expresses his conviction that the G*psy is now "a human being for the first time" (ibid., 30). Nováček pays lip service to official policy when he says that the "dispersal of the G*psy population" (*rozptyl c*kánského obyvatelstva*) was the logical response to this historically conditioned isolation, which serves to reproduce the "G*psy way of life" (*c*kánský způsob života*; ibid., 4). However, he perceives a double obstacle in such a process of assimilation. Firstly, there is the relationship of the G*psies to the "White" (*bílí*) population, as well as the attitudes of "others" to the G*psies (ibid., 37–38). On the one hand, Nováček puts a distance between himself and the racialising opinions rife in society, according to which "G*psies cannot be re-educated" and their "past and present way of life reflects their 'G*psy nature' [*c*kánská přirozenost*]" (ibid., 5). For this reason, in "resolving the G*psy question" he lays emphasis on the "re-education of the rest of the population in order to overcome their prejudices against the G*psies" (ibid., 6). However, he himself substitutes "G*psy nature" with a historically formed "G*psy psychology", which, he argues, makes building trust in the surrounding "White" population a long and fraught process:[25]

If a G*psy is disappointed in a person he trusted, he can hate him with all "G*psy sincerity", which is considerable. G*psies are, as a rule, a temperamental people, not infrequently impulsive, and very sensitive to possible injustice. They can rejoice boundlessly, and many of them are ready to turn their hand to a skirmish. This trait is, when all is said and done, not peculiar

---

25 In the end, a similar emphasis can be found in the texts by Tomáš and Miroslav Holomek (see Chapter Four).

to the G*psies alone, but to all collectivities at a lower level of development. (ibid., 38)

Nováček's text thus underscores the ambivalence of the concept of G*psyness discussed above. While elsewhere he puts a distance between himself and idea of a "G*psy race" [c*kánská rasa] or "G*psy nature" and interprets the "G*psy way of life" on the basis of social isolation and pathology, he nonetheless presents a generalised, highly racialising description of the collective "G*psy temperament" [c*kánský temperament]. He thus finds himself caught in a vicious circle (see ibid., 38): On the one hand, he speaks of "criminal and freeloading activities" as a characteristic of G*psyness (ibid., 37–38); while on the other, he wishes to put a distance between himself and the attitudes of a society in which "the G*psies are [...] indiscriminately regarded as a thieving, parasitic mass" (ibid., 22).

In an attempt to break down this "mass", Nováček offers a differentiation between G*psies that essentially divides them into "settled [usedlí], semi-nomadic [polokočovní] and nomadic [kočovní]" (ibid., 32–35). The way he uses this differentiation, however, approximates to the newly established administrative classification based on adaptability. Nováček suggests that nomadism is an inherent feature of the "backward G*psy way of life", and this in turn creates a scale of assimilation. According to this logic, "settled G*psies" are former nomads who have adapted to the dominant way of life. When accentuating the social character of G*psyness, Nováček stresses that the measures aimed at "resolving the G*psy question" do not apply to these "settled G*psies" and that, on the contrary, it would be an "unforgiveable error to organise educational work with a special focus just because they differ from the rest of the population by virtue of the colour of their skin and because their G*psy origin is evident from their physiognomy" (ibid., 32).

The social distinction Nováček postulates is, he believes, inscribed in the relationships between the G*psies themselves. According to him, many of them attempt to be "more like the 'Whites'" (ibid., 38), which leads to conflict "between G*psies involved in the labour force and the fluctuating and non-working G*psies" (ibid., 39). Though it is not entirely clear upon what data he is basing these claims, his thesis is interesting for at least two reasons. Firstly, for the author himself, it serves to confirm the relevance of the social definition of G*psyness and the way that the significance of shared ethnic traits has been overlooked. At the same time, however, it points to the potential power of a historically shaped dominant discourse that addresses the way that relations between the G*psies themselves are defined. Though Nováček does not elaborate on this further, in his work G*psies become active agents in the formation of this discourse. This is a not entirely self-evident emphasis that I also adhere to from a very different perspective, not only in this chapter, but throughout this book.

The ethnographer Eva Davidová, at that time working for the KNV in Košice, promotes a very similar discourse in her texts. This discourse was articulated most clearly in her monograph entitled *Bez kolíb a šiatrov* (Without Huts and Tents, 1965), as well as in undated "study material for workers of educational establishments" entitled "Cigánsky problém a jeho riešenie vo východoslovenskom kraji" (The G*psy Problem and its Resolution in the Region of East Slovakia), which she wrote in collaboration with Špiner, mentioned above, the secretary of the G*psy Commission at the same KNV.[26] Davidová had been researching the Roma in eastern Slovakia since the 1950s, focusing on themes typical of ethnography as it was then understood: livelihood, housing culture, folk religion, folklore, etc. In her monograph, she frames her somewhat complex explanation of these themes with claims of a "backward" and "anachronistic way of life", which had to be overcome. Like Nováček, she defines the G*psies as an ethnic group. However, she soon emphasises that the "G*psy question" (*c*kánská otázka*) must be resolved not as a national, but as a "social problem", "in the form of the gradual assimilation of the G*psies into the rest of the population" (ibid., 10). At this point, Davidová notes that there are "many G*psy citizens – families and individuals – whose way of life does not differ from that of the rest of the population as a whole", and expresses her conviction that the numbers of such people will continue to rise (1965, 11). At the same time, however, she no longer counts such assimilated individuals among the G*psies. On the one hand, Davidová reproduces the social pathologisation of G*psyness, while on the other, like Nováček, she attributes to it specific anthropological features that distinguish G*psies from the society surrounding them (ibid., 11).

Davidová, too, depicts the history of the G*psies primarily as the story of their persecution, with an equal status only being achieved after

---

26 ŠAKE Košice, f. Komisia Vsl. KNV pre cigánske obyvatelstvo, kart. 9, sp. 44. "Cigánsky problém a jeho riešenie vo východoslovenskom kraji", undated. Turčínová-Davidová was responsible for the chapter entitled "The G*psy Problem from a Historical, Ethnographic and Sociological Perspective".

1945. It was only then, according to Davidová, that suitable conditions were created for the "resolution of the G*psy question", which she herself defined as the "totality of the problems ensuing from the differences of the backward forms of the G*psies' way of life and culture, which must be eliminated on the basis of a change in their economic status during the process of socialist education" (ibid., 35). She describes the 1950s as a period of an "elemental solution" (*živelné řešení*), which only took on a unified form after 1958, when it was decided to put an end to the nomadic way of life as a "serious hangover from the past" (ibid., 42). Another key task in the assimilation of the G*psies, to which the very title of the monograph *Bez kolíb a šiatrov* refers, is, as Davidová says, the removal of the settlements as unhealthy environments that reproduce a "backward way of life" (ibid., 87–88). Davidová identifies similar obstacles as Nováček to the process of assimilation. The sought-after inclusion of the Roma in the regular work force is hindered by "ingrained attitudes towards work, which previously the G*psies regarded purely as a necessary evil", as well as certain "character traits" (*povahové rysy*), the list of which is highly reminiscent of Nováček's "G*psy psychology": "instability and a lack of stamina; a lack of responsibility towards work and the collective; unhealthy manifestations of temperament; and a feeling of inferiority and the hypersensitivity resulting therefrom" (ibid., 89). Davidová emphasises that there is a need to "combat not only the surviving misconceptions of many G*psies, but also the lack of understanding and aversion of the rest of the population" (ibid., 44). But though she believes it is necessary to "eliminate feelings of superiority towards G*psies", she also warns against "inconsistent" and "superficial" solutions to the "G*psy question", which she says leads to "some G*psies [...] craftily abusing the advantages that our society provides them". In this context she also warns against the adoption of only "external forms of a new life" without a "genuine" internal transformation on the part of the G*psies (ibid., 122–125).

Davidová's understanding of G*psyness possesses the same internal tension as Nováček's. On the one hand, she inveighs against racial prejudice. However, she does so in the name of the need to eliminate the characteristics of a "G*psy way of life" (namely parasitism and nomadism) and transform the "unhealthy thinking of G*psies", which is manifest in a particular mentality. This stance is outlined more explicitly in the study material referred to above, where she states directly that racial prejudice is a "serious impediment to a genuine transformation of the life and thinking of the G*psies" and has the effect of "provoking incorrect reactions in the G*psies themselves and making assimilation more difficult". She admits that such "antipathy is provoked by the G*psies themselves", which, she says, causes "upstanding G*psies to suffer needlessly". In addition to seeing racism primarily as an obstacle to the successful "re-education of the G*psies", Davidová ultimately describes it as a largely natural reaction to the behaviour of the G*psies themselves. In doing so she postulates a category of "upstanding (respectable) G*psies" (*pořádný C*kán*) which, as I shall show below, became ingrained in popular discourse, even amongst the Roma themselves. However, with the earlier definition of the G*psy as inherently "slovenly", i.e. "parasitical and backward", Davidová continues to blur the boundary between the socially pathological and the ethnic category, just as she obfuscates the answer to the question of who actually counts as a G*psy and who no longer.

2.1.3 "In the interests of all"

The representatives of the newly established Government Committee were also aware of the need to influence the wider "non-G*psy" public. They called out "anti-G*psy attitudes" in society as one of the main reasons for the failure of the existing policies and referred to earlier documents that evaluated the implementation of the government resolution of 1958 (see Jurová 2008, 996–999). In contrast to this resolution, the implementation of the resettlement policy was to be accompanied by a media campaign stressing the importance of the programme for the whole of society. To this end, a three-part television programme was broadcast, appropriately entitled *V záujme všetkých* (In the Interest of All). Right at the beginning of the first episode, broadcast on 26 October 1966, the voice-over implied the shared responsibility of viewers for the plight of the G*psies, so turning passive observers into important agents of the desired change:

What have you done to address the G*psy question? Why did you refuse to sell your house to G*psies? Would you marry a G*psy girl? Would you invite a G*psy into your social group? Every fifth child in eastern Slovakia is a G*psy. Each has a home, but few have a bed and toys. Few are taken out into the sun in a pram. The six-year-olds will be ready for school but will not attend. They will live in poor conditions. [footage from poor eastern Slovak settlements]. They will grow up and receive an ID card with Slovak or Czech nationality What will they do without education and qualifications? The boy will enter the army, where he will be taught skills and perhaps receive a qualification. The girl will give birth to children she won't care for.[27]

This introduction serves as a prelude to all three parts, which look at different stages of life and various aspects of the everyday life of the G*psies, i.e. those who represent the "G*psy way of life" as outlined in the introduction. But it also reveals the broader shift taking place in how social rights were understood in socialist Czechoslovakia. As Donert shows in more detail, during the 1960s there was a move away from providing paid work for everyone to issues revolving around care, family and everyday life, which inevitably included a gender dimension (Donert 2017, 143–153). This is clear not only from the introduction to the programme, but also in the texts discussed above. In several places, Davidová herself reminds her readers that given the traditional gender roles of the Roma, it is the "G*psy woman" who is the primary obstacle to the assimilation of G*psies due to a higher degree of social isolation (Davidová 1965, 80 and 159; Turčínová-Davidová [undated], 33;[28] see Donert 2017, 152). With an increasing emphasis on private life and, more generally, on its quality, attention turned to the high birth rate of the sexualised G*psy woman, who, according to the dominant logic, reproduced a deviant way of life. This theme regularly surfaces throughout the whole of the three-part TV series. "She became a mother. [...] A G*psy woman was born to bear children. She became a wife and mother when she was still a child herself," intones the voice-over introducing the segment entitled "Mother" in the first episode.[29] In addition to the possibility of birth control for G*psy women and the removal of G*psy children, subsequent episodes focus on hygiene, health, and the overall elimination of the "unhealthy" environment in which these children are socialised. "The environment shapes a person. Any of us would have a problem if we had been born in a dilapidated shack or grown up in the darkness of illiteracy and binding traditions. It's hard to break away and live differently," the voice-over persuades the viewer. Immediately afterwards, a television reporter visits "Mrs Marienka" in order to see for himself the facilities of her recently built house in one of the villages of

---

27 Archive of RTVS, Bratislava, idec: 766-7260-9000-0051, "V záujme všetkých 1.", 1966.
28 ŠAKE Košice, f. Komisia Vsl. KNV pre cigánske obyvateľstvo, kart. 9, sp. 44. "Cigánsky problém a jeho riešenie vo východoslovenskom kraji", undated.
29 Ibid.

eastern Slovakia. Mrs Marienka's husband is a welder and is at work. The camera takes in a flowerpot, a large wall clock and a double bass leaning against the wall in a corner. "Dirt and disorder are not an inevitable side effect of poverty," says the editor, pointing to the transformation in the living conditions and habits of the G*psies, proof that the systematic "liquidation of G*psy settlements" was the right path.[30]

The insistent message to the viewer that such changes are "in the interests of all" is part of a growing emphasis within central policy on the quality of the entire population. The "G*psy way of life" presented in the TV programme was not only a subversive element, but, given the high birth rate, posed a significant threat to the population even in the future. This securitising narrative, which accentuated the threat of a significant population increase of the G*psies as a deviant group, is characteristic of the entire discourse of that time, and culminated in the practice of sterilisation in Czechoslovakia, primarily on the basis of race (Sadílková 2019). This view of societal interest was formulated by Davidová herself, who co-authored the script of the first episode of the TV programme, in which she also appeared as an expert on the "G*psy question". She had warned against the direction social developments were taking in the study material cited above, writing that "the gap between the surviving G*psy way of life and that of the average citizen of our socialist society […] will widen, just as the relative number of G*psies in the Czechoslovak Socialist Republic will increase" (Turčínová-Davidová [undated], 36).[31]

Inasmuch as the primary motivation for eliminating racial prejudice was to allow for the re-education of the G*psies, the process of re-education itself was largely motivated by the desire to prevent any increase in the "G*psy problem". And inasmuch as the securitisation narrative was present, albeit implicitly, in official discourse and in nationwide television coverage, this concern was articulated explicitly in contemporary newspaper articles, which often warned of an "explosion in the G*psy population".[32]

The text "Smer: Morava a Čechy" (Direction: Moravia and Bohemia, 16 May 1967), published in the Bratislava Communist Party newspaper

30 Ibid.
31 ŠAKE Košice, f. Komisia Vsl. KNV pre cigánske obyvatelstvo, kart. 9, sp. 44. "Cigánsky problém a jeho riešenie vo východoslovenskom kraji", undated.
32 ŠAKE Košice, f. Komisia Vsl. KNV pre cigánske obyvatelstvo, kart. 20, "Výstrižky z tlače o cigánskej problematike", 1962–1968.

Lud (The People), opens with data on the number of G*psies, including their classification in accordance with the official categories. Referring to the second and third categories, the journalist wrote: "[w]e have to deal with both groups, not least because given a large population of G*psies they would quickly outnumber us. After all, by 1970 there will be at least a quarter of a million gypsies in the Republic!"[33] A text from the same newspaper simply entitled "Cigánska otázka" (The G*psy Question, 27 September 1967), which summarises the outcomes of a joint meeting of the Health Committee of the National Assembly and the National Council of the Slovak Republic's Health Commission, warns of a "population explosion" (*populačná explózia*). Dr. Ervín Mikula published an indignant article in the same newspaper (30 September 1967), claiming that it was "undeniable that we have managed to create a special caste, a privileged class, which knows only of rights and nothing of duties, out of the population of G*psy origin (lest we be accused of racism)". In explaining the higher birth rate of G*psy women, he repeats the widespread belief that this was primarily a source of livelihood thanks to the payment of child allowances: "It is almost inconceivable that a G*psy woman would use contraceptives. It would threaten the financial stability of the unit we consider a family". He also writes of a "population explosion" that can "unequivocally be declared poor quality [i.e. giving rise to a 'poor quality population']". "What is this explosion costing us?" he writes, only to recall the 11 million Czechoslovak crowns paid in 1966 for the education of G*psy children and the fact that one third of adult G*psies in Slovakia were in receipt of disability benefits.[34] Similarly, in a text entitled "Cigánské nokturná" (G*psy Nocturne), Adam Gajdoš illustrates the legitimacy of fears of the threat of an increase in the numbers of G*psies, citing a conversation he claims to have had with a "twenty-five-year old G*psy beauty" in an eastern Slovak settlement: "You have ten children. Would like to have more?" – "Of course. Ten more... so that my partner receives money!". In another text Gajdoš writes that "the G*psies are springing up like mushrooms after the rain [spreading like wildfire]".[35]

Though he declared himself to be against "compulsory sterilisation", Špiner, the secretary of the regional G*psy Commission, spoke about the need for "controlled parenthood and population reduction" in a lengthy

---

33 Ibid.
34 Ibid.
35 Ibid.

interview for *Obrana lidu* (Defence of the People) entitled "O cigánoch s porozumením, ale nie sentimentálne" (On the G*psies with Understanding but not Sentimentality). "After all, what is more humane: to allow psychically handicapped people give birth to degenerate offspring without feeling or love? Or to prevent it?" he asks, referring to the third official category of G*psy.[36]

2.1.4 "Let the councillors house them in their own home"

According to the prevalent narrative, the "population explosion" that threatened was contingent on the one hand upon the distinct sexuality of the G*psies, more specifically G*psy women, and on the other by a general pro-family welfare system that facilitated profiteering on the part of the G*psies as "work-shy freeloaders". This narrative can be seen in the broader popular discourse at that time. In my analysis of it here, I will draw on the response of viewers to the television programme discussed above, "In the Interests of All", more than a hundred of whom set forth their feelings in letters addressed to the television studios.[37] Notwithstanding the large number of responses received, this in itself cannot be seen as a representative sample of public opinion, since it involved only the voices of those viewers who felt the need to comment. Nevertheless, it is a relatively unique source from which to trace the complexity of the popular discourse surrounding G*psies at that time.

Adhering to the narrative described above, one of the viewers linked up ideas of deviant G*psy sexuality and criticism of the state family policy thus:

> It is true that all G*psies have children irresponsibly. However, the government indulges them in this respect by paying them family allowances, and generous ones at that. It is completely unacceptable that children have sex with other children without being punished, and that these children give birth to more children.[38]

---

36 Ibid.
37 NA Prague, KSČ-ÚV-05/3, f. KSČ – Ústřední výbor 1945–1989, Praha – oddělení – oddělení ideologické, sv. 37, č. j. 299.
38 Ibid.

Another warns that "with the continuing birth rate [of G*psies] there will soon be a national crisis".[39] The criticism of the state voiced in these letters relates not only to its welfare policy, but also to the assimilation policy as a whole, as presented in the television programme. Some viewers expressed a conviction that "nothing will change their [i.e. the G*psies'] minds", a statement they backed up by referencing the duration of their residence in "our" country: "They have been living here – in our and neighbouring regions – for centuries. They have seen our orderly way of life and have no desire to live like Whites."[40] In the shorter term, several of the letter writers cited as proof of the entrenchment of a different (i.e. "backward") way of life the twenty-year period of equal conditions under socialism: "I mean, they've had equal opportunities for twenty years and still live the same way," wrote one viewer.[41]

These assumptions form the basis for the prevailing opposition to the dispersional logic of the resettlement policy itself. Such attitudes are well illustrated by the letter signed by representatives of state-owned property in Železiovce in south-western Slovakia, who argued that the relocation of "[of G*psies] among ordinary working people [...] has a highly detrimental effect on the morale of the rest of the population and in several cases makes life more miserable." According to the letter writers, "those people who say: 'Listen, just tell me why I should have a G*psy family with multiple children as neighbours, who would make my life miserable every day, both by their way of life and by the way they destroy everything they see' – have a point [...] If senior public and political figures are so keen to re-educate the G*psies, why don't they have G*psy families as neighbours?"[42] The disconnect of central politics and politicians from the everyday lives of "ordinary" folks also featured in the comments sent in by residents of the housing estate in Nejdek in west Bohemia:

> Comrades, no matter to whom we lodge our complaints, most of the replies run as follows: 'They need to be re-educated'. For heaven's sake! Do any of the people who come out with this crap about re-education have to live in the same building as them? No, not one.[43]

---

39 Ibid.
40 Ibid.
41 Ibid.
42 Ibid.
43 Ibid.

It is telling that writers of letters framed in this way base the legitimacy of their attitudes toward the Roma on their own lived experiences. At the same time, the criticism of state policy is based on the conviction that everyone is aware of the "genuine" facts, the problem being that some people have fallen prey to a kind of political correctness. One of the many anonymous letter writers puts it perfectly:

> If I had written a eulogy to the G*psies, I could have proudly signed my name. But since I have written the truth about these parasites and freeloaders, I have deeply offended that noble race which has more care and concern lavished upon than the rest of the population. What I have written is not only my opinion, it is the opinion of all non-G*psies. [...] I am convinced that 100% of non-G*psies will agree with me.[44]

Some viewers criticised the television programme for only depicting "positive cases" amongst the G*psies, a policy that, in their view, distorted the dismal reality and created the illusion that the concept being conveyed could be successful.

And so inasmuch as the television programme reiterated the official discourse, according to which the "G*psy question" was primarily a social issue and its "solution" was to be "in the interests of all", the reactions of ordinary non-Romani citizens revealed both the embeddedness of racist ideas about the G*psies (see Hübschmannová 1968, also see the Ústav pro veřejné mínění 1971) and the ensuing scepticism felt towards the assimilation programme, as well as a marked unwillingness to answer the call to participate in its implementation. In a statement to be heard again and again calling for "officials to welcome them [the G*psies] into their own homes", there is a reliance on the oft formulated assumption that it was the policy itself that created a "privileged class" (*privilegovaná třída*) of G*psies to whom special "rights" (*práva*) are granted but to whom "duties" (*povinnosti*) do not apply. Present in such a narrative (whether explicitly or more implicitly) is the belief that G*psies live a better life in their "privilege" than ordinary citizens. This then becomes the starting point for proposed measures, which some viewers believe must be more repressive than those already in place, and others believe should be absolutely uncompromising.

---

44 Ibid.

Even those proposals that adopt the dominant logic of "dispersion", while conveniently omitting the dimension of voluntarism, count on a restrictive approach. Moreover, there is always an emphasis on distance. According to one viewer, the relocation of the G*psies should be carried out in the borderlands, while another proposed they be banished to the USSR because it was a "very large" country. Other viewers suggest their relocation exclusively to rural areas, where they would allegedly be subject to more rigorous social control. Otherwise, however, proposals that envisaged territorialisation and spatial segregation prevailed, whether this involved keeping the G*psies in eastern Slovakia ("Leave the G*psies in eastern Slovakia because they only bring shame to us in the Karlovy Vary region [west Bohemia], where there are so many foreigners passing through that we will acquire the reputation of being a G*psy nation."), relocating them to a single defined region on the border of Czechoslovakia, or expatriating them to Hungary (whence they allegedly originally came) or the Soviet Union.[45] Referring to the creation of the Jewish state, one viewer recommended the creation of a "strip of land" (unspecified) for the G*psies.[46] There were even calls for their internment in labour camps.[47]

The population growth of the G*psies was also to be dealt with using a restrictive approach. In more restrained proposals this involved limiting family benefits to a certain number of children or only paying them subject to conditions being met (e.g. the parents' permanent employment and the children's school attendance), while more radical schemes advocated the forced sterilisation of G*psy women. Several viewers wanted G*psy children taken into care and brought up in orphanages and correctional institutions in the belief that at least that way it would be possible to re-educate them. Some proponents of restrictive measures defended themselves against accusations of racism, maintaining that this was the only working solution to the problem as outlined by the television programme. One letter writer even described forced sterilisation as an act of solidarity, since as a mother of several children herself she was aware of just how exhausting the whole business of childcare was for women.[48]

These suggestions sent in by viewers largely corresponded to the results of a survey conducted by the Institute of Public Opinion.

---

45 Ibid.
46 Ibid.
47 Ibid.
48 See the discussion on the emancipatory character of sterilisation (Sadílková 2019).

A publication entitled "Opinions Regarding G*psies and the Resolution of the Gypsy Question" (1971) revealed that the majority of respondents wanted to achieve the social integration of G*psies[49] by coercive means ("control; punishment under existing laws or new laws; and forced labour by means of various measures"). In Czechia, 33 percent of respondents felt this way, while the figure in Slovakia was 59 percent. Other attitudes included the following: "expressions of resignation (nothing will shift the G*psies)" – 7% in Czechia /4% in Slovakia; "extreme opinions (coercive camps, the expatriation of G*psies from Czechoslovakia, isolation, restrictions on the size of the population of G*psies)" – 4%/10%; and the "concentration of G*psies (including self-government)" – 5%/6%. It was only at this point in the list that the option advocated by the central authorities appeared: "to distribute the G*psies amongst the rest of the population"– 4%/2% (Ústav pro veřejné mínění 1971, 51).

2.1.5 Disrupting the homogenous image of G*psyness?

It would be oversimplifying matters to view the discourse of that time as split between the official view of G*psyness as a social category (reproduced and developed further by Davidová and Nováček) and its popular racial definition. It is therefore worth dwelling on the voices that to some extent disrupted the dominant image of G*psyness. As Donert has shown in more detail, criticism of the logic of assimilation enshrined in the official policy, which shifted attention to the persistent racist structures of social relations, was voiced in the pages of *Literární noviny*, a monthly revue devoted to culture and politics (Donert 2017, 176– 178). Of the authors represented, it was Hübschmannová above all who pushed for the Roma to be granted the rights of an ethnic minority with a distinctive cultural legacy. By focussing on a description of specific Romani people, she sought to disrupt the homogenisation of the Roma as a group characterised by a backward way of life. She did this by drawing attention to university educated Roma and their ongoing efforts to achieve ethnic self-determination (Hübschmannová 1968), but also to the impasse faced by ordinary Roma, such as Mr Horváth from the settlement in Veľká Ida in eastern Slovakia, who was prevented from acquiring decent

---

49 The question was as follows: "In your opinion, what should be done to ensure that G*psies work permanently in some form of employment, live like other citizens, and take care of their children's compulsory schooling and their further preparation for practical life?"

housing by the racist attitudes of the local authorities and non-Romani residents, the administrative restrictions ensuing from the resettlement policy and the possibilities of new housing developments in general, but also by his (ethnically contingent) lack of social, educational and economic capital (Hübschmannová 1967). In a later text for *Sociologický časopis* (Czech Sociological Review), Hübschmannová turned the entire logic of the "G*psy question" on its head by shifting the emphasis away from the problem of the G*psies and reframing it as the responsibility of society as a whole. Furthermore, she maintained that this was not only a historical responsibility, as it had been formulated by Nováček and Davidová, but a contemporary one that included the discriminatory content of the central assimilationist policy (1970).

The approaches taken by Hübschmannová and Davidová differ in two respects. Firstly, they exhibit different attitudes towards existing state policy (although as early as 1966, Davidová was criticising the way the resettlement policy was not being sufficiently discussed with the Roma themselves; Sadílková et al. 2018, 150–155). Secondly, what they have to say is of differing relevance to the dominant discourse of that time. Unlike Hübschmannová, who published her texts in alternative outlets like *Literární noviny*, Davidová was part of an official media campaign to explain the importance of the policy, not only as co-author of the first episode of the TV show discussed above, but also as writer of the text "Bílé místo v našem svědomí: Cikánská otázka" (A White Place in Our Conscience: the G*psy Question), which was published in the Communist Party weekly *Kulturní tvorba* on 6 January 1966.[50]

The public opinion poll looking at the social integration of the Roma in Czechia and Slovakia respectively included suggestions for creating "suitable conditions" and "the same opportunities as others have" (9%/4%), the allocation of apartments (4%/1%), and the well received "general education of the G*psies (encouragement and training)" on 17%/9% (Ústav pro veřejné mínění 1971, 51). Also, the viewers' reactions by no means represented a homogenous view of the G*psies as a group of naturally deviant and inferior citizens, though it must be acknowledged that even the more liberal voices tended to confirm the dominant logic of G*psyness. A correspondent from northern Bohemia, for example, stated that "no people may deny another people the right to exist and to

---

50   ŠAKE Košice, f. Komisia Vsl. KNV pre cigánske obyvateľstvo, kart. 20, "Výstrižky z tlače o cigánskej problematike", 1962–1968.

live according to its customs."[51] The ambiguity contained in the letter is already present in its introduction, where the writer claims that he is neither "prejudiced against the G*psy race" nor is he "against a merger with our people", after which he goes on to offer a highly racialised description in which the "G*psies are of a cheerful disposition, they like to joke, they are hospitable, etc.", and perceives the "the main danger from their side" to be "their way of life and their rapid reproduction".[52] Another viewer, in line with the official discourse, sees a significant problem in "entrenched racial hatred", only to go on to propose enacting repressive measures against the G*psies. In the area of housing, which he says is in their case "truly beneath human dignity", he proposes moving the G*psies into "five-storey blocks with multiple entrances, i.e. 150 metres in length". He suggests covering the floors of individual apartments with "non-flammable material to prevent fires [and] during the relocation process lorries with several people would destroy the shacks. Anyone who did not want to move would be subject to sharp and decisive action".[53] Another viewer notes that "we are fighting against discrimination against Black people in America and yet we are guilty of it ourselves in our cohabitation with G*psy citizens", a point he illustrates by citing a situation on a train that he witnessed. In the same breath, however, he admits that the G*psies need to be "settled down" and "civilised" as soon as possible. In doing so, he reproduces the centralised categorisation of the G*psies by dividing them into those "who catch on quickly and are capable of being trained more rapidly, those who are slower, and [those] who are incapable of being re-educated".[54] In a similar vein, several viewers call for the involvement of the G*psies themselves, in particular the "more educated" and "more civilised" ones.[55] At the risk of over simplifying, the two different attitudes expressed in the accompanying explanation given can be paraphrased as follows: "let the G*psies fend for themselves"; and, more often, "the (more educated) G*psies know best what methods of re-education work on other G*psies".[56]

51 NA Prague, KSČ-ÚV-05/3, f. KSČ – Ústřední výbor 1945–1989, Praha – oddělení – oddělení ideologické, sv. 37, č. j. 299.
52 Ibid.
53 Ibid.
54 Ibid.
55 Ibid.
56 Ibid.

2.1.6 The figure of the "respectable G*psy"

The truth is that, in contrast to the earlier involvement of ideologically trained Roma (Donert 2008), as far as the technocratic conception of the policy towards the Roma was concerned (see Sommer et. al 2019), the official participation of the Roma as representatives of the affected population group in shaping state policy was basically rejected by the central authorities (Donert 2017, 154). This does not mean, however, that the Roma themselves did not engage in the public debate. Apart from the ongoing efforts of some of them to assert the rights of the Roma as a group (ibid., see also Sadílková et al. 2018, 2024), individual Roma became actors in the centrally promoted policy in their role as local councillors (examples of this are given in the following chapters). At the same time, the Roma participated in the shaping of the public discourse, for instance as authors of numerous viewer reactions to the television series under discussion. Of these, the figure of the "respectable (i.e. adaptable, civilised) G*psy" (*slušný C*kán*) stands out, and resonates strongly with the official classification based on the level of social assimilation.

The figure of the "respectable G*psy" was to a large extent also present in the letters sent to the TV station by non-Romani viewers, who distinguished between "backward (and at the same time privileged) scroungers" and "decent" and "civilised G*psies". The latter were to be spared the restrictive measures being proposed, as in the example of one rather extreme proposal from an anonymous writer who suggested returning the G*psies "to their original homeland of Hungary" if they were unwilling to submit to coercive re-education. At the end of this letter the writer concedes that "the small percent of full-time workers who have integrated themselves into normal life can be allowed to stay /as they see fit/".[57] It becomes clear that the figure of the respectable G*psy represents an attempt to reframe racist attitudes into a rational response to a different (i.e. deviant) way of life. The respectable G*psy here functions as evidence that it is not society that determines the deviant actions of G*psies and that anyone can conform to a "proper way of life" if they put their mind to it. In other words, the respectable G*psy becomes the exception proving the rule of the racialised image of the "G*psy scrounger", just as the official category reproduces the socio-pathological image

---

57   Ibid.

of G*psyness when it no longer even deems "integrated" G*psies to be G*psies (see Davidová 1965; Nováček 1968).

In her book, Donert demonstrates how the Romani elite, which in the latter half of the 1960s came together in the newly created Svaz Cikánů-Romů / Zväzu Cigánov-Rómov (Union of Gypsies-Roma), also participated in the reproduction of the image of poor "backward G*psies" (locating them primarily in eastern Slovakia). Donert (2017, 193) illustrates the attitudes of some of the organisation's representatives by a letter from a musician from Košice, who declares that as a "citizen of G*psy origin" who speaks "G*psy", he knows the life of "our G*psies almost all over Slovakia". He goes on to divide the Roma into three categories: "musicians" (barikane, i.e. "conceited" [namyslení; his own translation from Romani]), "workers" (munkáša) and "ne'er-do-wells" (degeš or "degenerates"). The last category he characterises as comprising people who "cause severe problems" and suggests the application of restrictive measures, such as placing older people in retirement homes (so that no one else has access to their pensions), and in the case of women various forms of birth control including sterilisation.[58]

Of the more than 100 letters received from viewers, just under a quarter were from correspondents introducing themselves as a "G*psy citizen/citizen of G*psy origin" (c*kánský občan/občan c*kánského původu). None of these writers ranked themselves among an "elite class" (however defined), and some of them were themselves from poor backgrounds in eastern Slovakia. Even so, like the musician from Košice, they put a distance between themselves and the "problematic G*psies" and expressed dissatisfaction with the fact that the latter were the people representing the Roma in the media and broader societal discourse. The letter writers objected to the tone of the TV show itself (as opposed to several of the non-Romani viewers, who were unhappy with the emphasis placed on positive examples, see above), and self-identified as G*psies living "respectable" and "orderly" lives. Thus they, too, reproduced the dominant logic of G*psyness, and in addition they expressed gratitude "to the Czechoslovak government and Party, which had managed to turn the G*psies into semi-respectable people", as one of them put it.[59] The image of G*psies who remained trapped in their "backward"

---

58 ŠAKE Košice, f. Komisia Vsl. KNV pre cigánske obyvatelstvo, kart. 18, sp. 50, letter of Július F., 18 March 1968.

59 NA Prague, KSČ-ÚV-05/3, f. KSČ – Ústřední výbor 1945–1989, Praha – oddělení – oddělení ideologické, sv. 37, č. j. 299.

ways despite the new "egalitarian" conditions was confirmed by the same correspondent:

> I have five children, and when these children of mine watched your show, I was embarrassed in front of them. Because they asked me if we lived like that, and I told them that we didn't, but that my parents did because they hadn't had the opportunities back then that they have today.[60]

The restrictive measures proposed to deal with the "backward G*psies" were based on this logic. Some of the letter writers were emphatic that the socialist state should not be "so generous to the G*psies", and voices were heard advocating limits on family benefits as well as well as sterilisation and internment in labour camps.

It would be oversimplifying matters to view these opinions as merely examples of the internalisation of the dominant discourse on G*psies. Although the arguments given reproduce its logic, in my opinion they must be seen as the expression of a particular lived experience and position in socialist society, not least experience of the anti-Roma measures introduced during the Second World War.[61] This is clear in a letter written by a woman who frames her surprise at "the fact that they [the Roma] can still live in such a backward way" within the context of her own wartime experience. She had been imprisoned in Auschwitz, where the Nazis killed her four children, her parents, her siblings and her first husband. Her belief that "everyone today has the opportunity to live like a decent citizen" she illustrates by the fact that from 1945 onwards she held down two jobs.[62] While this emphasis on inclusion on the labour market is tied up with the official discourse of social legitimacy and implicitly places a distance between it and "scroungers", it would be cynical to see this as simply the internalisation of the dominant logic of G*psyness. Even within the context of the tragic wartime fate of the woman's entire family, her letter must be read as the expression of a lived and fairly unique experience of social acceptance.

---

60 Ibid.
61 On the basis of long-term anthropological research, I have previously looked at the narrative of "harmonious existence" in a particular eastern Slovak village, which also reproduced the figure of the "problematic G*psy" while also testifying to the self-identification of the local Roma, their mode of belonging to a locally anchored community, making reference to a certain social practice and ultimately reflecting critically upon it (Ort 2022b).
62 NA Prague, KSČ-ÚV-05/3, f. KSČ – Ústřední výbor 1945–1989, Praha – oddělení – oddělení ideologické, sv. 37, č. j. 299.

In discerning the dominant logic behind the shared figure of the "respectable G*psy", we must therefore tease out the social contexts in which this concept is embedded. In their letters, the Romani viewers used said logic to express their lived experience of social belonging, whether on a societal or local level, but also of social mobility more broadly understood, defining different types of axes of differentiation. Sometimes this involved an intergenerational relationship, as in the case of the viewer who acknowledged what he called the "backward way of life" of his grandparents. Furthermore, there was a geographical element in play, such a lifestyle usually being associated with the region of eastern Slovakia (which could also be related to the sub-ethnic labelling by Bohemian Moravian Roma of post-war immigrants from Slovakia, see also Slačka 2015). However, the Roma from eastern Slovakia themselves also spoke out against the homogenisation of the way of life of the Roma in this region.

2.1.7 Reflections upon the limits of social acceptance

However, when observing the lived experience articulated by the Romani viewers, what emerges is less the expression of a degree of social belonging than the articulation of its limits. Inasmuch as Davidová and Nováček, in line with official discourse, viewed racism primarily as an obstacle to the "re-education of the G*psies", downplayed and inverted in the broader popular discourse by means of an image of G*psies as a "privileged race" (*privilegovaná rasa*), the Roma themselves were more inclined to reflect upon its everyday manifestations. In addition to frequent allusions to specific examples of discrimination on the part of the authorities, often when trying to obtain accommodation, several viewers also articulated the humiliation and helplessness they felt in everyday relationships. For example, one of the letter writers called for the greater involvement of the Roma on the level of the local councils, since they needed and deserved representation when communicating with the authorities:

For example, I'd be willing to get involved in sorting out G*psy issues, disputes between the G*psies and the Municipal Committees. We would all like to help in some way [...] but they don't offer us the opportunity. And that's why the G*psy goes under, that's why he thinks the way he does. No one ever believes us. He [the G*psy] gets nervous. And being sometimes illiterate, he can't help himself. And when he asks his friends, they laugh at him. So far they have ridiculed the fact that G*psies have come to Holland, to the Sudetenland, that they would be exterminated. And now they mock us saying we will be sent to Siberia. [...] They should stop with the mockery. [...] I've been working for five years at Váhostav. The construction foreman makes fun of me for going to the Netherlands and calls me a Jew. [...] The other workers also make fun of me.[63]

This passage reveals the psychological powerlessness experienced in the face of everyday displays of racism, a powerlessness reinforced by a marginalised social status with limited social and educational capital. The very taunts aimed at the Roma indicate a degree of normativity and continuity of ideas regarding what forms their resettlement might take, which, in turn, policies at that time built on, consolidated and then reproduced.[64]

Another viewer refers in the introduction to his letter to the social demand for "respectability", but then turns his attention away from the natural "backwardness of the deplorables" to their material conditions and existing structural barriers: "I'd also like to live a respectable life like everyone else but I can't get my hands on either an apartment or a job."[65] He described the reality of his life alternating between Czechia, where he travelled for work, and his home village in eastern Slovakia, as follows:

I'm young, 24 years old. [...] I'm a Czechoslovak citizen and I can't find a job or buy a house, though I was good enough for military service. I was only 18 years old and I served 26 months without any payment. And I came home from military service and didn't have a single pair of trousers. [...] Since I came back from the army, I still go to work at the State Assets and receive 800–900 crowns a month and have to take care of my wife and child and take care of myself so that I don't die of hunger. And I've been married for two years now, but when my wife and I had the chance to spend just six months together, it seemed like a long time. So what's in it for me?[66]

---

63 Ibid.
64 The taunts referencing the resettlement of Roma to Holland apparently stemmed from an article published in the press at that time, which reported on the plans of the "G*psy King" to establish a Romani state to which Romani people from all over the world would move. The newspaper's editors subsequently released a statement distancing themselves from the taunts. They conceded that the article had exacerbated matters and, pointing to the wartime internment and deportation of Roma, condemned the taunts as inappropriate. See ŠAKE Košice, f. Komisia Vsl. KNV pre cigánske obyvateľstvo, kart. 20, "Výstrižky z tlače o cigánskej problematike", 1962–1968.
65 NA Prague, KSČ-ÚV-05/3, f. KSČ – Ústřední výbor 1945–1989, Praha – oddělení – oddělení ideologické, sv. 37, č. j. 299.
66 Ibid.

Both the letters quoted above describe the reality of the marginalisation of Roma in terms of discrimination by the authorities, various forms of humiliation in everyday relationships, the general unavailability of decent housing and work, and even the input deficit in respect of various forms of capital (economic, social and educational) ensuing from the marginalised environment itself. However, they are not merely simple descriptions of each writer's plight, but in terms of the sense of helplessness expressed and the absence of any support, they represent a call for help from outside. It is clear that the television programmes depicting the situation of specific families triggered not only a need for the letter writers to distance themselves from the "backward G*psies", but also the hope that they would be able to solve their own problems. For example, the writer of the two quotations above ended his letter with a description of his application for the allocation of a building plot. After recording the rejection of both the municipal and district National Committees, he added ironically: "We could turn to the lord God".[67] At the very end of the letter, using official language, he appended a personal wish: "I would like you to come and see me and solve the issue I have [*vyriešiť aj moju otázku*]."[68] The television viewer from eastern Slovakia, in turn, stated in his short letter that in 1965, in the settlement, they "installed power points for eight homes but have not yet connected them up", and asked that they "send someone so that they would know whether they were going to be connected or not".[69]

Perhaps it is an awareness of the limits of social belonging that gives rise to another point often made in the letters of Romani viewers, a point that marks a sharp delineation between them and non-Romani viewers and that is specifically related to the "dispersive" logic of the resettlement policy. While suggestions from non-Romani viewers for the relocation of Roma appeared in isolated (and, as I have shown, relatively specific) cases and, on the contrary, an emphasis on their territorialisation or complete displacement prevailed, the Romani viewers consistently welcomed the logic of "dispersal". This applied to both those Roma who declared a relatively higher status and proposed distribution among the non-Romani population as a solution to the problem of "backward G*psies", and to those who were themselves part of a marginalised environment

---

67 Ibid.
68 Ibid.
69 Ibid.

and saw dispersal as an external source of assistance in overcoming existing barriers to social mobility (see Chapter Four).

From the brief analysis above of the position of the Roma as agents in the co-creation of the period discourse around G*psyness, it is clear that this involved complex feelings that, in line with what I have written in the previous chapter regarding the ambivalent social position of the Roma during the period of socialism, cannot be explained either by the internalisation of the dominant discourse, or by its pragmatic instrumentalisation in order to achieve one's own interests, or by resistance to it. Although the Roma did to some extent confirm the dominant understanding of G*psyness through their own logic of social mobility and their depiction of relations to other Roma, they also left themselves space for formulating their own specific experiences and requesting the satisfaction of their own interests.

2.2 Roma and G*psies in Brekov

2.2.1 The story of the exceptional Roma of Brekov

During my first visit to Brekov in May 2019, I received from the municipal authorities both a comprehensive monograph on the history of the village (Molnár 2017) and a recommendation to meet with Mr Koloman Gunár, who took a keen interest in the history of the local Roma, of which he himself was one. As we sat down to talk in his house, his wife Agáta urged him to show me a book he had written about the history of the Roma of Brekov based on the stories of older Romani men and women. His text, which he had had bound in four copies, was all the more valuable because at the time of my visit the people he had spoken with were not longer alive. The text appealed to me above all for its detailed treatment of the genealogies of individual families, supplemented by everyday stories of specific individuals, as well as descriptions of traditional Romani customs and crafts. What really caught my attention was the strong anchoring of the Roma of Brekov in the local community and the significant degree of social mobility, represented not only by the emphasis placed on continuity of employment, but also by the list of Roma who had successfully graduated from university or completed secondary school. Mr Gunár had himself received a university education. He had been politically active since the early 1990s, both as a founder and member of one of the newly established Romani political parties and as an activist who openly advocated for the rights of the Roma as a group (see Gunár 2020). He strongly emphasised the successful social integration of the Brekov Roma throughout our conversation. This was further underlined by the fact that Gunár spoke only Slovak, not Romani, the language of everyday communication in Romani families in many of the surrounding villages. At the very start of our conversation, Mr Gunár pointed out that not even the oldest generation of Roma in Brekov, which included his good self, spoke Romani.

The narrative of integration can best be illustrated by quoting from the preface to his book:

> Neither in the past, nor in the present day, do the Roma of Brekov hold out their hands in supplication to the state. Instead, following the example of their fathers and forefathers, they face life head-on, determined to be a part of majority society. In their everyday dealings, they have come to terms with the life led by the majority population of the village. In the previous regime, the Municipal National Committee (MNV) did not register members of the G*psy ethnic group in the village in its statistics (Gunár 2010, 2)

The "registration of G*psies" did in fact take place at the level of the Municipal National Committees at various stages during the communist regime, and it is not entirely clear to which period and context Mr Gunár was referring in his book. Unfortunately I did not have the opportunity to ask him myself, since he died about a year after our meeting. However, as regards the discourses around G*psyness being discussed, the very fact that the framing of the social mobility and local belonging of the Roma of Brekov resonates with the dominant logic at that time, according to which mobility depended on a person adopting the characteristics of the "majority" way of life and "integrated G*psies" were no longer understood as G*psies as such, is significant.

During my ongoing archival research, though I did not come across specific "records of G*psies" in Brekov (apart from a list of "nomadic persons", to which I will return below and the wider context of which I will discuss in Chapter Four), many documents from the 1950s and 1960s make mention of G*psies in Brekov. Although Mr Gunár did not himself work with archival materials, these documents largely support his retrospectively applied narrative.

As far back as 1958, the "Report on the Resolution of the G*psy Question in the District" included the claim that the settlement in Brekov "should be deemed a closed case in accordance with the Resolution of the Central Committee of the Communist Party of Czechoslovakia".[70] The report contains a description of the situation of the G*psies in Brekov that already bears a striking resemblance to Mr Gunár's narrative:

> The settlement [in Brekov] is closely connected to the village to the west. All of the houses are properly built with resilient building material. The inhabitants are acclimatised with the local population. The dress, behaviour and housing culture often exceeds that of even the local population. The young generation no longer speak G*psy [the Romani language]. The citizens are duly integrated into party and public life and are members of the MNV. Illiteracy is not a problem amongst the adults.[71]

However, other documents refer to ongoing problems with "housing culture". The section of the report on the regional survey of Romani settlements of June 1956 on Brekov notes the "unsatisfactory" condition of ten of the nineteen local dwellings.[72] In February 1961, a survey of the settlement in the presence of a representative of the district sanitary station observed, inter alia, that "[t]he residential buildings on the outskirts of the village comprise a G*psy quarter: they are clustered together and consequently they lag behind in respect of the general development of social order." Meanwhile, further construction was intended to "allow citizens of G*psy origin to be dispersed amongst other residents", something the survey claimed was a demand made by the "citizens of G*psy origin" themselves, who, in other respects, were found to enjoy a "sufficient standard of living" (with a reference to school attendance and employment).[73] The same findings are to be found in a report based on a "tour of the settlement" with the regional activist (an official function at the ONV) Štefan Fabián that took place in July of that year, according to which its residents live an "orderly life" (usporiadaný život) and the

---

70 ŠOkA Humenné, f. Odbor vnutorných vecí ONV Humenné, kart. 22, sp. 122, "Zápis prevedený dňa 14. Októbra při prieskume osady v Brekove", 14 October 1958. The document authors (members of the "survey commission") are referring to the resolution on Work amongst the G*psy Population from April of that year, in which the assimilation programme is formulated more comprehensively for the first time (Jurová 2008, 688).

71 ŠOkA Humenné, f. Odbor vnutorných vecí ONV Humenné, kart. 23, sp. 134, "Zpráva o riešení otázky občanov cigánského pôvodu v okrese", 20 December 1958.

72 ŠAPO Nižná Šebastová, f. Odbor vnutorných vecí KNV Prešov, kart. 219, inv. č. 53, "Zpráva zo služobnej cesty konanej v dňoch od 8 do 12 júna 1956", 1956.

73 ŠOkA Humenné, f. MNV Brekov, kart. 14, sp. 160, "Zápis na základe prieskumu obyvateľov cigánského pôvodu", 12 February 1961.

"housing culture" is "quite good" since "almost all of them have their own detached houses".[74]

The documents of that time, therefore, describe the position of the Roma in Brekov as somewhat ambiguous. On the one hand, they speak of a high standard of living that, in implicit comparison with the dominant figure of the "backward G*psy", is evidenced primarily by employment figures and school attendance, but also by the abandonment of the Romani language as a "deficient" linguistic code from the dominant perspective (see Davidová 1965; Nováček 1968). However, references to a lagging "cultural level" also emerge from these descriptions, mainly in reference to the housing and sanitary situation in the settlement and the (sometimes explicit) comparison with the situation in the village as a whole (even though according to one optimistic description, the standard of living of the Roma was at times even "superior" to that of the "majority" population).

2.2.2 Attitudes of the Brekov Roma in documents of the time

The period documents do not only include an external description of the situation in the Brekov settlement, but also capture the specific attitudes and agency of its inhabitants. Particularly noteworthy are those texts written by the Roma themselves. Most of them concern the housing situation and its development at the turn of the 1950s and 1960s. For instance, a document dated November 1960 notes that in 1956, one of the Roma purchased a plot of land in the village (i.e. outside the settlement) from a non-Romani villager and built a detached house on it in the same year, where he and his family have lived ever since.[75] However, the housing situation was to change in the settlement itself, when in 1959 and 1961, building permits were granted for the conversion of one detached house and the construction of another.[76]

According to a report by the Municipal National Committee (MNV), in 1962, Bartoloměj S sought to build a detached house for his family in

---

74 ŠOkA Humenné, f. MNV Brekov, kart. 14, sp. 161, "Zápis za prítomnosti krajského aktivistu pre otázky občanov *cigánskeho* pôvodu." 3 July 1961.

75 ŠOkA Humenné, f. MNV Brekov, kart. 14, sp. 157, "Kupnopredajná zmluva", 17 November 1960.

76 ŠOkA Humenné, f. MNV Brekov, kart. 14, sp. 157, Building permit, 3 June 1959; ŠOkA Humenné, f. MNV Brekov, kart. 14, sp. 157, Building permit, 28 January 1959; ŠOkA Humenné, f. MNV Brekov, kart. 14, sp. 160, Building permit, 29 February 1961.

the "developed part of the village" (due to the unsatisfactory housing in the settlement),[77] and in the same year Štefan D applied for the allocation of a specific building plot in the village and was advised by the MNV to arrange the sale himself with the landowners.[78] In neither case do the archive materials provide information on further developments. However, the archived application of Štefan D is itself important authentication of how the Roma themselves viewed their own social position, even in relation to a specific location. In the application dated 24 March 1962 and addressed to the MNV in Brekov, Štefan D states the following:

> I would like to request the allocation of building plot no. [xy], part of [xy] and [xy]. This land is located in the developed part of the municipality of Brekov [...]. My reasons are as follows: I am the father of six dependent children with whom I live in a G*psy colony. My children travel to a school that is located quite far from my family home. In order for my children to learn to live and work more culturally, they need to socialise with more mature and thus more cultured peers. It is for this reason that our [Communist] Party and government is taking great care of people of G*psy origin. This is a priority issue and I therefore believe that the officials of the MNV and ONV will take this matter into consideration. This is why I am requesting that you allocate to me the building plot I have specified above. I trust that this matter will be taken into consideration and that I will not encounter any difficulties with the officials of the MNV in Brekov or the ONV. For my part, I will do my best not to disappoint the faith placed in me by officials and will continue to be receptive.[79]

The language of the entire application is strongly in synch with the contemporary discourse of G*psyness, as I analysed it in the first part of this chapter. The writer accepts the dominant demand for a more "cultured life for G*psies" and cleaves to the official view of the "G*psy settlement" as a space of "cultural backwardness". He also reproduces the discourse according to which it is above all the new political regime under which the "Party and government" made possible the all-inclusive

---

77 ŠOkA Humenné, f. MNV Brekov, kart. 14, sp. 161, "Zápisnica pri príležitosti vyhliadnuti stavebného pozemku", 27 January 1962.

78 ŠOkA Humenné, f. MNV Brekov, kart. 14, sp. 161, "Žiadosť o premiestnenie z cigánskej kolónie – oznámenie", 17 April 1962.

79 ŠOkA Humenné, f. MNV Brekov, kart. 14, sp. 161, "Žiadosť o premiestnenie z cigánskej kolónie", 24 March 1962.

belonging of Roma within socialist society as a whole. Yet it is also clear that within the context of the application, this discourse is being instrumentalised, at least to some extent, in order to achieve specific objectives. Nevertheless, however much one allows for a degree of instrumentalisation of the language of that time, the applicant's desire to live a more "cultured life" must be taken seriously. Moreover, the very emphasis on the allocation of building land points to a shared idea of the settlement itself as the location of "cultural backwardness" or, more generally, as a "bad address" (see Ort 2022b, 79–119).

A similar emphasis on the key role of the "[Communist] Party and government" from the perspective of the Brekov Roma themselves is strongly present in a different context. In a discussion at the first district meeting of "citizens of G*psy origin" in October 1958, Mr K, himself from Brekov, stressed that the Roma of Brekov had always found gainful employment, even under the "capitalist state", when "they did [...] very important work, namely, they produced [...] building materials, specifically lime". The same individual also drew attention to the children's regular school attendance. He formulated the significance of the new socio-political order as follows:

It is clear that our life has progressed considerably. Many of us well understand the precepts of socialism, what the party and the government mean. It was never even heard of for G*psy children to have the opportunities they have now.[80]

Mr K also situates the individual efforts and mobility of his own children – his son, a student at the teacher training college in Michalovce, and his "properly employed" daughter – within this framework. In the case of his daughter, he reiterates that it was the "Party and government" that had offered her such an opportunity, while the future of his son was yet to test the veracity of the much vaunted egalitarianism: "We will see if he attains the kind of position a person of the White race can." He notes certain limits placed on equal opportunities in the housing sector too. He observes the unavailability of suitable building plots and the inadequate sanitary situation in the Brekov settlement, especially with regard to a lack of water and the limited number of toilets. From this perspective he states

---

80 ŠOkA Humenné, f. Odbor vnutorných vecí ONV Humenné, kart. 22, sp. 122, "Zápisnice z I. Okresného aktívu občanov cigánskeho pôvodu", 26 Ocotober 1958.

that the inspection of the settlement aimed at discovering if it "met health requirements" in the presence of representatives of the MNV and ONV was initiated by the inhabitants themselves. "We want our house to be such that it would not be possible to tell who lives in it," he concludes his contribution, and it is clear from the context that he is referring to the automatic association of G*psies with a deficient housing culture.[81]

As in another eastern Slovak village I analysed within a different temporal context, so in Brekov the (self-)image of the integration of the local Roma was based on the dominant discourse of G*psyness (see Ort 2022b). At a district meeting of representatives of the individual authorities with the participation of the Roma held in 1966, this was voiced explicitly by one of them. Mr D, though he himself lived on a housing estate in Humenné, spoke of "the standard of living of the G*psy population in the settlement of Brekov" whence, it seems, he hailed. According to the minutes of the meeting, he stated that "he and his family are completely civilised and as such **he no longer feels himself [to be] a G*psy**" [emphasis J. O.].[82] This statement, which was downstream of the logic of the entire assimilation policy, he supplemented with a reminder of certain limits as regards social acceptance. While Mr K wondered whether his son would enjoy the same opportunities as a "person of the White race", Mr D ended by articulating his lived experience of the "discourteous" way he was treated by the authorities as a Rom.[83]

When reading these documents, one cannot help but reflect upon the relationship of Romani people to the dominant logic of "dispersal" behind efforts to "liquidate undesirable concentrations". In addition to their explicitly formulated desire to leave their own settlement, they also sought to transform said settlement into a more dignified place to live. I will address this question, in which the strategy of escape versus acknowledgement of the existing environment and efforts to cultivate it are juxtaposed, in the following chapter (Chapter Three). However, given the exceptionalist narrative of the Brekov Roma it is telling that, in their conversations with me (see below), the Roma witnesses from the village did not use the largely stigmatising term "settlement" (*osada*; which, however, did appear in period descriptions of the area), but replaced it with the term "street" (*ulica*). Moreover, they pointed out that some

81 Ibid.
82 ŠAKE Košice, f. Komisia Vsl. KNV pre cigánske obyvatelstvo Košice, kart. 10, sp. 104, "Zápisnica", 23 June 1966.
83 Ibid.

non-Romani families also lived in this street, thus defining themselves in opposition to the idea of a segregated "G*psy concentration".

Finally, the documents presented here link up to the discussion of Romani agency in relation to state policies. In a situation in which the dominant discourse viewed the marginalisation of the Roma as the natural outcome of their G*psyness on the one hand, and the result of historically rooted racism of previous regimes and non-Romani society in general on the other, there was not much space left within which the Roma might track their own agency. Even in statements made by the Roma themselves, notwithstanding the fact they were made within a particular context and with a specific aim, the focus turned, alongside their own agency, to the role of the "Party and government" that had made social inclusion for the Roma possible in Brekov. This is fully in line with the discourse under examination, in which it was mainly the newly installed regime that enabled the Roma to live a "decent" and "civilised" life. As other documents show, it was through the lens of an egalitarian society that some of the demands being made by the Roma could be rendered illegitimate. In October 1964, Štefan D, together with other citizens, filed a complaint with the Regional National Committee (KNV) against the chairman of the Brekov MNV and relationships between other local councillors. The complaint was dealt with by the head of the control department and secretary of the G*psy Commission (Špiner, already quoted above), who declared it to be unfounded. The extensive justification of the decision included a comment regarding the illegitimacy of complaints submitted by "citizens of G*psy origin" with regard to their living conditions in the municipality:

> It is perhaps incomprehensible why such a substantial number of the complainants are citizens of G*psy origin, who enjoy almost the best conditions in the village in terms of housing, employment, the general environment, etc. The MNV has devoted great attention to these issues, not only now, but in the past. Today in Brekov there is no distinction made between citizens of G*psy origin and other citizens, and here it should be said that the National Committee has played a decisive role. The citizens themselves are aware of this fact and confirmed it during the interview. However, they did not even realise it when drawing up their complaint, a fact that was confirmed by Mr Štefan D himself.[84]

---

84 ŠAKE Košice, f. Komisia Vsl. KNV pre cigánske obyvatelstvo Košice, kart. 4, sp. 45, "Vyjadrenie k sťažnosti", "Zápisnica", 7 March 1964.

The authors of this text, too, played down the individual efforts of the Roma themselves, since it was the local authority that had apparently ensured they enjoyed the "best conditions". However, the document also shows that narrative of social equality, which was maintained from a position of power, preserved the existing hierarchy of relations and thus de-legitimised those voices that questioned the existence of such equality (see Ort 2022b).

2.2.3 The social position of the Roma in Brekov

Though the position of the Roma in the hierarchy of socio-economic relations in Brekov reveals signs of their firm embeddedness in these systems, one can also speak of a certain asymmetrical belonging. It was precisely through association with the category of G*psyness that a specific socio-economic position was fabricated for the Roma, relegating them to a subordinate position (see Hübschmannová 1998, Ort 2022b). Both the municipal chronicle[85] and a relatively detailed monograph on the history of Brekov (Molnár 2017) are essentially silent on the history of the Roma, and both texts thus present a largely homogenised picture of the local population. Gunár's text recounts the history of the Roma in the village in a way that is familiar from other locations: the beginnings of the Romani presence in the village date back to the very start of the 20th century and the invitation extended to the family of a Romani blacksmith from another nearby village (see Mann 2018, Ort 2021, 2022b). Gunár cleaves to the dominant image of the Roma in the eastern Slovak countryside by describing their key sources of livelihood, be this music or basket-making.

However, two sections of Gunár's text stand out. The author states that even "[p]rior to the arrival of the Roma, Juraj K had settled in the village, [...] [who] worked as a civil servant on the railways [and] was generally considered the wealthiest Rom in Brekov." This Juraj K apparently arrived in the village upon marrying a local, one Anna O, who Gunár speculates was from a poor non-Romani family or whose father might have been Rom. The story of the "first Rom in the village" constructed in this way implies a degree of interdependence between the Roma and the "local" (i.e. non-Romani) population, and thus disrupts

---

85 *Kronika obce Brekov* (Chronicle of Brekov Municipality).

the dominant idea of the Roma as a newly arrived isolated group (see Ort 2021, 2022b), while at the same time it contributes to the debate around the ambiguous question of who actually was a Rom in the local context.

The second feature that catches one's attention concerns a particular economic practice by means of which Gunár himself reinforces his exceptional status among the other Roma in the region. This involved the local production of handmade and fired bricks, as opposed to the unfired bricks produced by Romani people in many other places (see Horváthová 1964). It is said that the Roma produced these bricks from the pre-war period until the mid-1960s and supplied them to the non-Roma throughout the area. However, apart from the production of a "G*psy brick" (*c*gánska tehla*), as it was called by the non-Roma (Molnár 2017, 225), it also involved work in the local lime works, and this supposedly symbolised Romani embeddedness in local relations. In an online memoir, one non-Romani witness[86] documented the exceptional status[87] of Brekov's Roma by claiming that they all worked in the limekiln, not only before the war, but also during the period of the Slovak state, when the factory was confiscated from its Jewish owners.[88] In addition to the participant of the district meeting quoted above, the Romani witnesses Bartolomej and Jozef Demeter also refer to the work of the Roma in the limekiln in their published memoir of the Second World War (Fedič 2001, 39–40, 42). The former describes the economic relationship between the Roma and the Jews in more detail: "You worked only until October, because no one needed lime in winter. So we spent the whole of winter at home. The Jews gave us flour, sugar, oil and other foodstuffs, without which we would have perished." (ibid., 39). However, although the Jews were taken to concentration camps during the war and never returned to the village (according to the monograph on the history of the village, there were two families [Molnár 2017, 138]; the 1942 census of Jews listed nineteen individuals out of a total population of 711[89]), as elsewhere in Slovakia, the Roma were spared such a fate. However, the Second World War revealed the clear limits of local belonging for the Roma themselves, as the witnesses referred to above recalled their harassment by their non-Romani neighbours, members of the Hlinka Guard (Fedič 2001, 39–40 and 42; see Molnár 2017, 135–137). Nevertheless, one

---

86 The name, year of birth and date on which the interview took place are not specified.
87 He literally stated that "we can safely say that the G*psies of Brekov are the tops".
88 *Vápenka Brekov* [online]. Accessed 17 July 2023.
89 *Súpis Židov* [online]. Accessed 19 October 2019.

of the witnesses stated that "we had no beef with the others in Brekov, they were good people" (Fedič 2001, 42).

2.2.4 "Local" and "foreign G*psies"

The position of the Roma in Brekov was not based solely on their relationship with the non-Romani neighbourhood or the general category of G*psyness. There were other forms of classification that led to a sharper differentiation between the Roma in the region, whether applied from the outside or formulated by the Roma themselves. Tracing these forms helps us understand how the category of "civilised Brekov Roma" was created and maintained and how it came to play an important role in the way that the resettlement policy was implemented on the ground.

The external differentiation amongst the Roma themselves is mentioned in one of the few references to them in the monograph on the history of the village. In the chapter "The Crafts in Brekov", though the author is concerned mainly with the activities of a Romani blacksmith native to Brekov, he adds a paragraph about "Romani trough makers" from Podčičva (see Agocs 2003), some of whom had settled within the village boundaries close to the River Laborec. According to a non-Romani witness, who was perhaps still referring to the pre-war period, these Podčičva Roma lived "in makeshift dwellings and tents, with only the most basic facilities" (Molnár 2017, 217). The description of these periodic neighbours contains an implicit differentiation from the Roma living permanently in Brekov, while drawing on the popular image of the G*psy as nomad.

This latter figure in turn contributed to the external differentiation of the Roma living in Brekov within the context of the 1959 census of "nomadic persons" (*kočovné osoby*). In Brekov itself, four families totalling eighteen people were included in the census.[90] As in Kapišová (Ort 2022a), though these were exclusively Romani families judging by their surnames and Gunár's chronicle, by no means all of the Romani families living there were included in the census (according to the description of the situation of the Roma in Brekov, two years later there were a total of 176 people living there).[91] It is evident that, as in Kapišová, the way

---

90 ŠOkA Humenné, f. Odbor vnutorných vecí ONV Humenné, kart. 23, sp. 137, "Zpráva o priebehu súpisu osob kočujúcich a polokočujúcich", 12 February 1959.
91 Ibid.

the census was conducted reveals the ability of the local authority to distinguish between Romani families and to attribute to them and reflect different degrees of embeddedness in local socio-economic relations.

While conducting my research amongst the Roma in the vicinity of Humenné and attempting to contact surviving witnesses from the period under consideration, I observed several ways in which the Roma defined themselves according to the logic of local (self-)identification at the level of individual villages. This was particularly noticeable in the relationship between the Roma from Brekov and those from the Podskalka settlement in Humenné (see Chapter Three), especially given the geographical proximity of the two locations (Brekov is only a few kilometres from Humenné). The Brekov Roma pointed to the high level of social integration they enjoyed and in certain contexts referred to the Podskalka Roma as "backward". The latter claimed the Brekov Roma displayed arrogance towards other Roma, above all through their ignorance of the Romani language, which in Podskalka was the living language of everyday communication. The differences between the two locations were also reflected in what the regional authorities had to say of them at the time. In contrast to what were described as the "civilised G*psies" of Brekov, during the 1950s Podskalka was already cited as being the largest "G*psy concentration" in the district, with a population of around five hundred (as opposed to fewer than two hundred Roma in Brekov; see Chapter Three). Gunár, too, recalled conflicts with the Roma from Podskalka in an interview with me, stating that they took place while he was a youth, perhaps around the time of the resettlement policy (he was born in 1948):

> They knew we were from Brekov, we [knew] that [they] were from Podskalka, so we didn't speak to each other because they spoke Romani. We didn't understand Romani and they beat us up. [...] We boys, maybe 14 or 15 years old, used to go see a movie on Sunday. [...] We would get there and then they would arrive from Podskalka, they lived in Humenné too, and they started to speak to us in Romani. We told them that we didn't understand and that they should speak Slovak. And so we're being snooty, like people today say conceited, how do you know that we're Roma, G*psies, and why can't you speak Romani? And we replied that we don't speak it, neither do our fathers or our grandfathers, so neither do we. So they set upon us and we had to run to the train station. We never became friendly with them.[92]

---

92   Interview with Koloman Gunár (b. 1948), *op. cit.*

Elsewhere, Gunár extends this definition of the Brekov Roma in relation to other "G*psies" to the entire region:

> Well, you know, our Roma, our grandfathers and great-grandfathers, at the time when they were of productive age, they didn't even want to talk to other G*psies. There were G*psies who were on the lowest level, then higher and higher, until the highest level. [...] That was the village of Brekov, and the rest were so much weaker.[93]

This description, which in the main continues to copy and reproduce the dominant logic of G*psyness, cannot be understood purely on a discursive level, but as part of a set of specific strategies for shaping one's own social position. Gunár himself described the special status of the Brekov Roma as the result of historically continuous social control, which, he maintained, was also in part institutionalised:

> Our fathers and grandfathers had the final say. So that when, for example, someone [a Rom from the surrounding area] took a girl from Brekov as his wife and wanted to live here, they had to give their consent to the mayor. If they said no, we don't want him here, the mayor wouldn't register him.

And that used to happen?

> It did indeed. And that was a good thing too. These days everything is so free and easy that anyone can come here and take a wife and live here and cause us shame because they don't know how to behave. [...] I approved of it, I wanted it reintroduced. But voices were heard saying it was a bad thing, why shouldn't his daughter live here with her husband. Well, because we didn't want that man here, that's why.[94]

Although Gunár dated such an agreement with the local authorities to the pre-war period, other Romani witnesses from Brekov, Koloman S (born 1946) and Cyril D (born 1956), felt that this had in fact been a feature for the entire duration of the communist regime.[95] All of the witnesses I interviewed in Brekov (including Olga O, born 1938 in

---

93 Ibid.
94 Ibid.
95 Interview with Romani man Koloman S (b. 1946) and Romani man Cyril D (b. 1956), recorded by the author in June 2022 in Brekov in Slovak (recording in the possession of the author).

Brekov), at the same time as assuring me that "the G*psies of Brekov were always the best in the district" (or "the best in Czechoslovakia" according to Cyril D), expressed disappointment at the fact that "today" (i.e. when the interviews were being conducted) there was no control or selection of newly arriving Roma and that "problematic" (*problémoví*) and "filthy" (*špinaví*) Roma were moving into the village and blemishing the historically formed good name of the Brekov Roma as "respectable G*psies". At the time of my research, the narrative of their own excep- tionalism persisted amongst the Roma of Brekov (who identified with the original Brekov Romani families), who distanced themselves not only from the dominantly understood category of G*psyness, but also from those who were associated with it in the surrounding villages and from some of the newcoming families in Brekov.

However, the Roma in Brekov never formed a completely isolated community in relation to other Roma in the surrounding area. Despite their strong embeddedness in local relations described above, inter-ethnic marriages within Brekov were rare, and the local Roma usually chose Romani partners from other villages in the region. Although my inter- viewees named specific villages in which the Roma were said to have lived on a certain "level" (*úroveň*), even back then they also stated that pressure (direct or indirect) was exerted on the Roma who moved to Brekov to adopt a proper "way of life", for example, by relinquishing Romani as their everyday means of communication (see Hajská 2012, 2015). Given the prevailing practice of virilocal post-marital residence, it was usually women who moved to Brekov and the Romani women of Brekov who were expected to move to be with their husbands, possibly outside of their home village. Thus, the image of the "local Roma" was being reshaped on an ongoing basis and was to a large extent gendered (see Ort 2022b).

Although I have not been able to discover any more detailed infor- mation regarding the alleged agreement between the Brekov Roma and the mayor regarding the (non-)acceptance of newly arriving Roma, the archive of the MNV in Brekov does contain one document that suggests similar pattern. According to the minutes of a meeting of members of the Brekov MNV in 1953 regarding the "admission of outsiders of G*psy origin to our village",[96] one non-Romani villager (a widow) had decided to sell her building plot to "people who are not members of our village,

---

[96] ŠOkA Humenné, f. MNV Brekov, kart. 14, sp. 152, "Prijatie cudzích príslušníkov do našej obci, cigánskeho pôvodu", 1953.

of G*psy origin, who want to move to our village and build houses here". The MNV committee and its members, as well as other individuals, were against this move. They requested that "the ONV in Humenné vote against the relocation of three foreign families into our village and that these families remain where they are at present." They pointed out that "if the person in question is obliged to sell this land, then let them sell it to someone from our village and not to someone with whom the village is not satisfied." "[W]hy should these families move into our village and create havoc?", the minutes say, and conclude by stating that "[t]heir ancestors have never lived in our village and we are therefore against them being amongst us".

There is nothing in the minutes of the meeting of the MNV to indicate that this objection was raised (or supported) by the Roma living in Brekov. Similarly, the wording of the minutes does not explicitly state that the would-be buyers are to be prevented from moving to the village primarily on the basis of their ascribed G*psyness. However, as I have shown elsewhere, the categories of "foreign" and G*psy for the most part intersected and reinforced each other (Ort 2022b). The identification of these citizens as G*psies lent support to their being seen as foreign, and the way of life ensuing therefrom, which would supposedly cause "havoc in the village", resonates strongly with popular characterisations of "inadaptable G*psies". In the broader context, there is also an unspoken distinction between "local/our G*psies", who are in part excluded from the more general category of "problematic G*psies" (see Grill 2015b, Kobes 2012, Ort 2022b), and "foreign G*psies", who are included in said category (see also Hübschmannová 1998). The archival materials are silent regarding the outcome of this particular case. However, the attitudes of the MNV towards the family of "foreign G*psies" fit snugly into the way that the Brekov Roma viewed their own situation.

2.2.5 Displacement of a foreign G*psy

These mechanisms in the formation of the social position of the Roma in Brekov come together to create an important context for understanding the implementation of the resettlement programme in the village. This involved the eviction of Regina D's family, which occurred after her husband Rudolf returned from prison, where he had spent over ten years for the murder of a non-Romani villager. When two of my interviewees, Koloman S and Cyril D, recalled Rudolf D and the circumstances around which his wife Regina sold her house and the couple and their children moved out of Brekov, they attributed to him characteristics featuring strong associations with the figure of the "inadaptable G*psy". They emphasised that "he was not a Brekovian". As Cyril D explained, the different "mentality" was the result of a different origin:

> There was a different mentality where he came from. Not like ours. Where they lived they still had no relationship with the Whites. They fought and stole and everything you can think of. And then he came here and thought that things would be the same as they had been there. And they weren't. Because we and our fathers used to visit the pub together, as one family. And he arrived and he wanted something more.[97]

In light of this testimony, the resettlement of the family of Rudolf and Regina D fits well into the narrative of the history of the Brekov Roma as "respectable G*psies", who were able to assert themselves within the local structure of socio-economic relations, and, with the cooperation of their non-Romani neighbours and the local authorities, were able not only to define themselves in opposition to "problematic G*psies", but to separate those who belonged to this category from the local community. Rudolf D conformed to such an image, firstly by marrying into Brekov from a village where the Roma were deemed perfect examples of "backwardness", and above all by confirming his position as a "criminal" by shooting dead one of the local non-Roma. From this perspective, Rudolf D did not meet the tacit requirement to "adapt" to the local way of life and, as Koloman S and Cyril D pointed out, the local Roma never really accepted him into their community. According to the recollections of my interviewees, Rudolf D's family was forced to leave the village mainly under pressure from the family of the murdered villager, a family, moreover, that lived in a street inhabited mainly by Romani people (referred to in the documents as the settlement) only some two hundred metres from Regina and Rudolf D's house.[98] In light of the above, however, the family's departure could also make sense in terms of how the status of the local Roma themselves was shaped and maintained.

Such a framing of the practice of the resettlement policy in Brekov, which helped resolve a particular conflict and reproduce the relatively

---

97 Interview with Koloman S (b. 1946) and Cyril D (b. 1956), *op. cit.*
98 Ibid.

higher status of the Brekov Roma, has a clear legitimacy and demonstrates how the state policy was connected to locally specific and historically created contexts. Nonetheless, one must not fall into the trap of over-simplifying matters. Reading the testimony given by Cyril D, backed up by that of Koloman S, it should not be forgotten that the former was born in the same year that Rudolf D was convicted of murder, while the latter was only ten years old. I certainly have no desire to question the reliability of their testimony. My point is rather that both witnesses, whom I ended up interviewing together (something I had not planned – Cyril D joined the conversation I was having with Koloman S in the garden of his house), also set the event being discussed within a certain narratival framework. It was within the prevailing emphasis on the exceptionalism of the Brekov Roma that the description of convicted murderer Rudolf D as "foreign" made sense. However, other interviewees throw doubt on an unambiguous association of Rudolf D with the category of "foreign" and "inadaptable". Olga O, sister of Regina D, in particular, recalled that Rudolf D had been a "warm, gentlemanly and reasonable person", who, in a moment of weakness, had reacted badly to being humiliated by one of the non-Roma and had himself been the victim of "great misfortune".[99] In his book, Gunár described Rudolf D as follows (no doubt drawing on the stories of some of the older Roma):

Rudolf D [...] killed a *gadjo* and was sentenced to twelve years in prison. He ended up serving about seven or eight years for good behaviour. Rudo D was a musician and played the bass. He was a member of Gustáv O's band, but was also an avid chess player. He was a member of the Humenné Chess Club. [...] In 1956, one evening in a Brekov pub Rudolf D shot [...] Andrej D [who] lived in the locality of Hušták [i.e. in a Romani street] in Brekov. [Andrej D] [h]ated the Roma and treated them badly. Rudolf D [...] was not physically equal to Andrej D. He became very angry and could not bear the humiliation he suffered at the hands of the *gadjo* Andrej D. (Gunár 2010, 49)

And further on he writes:

[Rudolf D] [p]layed chess and cards in high society. He knew how to present himself, and Regina adored him for it. He could not bear insults and

---

humiliation, and so, provoked by anger and physical weakness, he committed murder. (Gunár 2010, 105)

Though these descriptions do not contradict the "different mentality" ascribed to someone from a different village, as Cyril D put it, it is clear that the image of an "avid" and "reasonable" chess player and musician is not fully compatible with a "culturally backward G*psy", while Rudolf D's membership of a local Romani band throws doubt on the idea of his non-acceptance among the Roma in Brekov and indicates a degree of embeddedness in local relations. According to the detailed genealogy in Gunár's book, Rudolf D must have lived with Regina, a native of Brekov, since at least 1944, when their first son was born (probably in Brekov). This is backed up by the recollections of another of Rudolf and Regina's sons, Aladár (born 1950),[100] who stressed that his father enjoyed good relations with the other "G*psies" (Aladár refused to call himself Rom, see the previous footnotes), something borne out, as in the case of Koloman G, by the fact he played in a local Romani band. However, Aladár referred to wider social participation over and above relations with the Roma of Brekov, and said that his father Rudolf was a "highly intelligent person" who had founded the Limeworks Physical Education Club with a local teacher. Aladár also recalled that when young they used to play with the children of the murdered man Andrej D and that the tragic conflict of their respective fathers to some extent passed them by.

It is clear that Rudolf D had an ambivalent status in the locally defined community. He was connected to the village by familial relations (through his relationship with the family of Brekov native Regina), socio-economic factors (being a member of the local band) and cultural ties (as a member of the chess club in Humenné and co-founder of the sports club). These bonds were also gendered. As a man he participated in the social life of a patriarchal village community, whether as a member of a traditional

---

100 Aladár D (b. 1950) remained in Czechia and no longer maintains contact with the Roma in Brekov. Due to the Covid-19 pandemic, he conducted one online interview via Skype, but later refused my request for another interview, saying that he had no desire to talk about the Roma or Brekov. He had fond memories of Brekov and said that he had not wanted to move away, but that he had now begun a new life for himself in Czechia. In terms of the focus of this chapter, it is interesting that right from the start of our conversation, he refused to call himself Romani, going so far as to claim that the Roma had never lived in Brekov. He was prepared to use the term "citizens of G*psy origin" and thus draw on the dominant logic, outlined above, of G*psyness as a socio-cultural and not an ethnic category (Interview with Aladár D [b. 1950], recorded by the author in September 2021 online in Czech [recording in the author's possession]).

Romani band or, for instance, through meeting other men in the local pub. However, there were circumstances that had the potential to exclude him from the local community. His origins in a different region of eastern Slovakia distinguished him from the local Roma and he could therefore be singled out and deemed to be "foreign". However, along with other Brekov Roma, he might have been relegated to an inferior status through his association with the racialised category of G*psyness. This level of relations is accentuated by Gunár, who recounts the story of a musician who played "chess and cards in high society", and who "murdered out of great anger and physical weakness", when he could no longer endure the humiliation provoked by a *gadjo* who "hated the Roma". This is therefore a powerful account of one man's experience of anti-Roma racism and its affective level. In the mid-1960s, the category of G*psyness comes into play once again in connection with Rudolf D and his family, this time within the context of the centralised resettlement policy. Her association with this category allowed Rudolf's wife Regina D, owner of a house in Brekov, to sell her property as part of the "liquidation of G*psy shacks", and to move to Czechia, given that it was now impossible to remain in the village following Rudolf's return from prison.

2.2.6 Eviction as a resolution of local conflicts

In order to understand the dynamics of the negotiation of the category of G*psyness and to try and make sense of the fact that the incident in Brekov resulted in the relocation of an individual family, I would like to place the entire case within the context of similar conflicts being played out at that time in other villages in eastern Slovakia for which there is evidence. These examples include the village of Vlachovo in the district of Rožňava, where a non-Romani villager was killed in February 1966, and the village of Hostovice in the district of Snina (then Humenné), where a non-Romani villager ended up in hospital with injuries sustained in a fight around the same time. It must be stressed that bringing these events together must not and cannot justify the period discourse of the criminalisation and securitisation of the Roma. Indeed, one might say that the opposite is true. I present these examples here partly in order to show how the dominant discourse of the securitisation of Roma outlined above was co-constructed, but also to reveal the different forms it took in individual locations, partly in relation to the resettlement policy with which all the cases intersected at some point.

The case of the killing in the village of Vlachovo is interesting, not least because in addition to the record in the Security Services Archive (see Zapletal 2012, 61), there exist several sources of Romani provenance that deal with it. These include a complaint addressed to the KNV in Košice, in which a Romani family from Vlachovo demanded they be allowed to return from Czechia to their home district;[101] a similarly phrased viewer's reaction to the television programme discussed above;[102] an archived transcript of an interview that Hübschmannová conducted with a Romani woman from Vlachovo then living in Czechia;[103] and one of my own interviews, recorded by chance with a relative of the Roma from Vlachovo during my research in Humenné.[104] An excerpt from the first example cited, the complaint, will suffice as a summary of the entire event:

> We are originally residents from Vlachovo in the district of Rožňava, where in February of 1966, citizens of G*psy origin rioted during the annual meeting of the JRD [Jednotné zemědělské družstvo or United Agricultural Cooperative]. This resulted in a fight, during which one member of the JRD was stabbed with a knife. He died, and the citizens of Vlachovo, in retaliation, demolished the houses of many citizens of G*psy origin, as a result of which we were forced to relocate to Olomouc [Moravia].[105]

The incident in Vlachovo involved the actions of an individual. A document from the Security Services Archive describes the murder of JRD member Jozef O by the "G*psy" Martin G (Zapletal 2012, 61). In his reaction to the television broadcast, Karol C, himself a Rom from Vlachovo, writes that "three G*psies fought with the whites and killed one of them".[106] The difference between this case and the one discussed above is clear. In Brekov, the killing of a non-Romani villager was framed as

---

101 ŠAKE Košice, f. Komisia Vsl. KNV pre cigánske obyvatelstvo, kart. 19, sp. 100, Complaint – Ondrej G., 14 November 1968.
102 NA Prague, KSČ-ÚV-05/3, f. KSČ – Ústřední výbor 1945–1989, Praha – oddělení – oddělení ideologické, sv. 37, č. j. 299.
103 Archive of MRK, Brno, f. Pozůstalost Mileny Hübschmannové, kart. 11_ET, sp. Transkripty77-83_MH, č. 11.
104 Interview with Romani man Dušan K (b. 1965), recorded by the author in May 2019 in Snina in Slovak (recording in the author's possession).
105 ŠAKE Košice, f. Komisia Vsl. KNV pre cigánske obyvatelstvo, kart. 19, sp. 100, Complaint – Ondrej G., 14 November 1968.
106 NA Prague, KSČ-ÚV-05/3, f. KSČ – Ústřední výbor 1945–1989, Praha – oddělení – oddělení ideologické, sv. 37, č. j. 299.

the act of an individual and the sanctions extended "only" to his nuclear family, one reason perhaps being that Rudolf D could be separated from the category of embedded Brekov Roma given his origins in another village. In Vlachovo, on the other hand, the principle of collective guilt was applied, whereby the category of criminalised and securitised G*psies was used to cover all local Roma in accordance with ethno-racial criteria. As Karol C's letter continues: "they drove us all out of the village and we had to leave our region and travel to Czechia, which made us all sad because our houses were worth 50 thousand and we had to leave them behind because of three evil G*psies".[107] In an interview with me, a contemporary witness named Dušan K testified that the collective guilt was indirectly extended to all the Roma in the area, against whom anti-Roma racism and manifestations thereof had become noticeably more pronounced. At the same time, he said that such attitudes still persisted in Vlachovo at the time our interview was conducted (spring 2019), that the local authorities and the residents themselves were doing their best to ensure that no more Roma moved into the village, and that Romani people themselves sought to give the village a wide berth.[108]

In this context, however, it is worth nothing that the dominant logic according to which the murder of a JRD member in Vlachovo was framed as a collective act involving all the (local) Roma was also adopted by the parties submitting the complaint, in which they used the plural "citizens of G*psy origin [...] stabbed a member of the JRD with a knife".[109] Mrs G reached for a similar formulation in her interview with Hübschmanová. When asked "Why did you come to Olomouc?", she replied "Because the Roma killed a *gadjo* in Vlachovo", though she added in passing that "we all had to come here, all of us, all because of one person".[110] One cannot draw broader conclusions from these two testimonies, nor am I interested in "accusing" the Vlachovo Roma of internalising a criminalising view of the Roma as G*psies. In contrast to the strictly individualised description of the murder in Brekov, these

---

107 Ibid.
108 Interview with Dušan K (b. 1965), *op. cit.* Similar conclusions were drawn by fellow linguist Viktor Elšík on the basis of his field research in the region focusing on the dialectology of Romani. I would like to take this opportunity to thank him for sharing these unpublished findings with me.
109 ŠAKE Košice, f. Komisia Vsl. KNV pre cigánske obyvateľstvo, kart. 19, sp. 100, Complaint – Ondrej G., 14. 11. 1968.
110 Archive of MRK, Brno, f. Pozůstalost Mileny Hübschmannové, kart. 11_ET, sp. Transkripty77-83_MH, č. 11.

stories may rather serve to symbolise the diversity of the situation in both villages. In Brekov, the entire narrative was constructed on a proclamation of the collective identity of "civilised Roma", from which group a specific individual was singled out. In contrast, the letters written by the Roma of Vlachovo represented the demands of individuals trying to break free of the collectively applied category of G*psyness and to return to their home region (see also Chapter Four and a letter from Ondrej G).

The second case for the purpose of comparison concerns a conflict that took place in the village of Hostovice, which we learn of only from the testimony of witnesses. There is no complete agreement regarding the details and the precise date is uncertain. One of the witnesses is Margita Hlaváčová (born 1954), who herself grew up in the Hostovice settlement and described her family's departure to Czechia as follows:

> Dad got into a fight in Slovakia, so we had to up sticks and flee [from Hostovice] here [Czechia]. They had a fight and were looking for my dad, saying they wanted to kill him. There were three brothers who had to run away, because the youngest had got into a fight with some bloke at a party and stabbed him with a knife. [...] And he told us to move out immediately and that he wanted to kill my uncle. So we all had to flee from Slovakia to Czechia at midnight. [111]

It is not entirely clear whether Mrs Hlaváčová is referring to an event (or two different events) in which both brothers were involved, or to a single event regarding which at one point in her narration she confused the actors involved. It is also not clear whether *all* the Roma had to leave the Hostovice settlement as a result of the conflict. Mrs Hlaváčová speaks of the families of three brothers, and the village mayor stated in an interview with me that all the Roma had to flee.[112] Nor is it clear what relationship this event had to the resettlement policy. It apparently took place sometime in the mid-1960s, and as late as 1968 (in June and September respectively) two families were compensated for the homes they had sold in the Hostovice settlement.[113] The "flight" of the Roma from the settlement and the demolition of these buildings cannot be definitively linked. However, it is possible that in this case, too, the centralised

111 *Pamět Romů* [online]. Accessed 24 July 2023.
112 Interview with the mayor of the village of Hostovice conducted by the author in August 2020 in Hostovice in Slovak (unrecorded).
113 ŠOkA Humenné, f. Finančný odbor ONV Humenné, kart. 16, sp. 100, Jan S. [unprocessed]; ŠOkA Humenné, f. Finančný odbor ONV Humenné, kart. 17, sp. 103, Mária T. [unprocessed].

resettlement programme was deployed in the resolution of the local conflict and the departure of "unsuitable G*psies" confirmed. The events of that time are not clarified even by the scant archival documents that touch on the situation of the Roma in Hostovice. In 1966, in a discussion at a district meeting of officials from various authorities, including the Roma, the chairman of the MNV in Hostovice was forced to explain a situation in which local Roma were hiding in the surrounding forest "due to malicious reports circulating in the village", and "the VB [public security services] were warning the G*psies that they would be taken to Sudetenland".[114] A resolution passed by the district G*psy Commission of 22 March 1967 also states that it is necessary to investigate complaints submitted by "G*psy citizens from Hostovice, who are demanding the liquidation of the settlement, since it is situated far from the village".[115]

From the testimony of contemporary witnesses it ensues that no Romani people had been living in Hostovice for decades at the time of my research, i.e. that all of the inhabitants of the former settlement left for Czechia sometime in the late 1960s. But here, too, the situation was more complicated. During the time I spent amongst the Roma in the village of Stakčín, by chance I encountered Mrs Mária K (born 1950), who herself was from Hostovice. However, Mrs K was born into a Romani family whose presence I had not learned about from other sources. There follows a transcript of part of our conversation.

So how many Romani families were there in Hostovice?

There were Roma living there, but two kilometres from us. They were far away.

So there was a settlement, but you didn't live in it?

No, not at all. There was no settlement. There were four houses, no more. As far as I remember. But the older people told me that there had been more of them living there, but that they all went to Czechia leaving only four houses. And they were so poor. The children walked through mud, they lived like pigs. They used to take wood there [the non-Romani villagers], transport it in

---

114 ŠAKE Košice, f. KomisiaVsl. KNV pre cigánske obyvateľstvo, kart. 10, sp. 104, "Zápisnica", 23 June 1966.
115 ŠAKE Košice, f. Komisia Vsl. KNV pre cigánske obyvateľstvo, kart. 15, sp. 71, "Uznesenie", 22 March 1967.

cars, and you know what it's like, there was mud from the forest... And there was flowing water there, the kids were like filthy pigs.

And your family lived in the village?

Yeah, we used to live in the village.

[...]

Then some of the Roma got into a fight and people chased them away. They left and now there are none of them living there, none at all.

[...]

You didn't have much to do with each other...

No, they used to come to ours, my mum was godmother, they came to mum or for vegetables, but then mum killed a pig. She used to give them tripe and stuff like that and they would come to us. Because she was godmother they came over to ours.

And you were related somehow?

No, we weren't related.[116]

Mária K's testimony does not shed much light on the circumstances surrounding the departure of the Roma from Hostovice, except to raise the possibility that there might have been two distinct phases, what might be called a voluntary and forced departure (with all due allowance for the problematic nature of such a distinction). However, it is interesting for a different reason, since it demonstrates another way of differentiating the Roma in a specific location, a form of differentiation the framing of which is in lockstep with the dominant logic of G*psyness. This ensues from the location of families in the layout of the municipality, with the space of the (non-Romani) village on the one hand, and the Romani settlement on the other. In line with the dominant discourse on G*psies, Mária K describes the life of the Roma living in the settlement in somewhat dehumanising terms ("the kids were as filthy as pigs") and homogenises their position and actions ("some of the Roma got into

---

116 Interview with the Romani woman Mária K (b. 1950), recorded by the author in May 2019 in Stakčín in Slovak (recording in possession of author).

a fight and people chased them away"). At the same time, however, she reproduces the automatic association of the "G*psy way of life" with the "unhealthy" environment of the settlements (see Chapter Three). The relatively higher status of this Romani family, which did not speak Romani according to Mária K and which had an almost paternalistic relationship to the Roma of the settlement (framed by the institution of godparenthood), went hand-in-hand with its situatedness in the non-Romani part of the village outside the space known as the settlement. Perhaps it was also thanks to this positionality that the family did not attract the attention of the authorities, which referred to the situation of the G*psies in the village, nor was it affected by the final departure of Romani families from the settlement, who were to be expelled as a result of the conflict described above.

To sum up, in Brekov the Roma were able to claim membership of the category of "civilised Roma" and the category of G*psyness was applied to an individual. In Vlachovo, on the other hand, all the Roma were collectively included in G*psyness and consequently expelled, while in Hostovice, it was one family that held onto its established status, while the dominant category applied only to inhabitants of the settlement.

One should, of course, bear in mind that this is a retrospective reconstruction which is also shaped through the testimony of my interviewees. However, the internal differentiation between the Roma based on their location in the layout of a particular municipality has been described in more detail for other villages in eastern Slovakia (e.g. Grill 2015b, Hrustič 2015a,b). Particularly relevant to the period in question is my own historical reconstruction of the politics of place in the village of Jolany (Ort 2021, 2022b). Here, one family managed to obtain housing in the village outside the settlement in the mid-1960s, as a result of which the MNV did not draw up plans for their resettlement in Czechia, a measure which, on the contrary, was proposed for all families from the local settlement (even though the programme was in the end not implemented here). In the case of Jolany, the mobility of this particular family was also woven into the application of the official classification of G*psies (see the introduction to this chapter). This family was the only one to be included in the first category of G*psies who were well on their way to complete assimilation, while the other Roma remained in category II, the category of primary interest in the case of the policy in question (ibid.).

2.3 Conclusion

When Guy writes about the categorisation of G*psies within the context of the resettlement policy, he makes it clear that the relatively vague definition of centrally regulated administrative categories allowed room for local authorities to pursue their own interests. He illustrates this using the example of Bystrany, a village in the Spišská Nová Ves district of central-eastern Slovakia, where the MNV classified all the local Roma as category II, i.e. people who were expected to leave for Czechia. According to Guy, the authorities reached this decision without any regard for the actual way of life of the local Roma and with the apparent aim of getting rid of "their" Roma (Guy 1977, 279). I have not been able to track down how the centralised classification of G*psies in the case of Humenné was implemented, which makes it difficult to examine how the delineation of G*psyness was handled by individual actors at the local level within the context of the resettlement policy. Inasmuch as in this chapter, and indeed throughout the entire book, I have shifted the emphasis to the agency of the Roma themselves and the negotiation of their position in local relations, linking up these two levels, i.e. the official categorisation of G*psies and the ways in which local relations were defined, would be of considerable benefit to such a discussion. This is confirmed by the example cited above from Jolany, where the spatial mobility of one Romani family within the layout of the village was reflected in the official classification of G*psies (Ort 2022b, see above).

Even without knowing how the Municipal National Committees of the district of Humenné classified the Roma into centrally defined categories for the purpose of preparing a timetable for their resettlement, the example of Brekov, set within a broader analysis of the discourse of G*psyness of the time, is interesting in several respects. Firstly, it supports Guy's argument that the selection of certain families for implementation of the entire policy reflected the interests of local actors rather than the outcome of any proper assessment of way of life as implied by the regulation overseeing resettlement. Whereas Guy examined mainly the position of the local authorities, the implementation of the central policy in Brekov points to the interests of other local actors. It seems the non-Romani villagers, led by the survivors of someone murdered more than a decade earlier, sought the eviction of a particular Romani family. The expulsion of this family may have intersected with the interests of the Roma themselves and the ways in which they defined their own position in the local community and, by extension, in the region as a whole.

Apart from the family of Regina and Rudolf D themselves, who, according to witnesses at the time, decided that it was impossible to remain in the village after the latter's return from prison, it was the other Roma of Brekov, for whom such a practice of central policy converged with a historically shaped and locally embedded identity of "civilised Roma", who shared the local way of life (see Ort 2022b).

However, the example of the eviction of a single family framed in this way also serves to illustrate well that the practice of the central policy always depended on locally specific and historically contingent contexts. Although I was unable to trace a direct relationship between the centralised administrative classification of G*psies and its application by the local authority in Brekov, I have shown how the officially promulgated logic of G*psyness came up against the mechanisms of its own definition within a specific location. In the official ideology, G*psies were categorised on the basis of the degree to which they were "civilised" and integrated within socialist society (their "adaptability"). The ways of defining the relations and self-identification among the Roma of Brekov were fully in line with such a concept since they included the category of "civilised" versus "backward", i.e. "adaptable" versus "inadaptable". The inscription of the dominant concept of G*psyness into the structure of relations between the Roma themselves has previously been described in anthropological texts that have traced the modes of sociability of the Roma in the societies of central Europe (see Abu Ghosh 2008, Horváth 2012, Kovai 2012, Ort 2022b). Although the research referred to was conducted in the period following the start of the new millennium and thus took place against a different socio-political backdrop, Horváth, for example, places the strategy of "silencing G*psyness" within the context of socialist policies that (as in Czechoslovakia) held out to the Roma a false promise that if they were only to rid themselves of the characteristics of G*psyness, they would become fully-fledged citizens (Horváth 2012). This framing of the affirmation of one's own status and social belonging is to be seen amongst the Roma in Brekov in the statement made by one that he no longer "even feels like a G*psy". However, while I have shown that similar statements, not only by the Brekov Roma but also by Romani people writing letters in response to television programmes, were framed in the language of the ideology of that time, including expressions of gratitude to the "[Communist] Party and government", the roots of similar strategies aimed at "escaping G*psyness" (Abu Ghosh 2008) or "emigrating from G*psyness" (Hübschmannová 1999a) run deep. This is because they resonate not only with the language of a centrally defined politics in which G*psyness was understood as a category of social deviance, but also with a broader popular discourse in which the acknowledgement and recognition of a category of "respectable G*psy", free from "backwardness" and "parasitism", legitimised an otherwise highly racialising understanding of G*psyness. By identifying with this category, the Roma of Brekov (and elsewhere, for that matter) sought to reframe relations of domination and marginalisation (see the previous chapter) and to break out of the position of G*psies, to whom an inferior social status was automatically accorded.

The category of G*psyness here functioned as a "sticky" category (see Ahmed 2014), which adhered to certain bodies, and the Roma attempted to keep it from sticking to them. The attribution of G*psyness was decided by their surroundings, which, by the selfsame logic, participated in its silencing. And so, depending on various criteria, the Roma in individual villages were either included in or, on the contrary, excluded from the framing of local conflicts and, consequently, from the practice of resettlement. On the other hand, within the context of the resettlement policy, an association with the category of G*psyness was a way of monetising one's property, an opportunity taken up by Regina D and other Roma (see Chapter Three). Thus the official categorisation of G*psyness come up against its ethno-racial definition on an unclear border during the period under consideration and entered in various ways into the structuring of social relations and the socio-economic strategies of the Roma themselves.

However, the story of the Brekov Roma should not lead us to imagine that the Romani people, through their choice of language and the configuration of their understanding of their own social status, uncritically reproduced the logic of centrally formulated assimilationist policies. In fact, however much the Brekov Roma pointed to the absence in themselves of the key characteristics of the dominantly understood G*psyness, including language, one cannot speak in this context of an effort to reject outright a distinctive cultural identity and to blend into non-Romani society. A few moments are worthy of emphasis. Firstly, when Gunár reconstructed the "history of the settlement of the Roma in Brekov", he treated it as the story of a distinct group, notwithstanding its strong embeddedness in local socio-economic relations. Secondly, at the start of the 1970s, the Roma in Brekov were active members of the local branch of Zväz Cigánov-Rómov (Union of Gypsies-Roma; see Donert 2017, 189–193), in which they again formulated not their individual interests but the interests of the Brekov Roma as a group. Finally, while some officials, in line with the dominant narrative, viewed the integration of the Roma in Brekov as the outcome of the agency of the local authorities (or of "the Party and government") in particular, the Roma themselves were more prone to emphasise their own merits, especially as regards employment. It is possible to observe, especially in the reactions of viewers to the television programmes referred to above, that it was from these positions that the Roma defined the limits of what was claimed to be an egalitarian society, and this is also perhaps the source of some of the disparate demands made of the centrally formulated policy, specifically, in respect of its "dispersive" logic. I will speak more about this last aspect in the next two chapters.

3. CHAPTER THREE
The Settlements: Between Marginalisation and Autonomy

In the archive materials pertaining to the "G*psy settlements" in the Humenné district (however its borders changed in the post-war period), the Podskalka settlement crops up again and again. It attracted special attention for several reasons. From the 1950s onwards, in the reports of what was then the KNV in Prešov, it was referred to as both the largest settlement in the region and as a location with highly unsatisfactory standard of living, above all with regard to housing conditions. As such, it was one of the settlements the "liquidation" (*likvidace*) of which was deemed a priority. Podskalka was regularly mentioned in reference to children's education, since an independent Romani school had been opened during the First Republic and then, after a period during which operations were suspended, had been reopened at the end of the Second World War. Many cultural and social activities were linked to some degree or other with the school. In addition to its own football team, the settlement had a fire brigade and the "Anglal" ("forward" in Romani) folk dance group. All of these characteristics converged from multiple directions on an image of Podskalka as a highly distinctive place.

The archival materials related to the situation at the Podskalka settlement also include some of Romani provenance. Mr Tokár, by this time already a resident of Ostrava, reacted to the fact that his native Podskalka had appeared in the 1966 television programme (see Chapter Two):

> I was very surprised that you filmed our village for television. You gave examples of both the good and the bad. It's good to come here, take photos and leave. But to live among them, to help them, that's beyond you. [...] There are people who are paid for the G*psy question. They arrive once a year and

then leave again. It's not enough simply to arrive by car, look around and leave again. [...] I realise that we are the ones who are mostly to blame for not understanding that we have opportunities and that our children could aim high. [...] But I think that if assistance remains at the level it has been up till now, it will be a long time before we arrive at a higher level. Without your help we couldn't have managed anything.[117]

Bearing in mind the findings laid out in the previous chapter, it is interesting that Mr Tokár includes the "G*psies" themselves when apportioning blame for the less than desirable living conditions. However, he believes they need help from outside and he acknowledges that the assistance received so far has been inadequate. Apart from this criticism, the most interesting thing about the whole letter is Mr Tokár's own life story, which includes his housing situation. Below are a few excerpts that connect up his lived experience with the regional and centralised housing policy as it related to Romani settlements.

In 1958, I had a lot of bother with my family when it came to the development of our village [Podskalka]. So only a few houses were built, and only by those with family contacts to the district authorities. Those who had poor houses remained. [...]
After I got married, it wasn't easy to begin with. I was working as a building labourer and earning 700 to 800 crowns. I was part of the best crew, and we worked up to 250 hours a month, sometimes more. Then winter began, the frost came, and the foreman told us to take unpaid leave for a month or two. So how were we supposed to survive? I saw I wasn't earning much and that my wife was struggling to make ends meet, so I decided to go to Ostrava. I began working at the VŽKG [Vítkovické železárny Klementa Gottwalda – Klement Gottwald Vítkovice Ironworks]. [...] I still work here and now have a three-room apartment. [...] I have my own little house at home [in Podskalka]. When I heard that our houses were going to be demolished, I went to the district authorities to have my house valued. They offered me a price of 12,000 crowns. I went to where they were buying off the buildings and submitted an application. The person on duty was really rude. He told me they'd have to look over the house and there was no saying what they'd find. And that I should return for a second visit. I told him I was from Ostrava and

117 NA Prague, KSČ-ÚV-05/3, f. KSČ – Ústřední výbor 1945–1989, Praha – oddělení – oddělení ideologické, sv. 37, č. j. 299.

wrote down my address. But I got no reply. That's how they treat us all over Slovakia, Moravia and Bohemia. He no doubt saw that I was standing in front of him with papers and he was sitting behind a desk and that I was a G*psy. No answer anywhere. That was in July and now it's November.[118]

Mr Tokár's letter raises several important points as regards the experience of the Roma in relation to the policy pertaining to the settlements. Firstly, the centralised attempt to eradicate settlements as part of the resettlement programme represented the continuation of earlier policies, whether formulated on the central, regional, district or municipal level. In the case of Podskalka, this involved mainly the construction of detached houses in 1958 mentioned above, a project that later found itself in conflict with the logic of liquidation since it preserved the segregation. This tension between the cultivation and eradication of the settlement will be discussed in more detail below. It is significant that Mr Tokár refers in his letter to the "municipality", when he is more likely referring to Podskalka itself as part of the municipality of Humenné. Although many of the Roma, like Mr Tokár, left Podskalka because of its dismal living conditions, they also participated in its formation as a distinct space, thus acknowledging their belonging to the location in question. This ambivalent relationship between belonging to the settlement as a location in its own right on the one hand, and, on the other, escaping from the settlement in light of its unsatisfactory living conditions, and viewing it as a "bad address", is one of the key motifs of this chapter. Podskalka offers a unique opportunity to observe this unclear relationship, not least because it was regularly the target of such contradictory approaches. I will first compare the situation in Podskalka with that in other settlements in the district at that time, while simultaneously contextualising it within the dominant academic discourse of that time and later.

Mr Tokár's complaint that only those families with connections were able to receive new housing in Podskalka again reveals that any possibility of benefiting from the policy towards the settlements depended on a certain status in the local hierarchy of socio-economic relations. In this case, positionality was not formulated in terms of G*psyness (see Chapter Two), but in respect of a certain social capital (in this instance kinship ties to specific officials). At the same time, it was the presence of

---

118 Ibid.

certain Romani people in local political structures, and not only those in charge of policy toward the Roma, that further disrupted the clearly dichotomous relationship between the state and the Roma as its significantly marginalised inhabitants (see Chapter One).

Mr Tokár's testimony also speaks volumes as to the actual business of purchasing houses within the context of the resettlement programme. As is evident from other documents and has been described to an extent in the literature, this process was fraught with administrative difficulties and left significant room for the agency (including the laxity) of specific officials.

As regards the debate surrounding the plurality of Romani agency, Mr Tokár's letter reminds us that the liquidation of the settlements under the government resolution of 1965, including the subsequent "transfer" and "dispersal" of the G*psy population", was intertwined with the migration of Romani people (here primarily from Slovakia to Czechia) as an independent strategy of social and economic mobility. Though I will look at this aspect in Chapter Four, it is impossible to encapsulate it within the confines of a single chapter and not consider it as an important context here too.

3.1 Central and Regional Policies towards the Settlements

In the territory of post-war Czechoslovakia, the highest percentage of Romani people was in the easternmost part of the country, i.e. in eastern Slovakia. Although there were Roma living in towns (often wealthier, relatively high status musicians), a significant number lived in villages, often in enclaves spatially and symbolically separated from the rest of the community, segregated to varying degrees and socio-economically marginalised. These places, whether in the local context or the broader popular or official discourse, were dubbed "settlements", depending on local dialects, including Romani itself (Slovak/Rusyn e.g. *osada, kolónia, vatra, vatrisko, tábor*; Romani e.g. *osada, vatra, taboris*). And it was mainly to these eastern Slovak settlements that the terms "undesirable G*psy concentrations" were used in central documents to refer to the resettlement policy, even though such settlements were not only to be found in eastern Slovakia and said policy was to affect all the regions of what was then Czechoslovakia in various ways.

The historian Donert shows that the attempt to "liquidate" these settlements under the terms of a government resolution of 1965 was not a purely top-down policy. It was instead a reaction to voices from the provinces, specifically from the region of eastern Slovakia, appealing to the central authorities to recognise that this pressing issue could not be resolved on a purely regional basis. According to Donert, it was representatives of the Central Committee of the Slovak Communist Party who convinced officials in Prague that the issue of the settlements must be addressed systematically on the central level, even resorting to photographs of the highly unsatisfactory living conditions (Donert 2017, 159–160). It should be added that this was not the first time that the eastern Slovak settlements had aroused the interest of the central authorities. Efforts to eradicate them had been one of the important points of the 1958 resolution on Work amongst the G*psy Population. However, in later documents reflecting upon the implementation of this resolution, failure on this point was noted and attributed mainly to the unsystematic organisation and laxity of the local authorities (Jurová 2008, 996–999). This was to change with a new resolution of 1965. A timetable was to be drawn up for the "liquidation of the settlements" in each district, and in a departure from previous practice, special funds were set aside (e.g. Haišman 1999). While previous efforts had been formulated as appeals addressed to the regional and local authorities, the 1965 government resolution allocated money from the state budget to be used both for the purchase and demolition of the "G*psy shacks" and for the provision of new housing for the families affected. Donert points out that in the context of post-war state-building, these settlements were sidelined, since the ethnic, religious and linguistically heterogeneous and long-standing socio-economically marginalised region of eastern Slovakia, which also formed a historically unstable state border, constituted an opaque space and potential security risk as a whole to the central authorities (Donert 2017, 85–89). It is here that we see the centralised acceptance of responsibility for what had been up till then more a regional problem, the solution to which had been formulated in resolutions drawn up by the Regional National Committee (then in Prešov) during the 1950s.[119]

Such a policy towards settlements sat well with the modern state's more general attempts to control its inhabitants and the framing of disorderly locations as a threat to security (Scott 1998). If what Scott describes vis-à-vis the functioning of the modern state is not merely the careful arrangement of space, but, in effect, the homogenisation of its

---

119 ŠAPO Nižná Šebastová, f. Odbor vnútorných vecí KNV, kart. 219 and 220, inv. č. 53.

own inhabitants for the purpose of exerting control, then in the case of the settlements, too, the priority became eliminating the deviant way of life associated with them.

3.2 Discourse of the G*psy Settlements

3.2.1 The logic of "liquidation"

For a more detailed insight into this logic, it is worth revisiting Davidová's monograph (1965), in which the social significance of the removal of the settlements is a key theme and the discourse of which is fully in line with the logic of the government resolution from October of the same year. According to Davidová, the settlements are characterised by a particular way of life that differs from that of the rest of the population (ibid., 87). In line with official ideology, Davidová understands this difference hierarchically, i.e. in terms of "backwardness". For Davidová, then, the settlements were not only an opaque space with inadequate living conditions, especially in the sphere of housing and hygiene, but also, overall, a space embodying a kind of social deviance. She understands this, inter alia, in terms of "parasitism" (*příživnictví*), where this "typical way of life" resists due inclusion in the labour process, something she sees as a key instrument of social assimilation and the main criterion of the legitimacy of belonging to a socialist society. In addition, Davidová understands the settlements (as well as the "G*psy way of life" associated with them) as a product and symbol of the racist approach taken towards the Roma on the part of previous political regimes. From this perspective, the legitimacy of the new social order is dependent on the successful disposal of the settlements. And so Davidová sees "liquidation" as right and proper, since it affects not only the material sphere, but involves the "overall transformation of the human being" (ibid., 96). In this context, she believes the construction of new housing for Romani families on the land of the old settlements is misguided and will lead, notwithstanding the transformation of material conditions, to the preservation of a locally anchored way of life. When offering an example of such bad practice, Davidová refers, among other things, to the construction of detached houses in Podskalka in 1958 mentioned above.

However, Davidová also believed it would be wrong to rush headlong into the wholesale removal of settlements and that the project needed to be approached systematically, taking into account the specific circumstances in each location. In line with the later timetable ensuing from government resolution 502/1965, Davidová states that it is not possible to remove all settlements by 1970, but only the "worst" ones. In other cases, hygiene had to be improved, typically by increasing the availability of drinking water by means of the construction of wells. If the entire process is rushed, there is a risk of the way of life not being completely transformed and only "superficial changes" (*povrchné zmeny*) being adopted by the original inhabitants of the settlements. Davidová illustrates this with a specific example in which, though the Roma were provided with new housing outside the settlement, they ended up sleeping in one room on the floor, which Davidová sees as a symbol of their reversion to the old way of life in the settlement (ibid., 95).

As an example of "successful liquidation", Davidová cites the relocation of all one hundred inhabitants from the Miklušovce settlement near the village of Hôrka in the district of Poprad to eight other villages in the same district in 1961. This is a good example of what Davidová terms the "total transformation of the human being". It also offers an insight into how she understands the association of the Roma with settlements as locations featuring "a different way of life". According to Davidová, Miklušovce was "the most backward settlement in the entire region, perhaps the whole country, with an incredibly low standard of living for its inhabitants", which made it all the more essential that its removal be planned in detail (1965, 104). Liquidation was to include the "delousing" (*odvšivenie*) and "bathing" (*vykúpanie*) of all the Roma, including a thorough medical examination and vaccination of the children. After being "clothed and fed" (*ošatení a občerstvení*), the Roma were taken by bus to their new homes, where representatives of the MNV and local population of each village waited for them in "neat apartments with basic fittings and furnishing", in order "to welcome them and in some places to help them overcome initial difficulties". Davidová also speaks of the natural tendency of the Roma to return to their original environment, i.e. to their original way of life:

> The old G*psy settlement was immediately set on fire after the departure of its inhabitants and its remains were razed to the ground in order to prevent some of the Miklušovce G*psies from returning. (Nevertheless, one of them, old Pompa, would come here in the evening and sleep on the ground, on the location of his former dwelling, all night. He was drawn to the old place, but eventually caught on.) And in a short time the whole place, with all the remnants of the miserable life of the "outcast" G*psies, grew over with grass

and its former inhabitants began to get used to a different life in their new homes. (ibid., 104)

The old way of life, which was to be removed as part of the comprehensive "transformation of the person", was seen by Davidová as involving an overall physical cleansing in line with an understanding of the settlements as a hygienic problem and the associated way of life as being on a fundamentally physical level. Of particular importance to this chapter, however, is the way that Davidová perceives the relationship between the way of life and the settlement as a specific location. She regards the settlement as the outcome of the historical isolation of the Roma as a consequence of racist policies and the attitudes of the non-Romani society, and sees one of the obstacles to the successful disposal of settlements in the anti-Roma attitudes of particular authorities and local inhabitants (ibid., e.g. 101). What is clear from the quotation above is not only the natural association of a way of life with a particular place, but also the strength of the emotional attachments Davidová attributes to the Roma in relation to such a place. This attachment had to be overcome if successful liquidation was to take place.

3.2.2 The settlements as a locus of Romani culture?

Hübschmannová, as another agent in the debate taking place at that time, does not offer as comprehensive an overview of Romani settlements and the policies being applied to them as Davidová. This must be inferred from her individual claims and her overall conceptualisation of a distinctive Romani culture, as well as from later texts. Though Hübschmannová, like Davidová, recognises the inadequate level of housing and overall living conditions, she does not associate it with the "backward way of life of the G*psies", but rather with the dynamics of broader social development. Hübschmannová speaks of Romani "settlement communities" that were originally defined by kinship on the one hand, and profession on the other. Though visibly poorer than the non-Romani part of a village, the communities were nevertheless part of local socio-economic structures (structures that Hübschmannová conceptualises through the lens of a caste system, see also Hübschmannová 1999b). She conceives of traditional settlements as functioning units in themselves, featuring both internal mechanisms of social control (e.g. Hübschmannová 1999a, 33) and the regulation of population size. Representatives of a new generation of occupationally and kinship defined community relocated to other villages, where they were needed and in a position to support themselves (e.g. Hübschmannová 1993, 23 and 36; 1998). She attributes the disruption of the admittedly subordinate but in some ways equilibrious position of the settlements in local systems to both industrialisation and the consequent broader social and economic transformations in the functioning of society as a whole, i.e. including rural east Slovakia, and the implementation of specific policies, be these the forced relocation of settlements further from the village during the period of the Slovak State (Hübschmannová 2005), or the social engineering policies of the communist regime (Hübschmannová 1999a).

Hübschmannová also wrote of the inhabitants of the settlements having a different way of life, but unlike Davidová, she did not understand this in terms of "backwardness", but in terms of cultural relativism. She did not see the manifestations of different customs in the new environment (typically within the context of migration to cities in Czechia) as something to be eradicated, but as an opportunity to understand a different culture and refute certain stereotypes about Romani immigrants in Czechia (1993, 42–44). And so when Hübschmannová wrote about the fatal undermining of the socio-cultural values of the Roma as a result of the assimilationist policies of the Czechoslovak communist regime (e.g. Hübschmannová 2000a), she placed these values within the settlements as the natural space for their realisation. Reading her criticism of the central policy, however, it is clear that Hübschmannová did not oppose the "liquidation of the settlements" as the removal of certain isolated outposts of Romani culture (see Hübschmannová 1967, 1968, 1970). In emphasising the criticism of freedom of movement, in terms of the settlements this meant more a criticism of the artificial social engineering intervention in the broader social dynamics that accompanied their functioning, specifically the natural movement of the Roma from the settlements, whether within the region of eastern Slovakia or to Czechia. In her article for *Literární noviny*, for example, Hübschmannová points to the impasse in which individual Romani families found themselves in the settlement in Veľká Ida (in the district of Košice). These families were not able to build new housing in the settlement itself, which would have been at odds with efforts to liquidate them, nor in the village, where new construction was forbidden because of the pollution of the atmosphere from the eastern Slovakian Košice ironworks, nor even in other villages, where "they have enough of their own G*psies", and could not move to join their relatives in Czechia, because this would have placed them outside the plans for controlled movement, which only allowed for the movement of Roma to selected partner districts. And the families themselves did not want to live in these partner districts because they had no contacts there and lacked the necessary social capital (Hübschmannová 1967). Similarly, in the case of the village of Rakúsy, Hübschmannová recounted how the Roma wanted to build housing in the settlement "amongst their own people", i.e. in an environment offering them a certain social security (see Skupnik 2007; Stewart 1997), but were prevented from doing so because of the state's stated goal of removing such "concentrations" (Hübschmannová 1970, 105). Drawing on the story of families in a particular settlement, she later wrote that the "manipulative 'integration' of the communist state [...] 'resolved the G*psy question' in a totalitarian manner, thus preventing [...] Romani families from spontaneous and natural upward social mobility" (Hübschmannová 1999b, 133). Using these examples, Hübschmannová reveals not only the discriminatory nature of the entire government resolution, which limited the freedom of movement of a specific group of the population, but also the pauperisation of the settlements as the paradoxical effect of efforts to eliminate them.

3.2.3 Marginalisation, stigmatisation, belonging

In contrast to Davidová, Hübschmannová shifted her perspective from an emphasis on a successful "resolution of the G*psy question" to that of the agency and life strategies of the Roma themselves. However, her dogged commitment to criticism of the assimilation policy prevented her from interpreting more precisely the agency of the Roma within the context of the practice of the resettlement programme. It appears that when conceptualising the Romani settlements, Hübschmannová had a tendency to understand them as a natural space for the realisation of a distinctive Romani culture. Although she also took into account the role of other actors besides the Roma in maintaining the existence of Romani settlements and therefore the continuity of territorialisation of the Roma, it was left to other authors to develop this aspect more systematically.

In his long dissertation based on research conducted in the region of Spiš in the early 1970s, it was Guy who viewed the status of the Roma in rural areas of eastern Slovakia in terms of racial segregation, i.e. including the territorialisation of the Roma and the overall marginalisation of their settlements. When analysing the reasons for the failure of the communist regime's efforts to assimilate the Roma, Guy points mainly to the persistent anti-Roma racism of the local authorities and non-Romani inhabitants, who opposed the disruption of the historically formed hierarchy of relations according to a racial key, i.e. the disruption of the naturally understood distinction between the (non-Romani) village and the "G*psy settlement" (Guy 1998).

Four decades later, on the basis of microhistorically inflected research, Sadílková (2017) recognised a similar attitude on the part of the local non-Romani actors. Sadílková unmasked the state as a homogenous whole and distinguished different actors with diverse, sometimes conflicting interests on its side, above all in respect of the relationship between the central and regional authorities (see Chapter One). Adopting a similar perspective, I recently looked at the formation of the continuity of a settlement as a specific site in the layout of an eastern Slovak village. Combining ethnographic and historical research, I examined the politics of place in a village in northeastern Slovakia (Ort 2021, 2022b). I traced the processes that historically shaped the settlement as a place that, conforming to the dominant narrative of the local inhabitants, was the product of a distinct "G*psy mentality" (*c*gánska mentalita*), or what Davidová described as a "G*psy way of life". I showed that historically this place functioned as a "bad address" and was therefore subject to what Wacquant describes as "territorial stigmatisation" (Wacquant 2007). Consistent with this concept, the notion of the settlement as a place of "cultural backwardness" was shared by all the local residents, including the residents of the settlement themselves, who, as in the study by Sadílková cited above, sought spatial mobility and expressed a desire to "escape" from the settlement to the non-Romani part of the village. Such efforts were in line with central policy and actively supported by the District National Committee (ONV) tasked with coordinating its implementation. However, even here they came up against the strong embeddedness of the territorial boundary and the reluctance of the local authorities and local residents to break it. Nevertheless, several families managed to obtain housing in the village outside the Romani settlement, i.e. "among the *gadje*" (*maškar o gadže*), thus achieving a relatively higher social status in the locally anchored socio-economic hierarchy (see Hübschmannová 1999a). However, their movement was framed in terms of G*psyness (see the previous chapter) in the sense of a shift away from the "G*psy way of life", which thus continued to be automatically associated with the space of the settlement and reproduced its stigmatisation.

In my study, however, I argue that while the stigmatisation of the settlement was a strong factor in the local politics of place at the time of my research and strongly impacted the life strategies of the local Roma, it was not their sole determinant. Firstly, the environment of the settlement itself was undergoing a certain transformation and after the construction of the council flats on the site of the original wooden shacks, residents reported significant improvements in their living conditions. Secondly, in the centre of a world of non-Romani dominance the settlement also functioned as a safe space, and in this respect, too, its inhabitants to a degree accepted popular ideas about Roma with a natural tendency to live together as a group and form concentrated settlements. Thirdly, the local Roma were able to confirm the continuity of local belonging, which formed a strong aspect of their sociability, not only *despite* living in the settlement as a segregated and marginalised space, but also *through* living in the settlement, with its particular location in the layout of the village (its unusually central position compared with other such segregated settlements) and its specific form (in addition to improved material conditions this would include the maintenance of cleanliness, which was in contrast with the idea of the naturally "filthy" settlements).

In this chapter, I examine the ambivalent relationship between Romani people's attempts to escape from the settlement as a marginalised and stigmatised place, and their embrace of a sense of belonging to said settlement within the context of efforts to liquidate them. I must reiterate that I do so in the knowledge that, in contrast to my ethnographic research referred to above, such a historical reconstruction has obvious methodological limitations. In tracing the practice of the policy towards the settlements in what was at that time the district of Humenné, I will be interested in the agency of the Roma and the ways in which they identified with the settlement as a distinct place, defined not only socially but also materially. In tracing the agency of the Roma during the practice of state policy, I will not seek to answer the question of whether or not the Roma wanted to live in the settlements, nor will I reach a conclusive decision as to whether such a policy coincided with their interests or represented the manifestation of symbolic violence against them. On the contrary, having examined various aspects of the policy in question and above all of the life strategies of the Roma and hence their modes of (self-)identification, what I observe is a state of ambivalence and tension. On the one hand, there is plenty of evidence of the efforts of individual Roma and Romani families to break out of the settlement and obtain housing outside it, as well as collectively formulated requests by the inhabitants to liquidate their own settlement (see Roma in the settlement in Hostovice, Chapter Two). On the other hand, it is impossible to ignore the evidence of their acknowledgement of belonging to the settlement as a distinct place, whether through requests for its modernisation, independent cultural and social activities, or its own self-government.

In this respect, one feature that stands out is a sense of relating to a settlement through the physical form of a given place. This feeling is usually based on recollections of the past contained in biographical oral-historical interviews (see Chapter One). Davidová hinted at such a relationship when, within the framework of a somewhat racialising and romanticising narrative, she described how "old Pompa" returned to sleep on the site of the removed "shacks", only eventually to realise that he, too, must submit to the process of civilisation (Davidová 1965, 104; see above). These recollections of contemporary witnesses will inevitably contain a degree of nostalgia and idealisation. However, their relationship to the settlement as not only a social but also a physical space cannot be ignored. In this chapter I seek to reconcile at least to some extent the seemingly contradictory impulses that accentuate the role of the dominance of non-Romani society in the territorialisation of the Roma on the one hand, and the agentive shaping of a distinct space on the other. In such a conception, an understanding of the relationship of the Roma to a particular place transcends established notions of the unity of place, culture and identity (see Gupta and Fergusson 1992) and moves toward a more complex grasp of Romani identity (see the ideas of Theodosiou discussed in Chapter One; also Ort 2021, 2022b). On the other hand, I will show that efforts to "liquidate the settlements" were also embedded in unclear, locally contingent processes and may have represented their partial discontinuity.

3.3 Disposal of the Settlements in the Former District of Humenné

The best evidence of the practice of disposing of the settlements in the district of Humenné is to be found in the archive of the Financial Department of the District National Committee. One hundred and seventy files cover the purchase and demolition of individual "shacks" between 1966 and 1972, which is also the period during which Government Resolution No. 502/1965 was valid in Slovakia (it was rendered null and void two years earlier in Czechia; Guy 1977, 273). However, similar attempts at liquidation can be traced further back. At the provincial level, the issue was systematically formulated in regional resolution No. 301 of 1956.[120] Subsequent initiatives were then based on the central resolution on Work amongst the G*psy Population of 1958, which was also to serve as the basis for the formulation of a timetable for future liquidation (Jurová 2008, 688). Plans specific to the district of Humenné are contained in materials from 1963. The numerical schedule identified 418 "substandard shacks" out of a total of 548 homes.[121] Their demolition was planned for the years up to and including 1970 by private housing construction (233 homes), cooperative housing construction (119 homes) and state housing construction (66 homes).[122] However, only the removal of the settlement in the village of Papín is referred to explicitly, which was planned for the same year (for more details of the settlement in this municipality, see below). By 1965, the District National Committee in Humenné was able to reflect upon the successful removal of two settlements (Oľka, Slovenská Volová),[123] and in February of the same year to confirm the planned removal of all settlements in the district by the end of 1970.[124] However, in the plan of November 1965, i.e. already at a time when the October government resolution No. 502/1965 had come into force, these ambitions were moderated, with only the "worst" settlements to be removed by 1970, and the rest dealt with at some point in the future, the emphasis now being on improving the situation in the settlements themselves.[125] Although the removal of four settlements and the compulsory purchase of twenty-nine shacks was carried out in the first half of 1966, the timetable was not met.[126] According to interim reports, individual members of the district G*psy Commission were not meeting their objectives, namely, assessing the value of the shacks

---

120 ŠAPO Nižná Šebastová, f. Odbor vnútorných vecí KNV Prešov, kart. 2019, inv. č 53, "Uznesenie 301/1956", 1956.
121 ŠAKE Košice, f. Komisia Vsl. KNV pre cigánske obyvateľstvo, kart. 4, sp. 25, "Plán úloh na úseku riešenia otázok osôb cigánskeho pôvodu", 3. February 1965.
122 ŠAKE Košice, f. Komisia Vsl. KNV pre cigánske obyvateľstvo, kart. 3, sp. 55, "Komplexný plán na riešenie cig. ot. do r. 1970", 2 March 1963.
123 ŠAKE Košice, f. Komisia Vsl. KNV pre cigánske obyvateľstvo, kart. 4, sp. 1, "Informatívna zpráva o riešení problémov osôb cigánskeho pôvodu". undated.
124 ŠAKE Košice, f. Komisia Vsl. KNV pre cigánske obyvateľstvo, kart. 4, sp. 25, "Plán úloh na úseku riešenia otázok osôb cigánskeho pôvodu", 3 February 1965.
125 ŠAKE Košice, f. KomisiaVsl. KNV pre cigánske obyvateľstvo, kart. 8, sp. 117, "Kontrolná zpráva o plnení opatrení o práci medzi cig. ob.", 13 November 1965.
126 ŠAKE Košice, f. Komisia Vsl. KNV pre cigánske obyvateľstvo, kart. 11, sp. 120, "Hodnotenie výsledkov za I. polrok", 1966.

in the individual settlements.[127] However, more fundamental problems appeared that are described in the literature as significant obstacles to the successful implementation of the resettlement programme in other places in Slovakia and Czechia too. This included the indecisiveness or dismissive attitudes of Municipal National Committees with regard to the sale of houses and the allocation of building plots to the Roma from the settlements, as well as poor cooperation with partner districts in Czechia, specifically Opava and Bruntál, which reported insufficient capacity to accept newly arriving Romani families (see Chapter Four). Given the difficulty involved in obtaining new housing in what was then Czechoslovakia, which for the Roma of eastern Slovakia was exacerbated by historically entrenched anti-Roma prejudice (Guy 1977, 308), most families eventually secured accommodation through recourse to their own existing connections, whether thanks to their own experience of migration to specific locations in Czechia or within the confines of Humenné itself (see Chapter Four).

Despite the ostensible continuity of post-war efforts to dispose of the settlements, a fundamental change took place to this policy with the adoption of the government resolution under consideration, namely, the allocation of specific funds from the state budget in order to ensure its comprehensive, systematic implementation. According to the policy, every shack identified for redevelopment was first to be valued and only after confirmation of new suitable housing for the family living there was it purchased by the District National Committee from the funds set aside. The relevant Municipal National Committee was then responsible for its demolition. In the event of these funds being insufficient to secure new housing (which was so in the majority of cases), the financial department of the ONV approved a dispensation, the purpose of which was to provide new housing (including the purchase of building materials), fittings and furniture.

Under the government resolution, not only the compulsory purchase of the shacks, but the entire resettlement programme, was to be carried out on a voluntary basis, though an educational campaign was to be conducted aimed at persuading even the most recalcitrant Roma of the importance of this issue. In many cases, however, it did not seem that the reluctance of the Roma was the main obstacle to the successful implementation of the entire project. Regarding the district of Spišská

---

127 Ibid.

Nová Ves, Guy describes how there was enormous interest in resettlement from the Romani settlements to Czechia, and that during the first stage, the District National Committee was overwhelmed by applications from Romani people hoping to be included in the resettlement project (Guy 1977, 278). As regards the district of Humenné, in many cases it was a matter of granting consent to the sale of shacks in Slovakia by people who were already living on a virtually permanent basis in various locations spread around Czechia, where they were either attempting to obtain new accommodation or had already secured long-term housing. For them, the sale of a shack (and the financial dispensation referred to above) meant both the possibility of achieving such housing and even, perhaps, a significant lump-sum payment. This is clear in the letter quoted at the start of this chapter from Mr Tokár of Podskalka, who sought payment for a building he had had valued at a time when he was already living in Ostrava. However, his letter shows that one could not take for granted that payment would be forthcoming for a shack that had been valued. Moreover, the life story set forth above, in which Mr Tokár recounted how he had moved to Ostrava in response to the unsatisfactory conditions in his home village, clearly demonstrates that migration in and of itself was the result of certain structural conditions which, even taking into account the historical development of the position of the Roma in specific locations, problematises the idea of the voluntary character of such relocations.

3.3.1 The position of the local authorities

On 13 June 1968, the husband and wife team Michal and Anna D from Čertižné (the district of Humenné) wrote a letter addressed to the Commission for the People's Control at the District National Committee in Humenné complaining about the demolition of their home. The letter is so eloquent, I am reproducing it in full:

> In the village of Čertižné we owned a wooden building that was plastered inside and had floors in all the rooms. The building was built over water and during rainy weather we were in danger of being flooded. We therefore asked the chairman of the MNV in Čertižné to assign us another building plot in the village so that we could build a new detached house. We made this request several times, but the chairman of the MNV informed us that, though he had no building plot he could give us, he would offer us a certificate allowing us

to travel to Czechia and live there. In the end, we agreed to this and for about three years we lived and worked in Beroun [Czechia]. Since my husband could not work in Czechia for health reasons, we had to move back to the village [Čertižné]. However, upon our return, we discovered that our home had already been demolished.

Now we find out at the ONV that our house was valued at 12,800 crowns. We are not satisfied with this valuation, since it was carried out in our absence and without the chairman of the MNV telling us that he intended to buy our house and demolish it for being a shack. I would point out that our house should not have been classified as a shack, since, as I wrote above, it was plastered inside and was built in about 1959.

Furthermore, the house of my mother, Anna G, which was valued at 8,000 crowns, was burnt down and I have impression that this was done by the MNV in Čertižné.

We request that our complaint be investigated and the valuation of the house we bought be increased.[128]

Other documents show that the writers of the above letter eventually gave way, perhaps under pressure from the Čertižné local authorities (or perhaps even the ONV in Humenné). On 15 June 1968, two days after the letter was written, a sale and purchase agreement was drawn up for the building in question, in which Michal D signed over the house at the price specified of 12,836 crowns.[129]

The contents of the complaint point to important broader interrelated aspects of the practice of the central policy. I suggested above that the Roma may have to some extent shared the idea of the settlements as culturally backward places and adopted parts of the language used to refer to such locations in the dominant discourse: the complaint above throws doubt on such a claim. Although Mr and Mrs D cite the inconvenient location of their house, which has led them to apply for a more suitable building plot, they resent its being called a shack and being included in the campaign to remove all such buildings. In other words, the demand for dignified living conditions was not necessarily made in the grip of a dominant logic that viewed living in shacks as a natural feature of the "G*psy way of life".

---

128 ŠOkA Humenné, f. Finanční odbor ONV Humenné, kart. 16, sp. 102, "D. Michal, Čertižné" [unprocessed].
129 Ibid.

The entire letter, however, throws into doubt the voluntary basis of participation in the resettlement project on at least two levels. Firstly, it implies that, at least in the case of the redevelopment of the shacks, preparations could go ahead behind the backs of the owners themselves. The letter writers even suggest that the actual extent of the damage done to specific buildings may have been the result of actions taken by the local authorities, as in the case of the fire that razed to the ground the house of the mother of one of the complainants (it is not entirely clear whether this involved the mother of Michal D or his wife Anna). However, in addition to the agency of the local authorities, which in other cases might have taken the less blatant form of coercion and persuasion, the complaint under discussion, like the letter from Mr Tokár from Podskalka, points to a broader structural problem that calls voluntary participation into question. It is clear that post-war migration to Czechia was not only the result of the socio-economic marginalisation of the badly war-torn region of eastern Slovakia as a whole, but in the case of the Roma was also the outcome of their marginalised position. In this respect, migration may not have been the preferred option. Moreover, as the complainants' own description of their situation makes clear, even Romani migrants who remained in Czechia could often count on maintaining their ties with their home village in Slovakia, which could thus to some extent function as a safe space for them, for example in the event of poor health. Such migration dynamics have been used to describe not only the situation of the Roma in socialist Czechoslovakia (see Guy 1977, 486), but also the post-Velvet Revolution migration of the Roma to Czechia (Ort 2022b, 186–187) or even to the West (Ort and Dobruská 2023). Seen from this perspective, the consent of Romani migrants to the sale and subsequent redevelopment of their homes in their original village in Slovakia may have been a rational economic decision, but was also the result of their complexly shaped long-term marginalisation and inferior position in the socio-economic hierarchy of the village in question, something that was often manifest in the sphere of housing (whether this involved the quality of construction or a building's positionality within the layout of the village).

3.3.2 "Successful liquidation": the settlement in Ľubiša

From this perspective, one can read not only the complaint cited above, but the situation in those settlements reported in the ONV materials as "successfully liquidated". A closer look at relations in specific villages – not least because of the nature of the archival materials – tends above all to encourage an examination of the agency of the Municipal National Committees, local policies towards Romani settlements and certain (dis)continuities of the territorialisation of the Roma. However, I consider a description of these matters to form an important context for tracing the positions, experiences and agency of the Roma themselves.

After the adoption of the government resolution, the settlement in Ľubiša was one of the first in which all the buildings were valued and purchased for the purpose of demolition during the course of 1966. However, according to the individual files of the Financial Department archive, the families of all of the building owners had already found housing for themselves in Prague. The Roma of Ľubiša departed for Prague immediately after the war: according to the MNV, as early as 1946.[130] This was confirmed by the testimony of contemporary female witnesses from the ranks of the original Roma of Ľubiša, who spoke of the Roma having become embedded in Prague by the 1960s, both in terms of housing and employment, and their relationships with people in the area, including other Roma who had come to Prague from the district of Humenné (Hudousková et al. [unpublished]). According to the records of the individual valuations in the Ľubiša settlement, these were buildings that had lain unoccupied for a long time and in many cases were no longer habitable.[131] In 1966, the building owners approved their sale for the purpose of demolition, and the ONV in Humenné was able to quickly tick the boxes of the "liquidated settlement" quite easily.

However, the situation as described was preceded by a somewhat ambiguous development. For a long time, Romani people regularly returned from Prague to Ľubiša, a fact evidenced not only by the recollections of contemporary female witnesses, but also by entries in the school chronicle, in which the attendance of children from these families was always recorded for only part of the year, before the footnote "left for Czechia" appeared.[132] One of the non-Romani villagers in Ľubiša recalled in an interview with me that the Roma always returned to their home village for the summer with great pomp thanks to the newly

---

130 ŠOkA Humenné, f. MNV Ľubiša, kart. 1, sp. 27, "Cigáni v Ľubiši", 1953.
131 ŠOkA Humenné, f. finanční odbor ONV Humenné, kart. 15, sp. 2, 3, 4, 5, 6, 31, 32, 36, 40, 87 [unprocessed].
132 ŠOkA Humenné, "Školní kronika Ľubiša".

acquired socio-economic capital they had won, especially as musicians.[133] This was confirmed in the testimony of the Romani women themselves, according to whom the men from these families were able to successfully apply their musicianship in Prague, where they began earning money by playing in wine bars (ibid.). Although in this case the migration of the Roma should certainly be seen as an agentive strategy leading to significant social mobility and social participation in the new environment (see ibid.), I will show that an important context that should not be forgotten was the continuity of the anti-Roma attitudes of the local authorities in Ľubiša, which were manifest in the sphere of housing and politics of space, and which, moreover, replicated the same (and explicitly framed) attitudes of other non-Romani villagers in Ľubiša. In this respect, the demolition of the Ľubiša settlement can also be seen as the outcome of an ongoing endeavour by the local authorities to territorialise the Roma or evict them entirely.

During a survey of "G*psy settlements" in 1956 in what was then the region of eastern Slovakia, with its headquarters in Prešov, eight buildings were recorded in the Ľubiša settlement, four of them uninhabitable and the rest inhabited by a total of 32 people. The authors of the report concluded that new construction work should take place in Ľubiša, with the aim of creating detached family houses and a fully functioning well.[134] However, the municipal authorities had already made their position very clear regarding the possibility of individual building projects overseen by inhabitants of the settlement in the previous year, when in July 1955 it dealt with a request submitted by Ján F to build a house bordering the state highway. The chairman of the council observed that "all of the citizens of Ľubiša are against this and do not want to allow him to build a residential building, because as a G*psy he will pollute the surrounding area".[135] The same argument was used by the Council of the MNV, which was asked to take a vote. In addition to observing that the applicant "as a G*psy will pollute the surroundings", the council noted that "[in] the village there is an entire G*psy settlement where they have suitable land for building houses, and so this Ján F can also build a little house for himself there, where he has

---

133 Interview with non-Romani villager Ján Š (b. 1933), conducted by the author in April 2015 in Ľubiša in Slovak (unrecorded).
134 ŠAPO Nižná Šebastová, f. Odbor vnutorných vecí KNVPrešov, kat. 219, inv. č. 53, "Zpráva zo služobnej cesty konanej v dňoch od 8 do 12 júna 1956" 1956
135 ŠOkA Humenné, f. MNV Ľubiša, kart. 2, sp. 39, "Zápisnica", 21 July 1955.

been living in an old house up till now".[136] As individual departments of the state apparat would later note, a dismissive approach on the part of Municipal National Committees when dealing with the allocation of building plots for Roma was par for the course (see Guy 1977, 278). In this case, however, it is worth noting the overtly anti-Roma, inherently racist motive, which was elsewhere present either implicitly or carefully concealed (see Ort 2021; 2022b, 90).

The MNV in Ľubiša drew on similarly blatant anti-Roma arguments when attempting the relocation of the entire settlement back in August 1945:

> There is no one responsible for health and policing in the present location of the G*psy settlement, since the enclave is located almost in the centre of the village. Its surroundings are polluted by sewage and disease-inducing garbage, a state of affairs caused purely by the G*psies living in the encampment, the result being that public interest demands that the situation be remedied without delay. The land on which the cottages are located is owned by the municipality of Ľubiša. The new site, according to the attached plan, is adequate to such purposes in all respects. (Jurová 2008, 92–95)

The plan referred to and the argument used to back it up were affirmed in the same month by the District National Committee in Humenné, which added that "the municipality has a duty to build cottages for the G*psies that meet health and fire safety regulations", that it must "provide the G*psies with adequate shelter without security after the relocation period" and that "the G*psies relocated by the municipality are obliged to help the municipality with such work as may be necessary" (ibid.). The representatives of the settlement themselves quickly filed an appeal (in September 1945) against the decision to relocate the settlement with the Slovak National Council for Internal Affairs in Bratislava. They pointed out that the new location would discourage their children from attending school given its distance from the village. Should the appeal be rejected, they expressed their concern that "in our People's Democratic Republic, the lowest class of the people is still being pushed away from the public". The Roma demanded a commission be set up tasked with selecting a new construction site for the "G*psy encampment", insisting:

---

136 Ibid.

that until a new G*psy colony is created, our existing houses must not be destroyed, since winter is approaching and there is at present a difficulty in obtaining building materials. It is clear that a colony cannot be built by winter and if our existing houses are destroyed, we and our families would be forced to live without a roof over our heads. (ibid.)

The response from the Ministry of the Interior, addressed to the District National Council in Humenné, only arrived in May 1946. In addition to asking that details of the planned resettlement be provided (its cost and the distance of the new encampment from the centre of the village of Ľubiša), it also questioned the wisdom of the entire project in light of the "considerable interference in the most basic civil rights of the socially weakest segment of the population" (ibid.). Although I found no evidence of any further communication between the parties, it is clear that the entire project was brought to an end by the departure of the residents of the settlement to Czechia, which was supposed to have taken place in 1946.[137] It has been suggested that the initial departure of the Roma from Ľubiša was influenced not only by the unsatisfactory living conditions in the existing settlement (even the Romani representatives envisaged the construction of a new encampment in their appeal), and the generally unstable post-war situation in eastern Slovakia, but also by the way the local authorities treated the Roma, especially since they relied on the opinion of the other villagers, something they themselves point out.

3.3.3 Disposal of the settlement in the village of Papín

In 1945, much to the dismay of the MNV and local residents, the Ľubiša settlement was still situated in the centre of the village. The situation was different in other villages, where the settlements tended to be relocated further away from the centre due to anti-Roma measures dating back to the period of the Slovak State (see Jurová 2002). This in turn became a factor in determining not only the post-war position of the Roma in the hierarchy of local relationships and their migration to Czechia (see Sadílková 2020), but also impacted on the follow-up policies pursued by the regional authorities. In the district of Humenné there is evidence

---

137 ŠOkA Humenné, f. MNV Lubiša, kart. 1, sp. 27, "Cigáni v Lubiši", 1953.

of the war-time relocation of settlements from Jabloň, Slovenská Volová (see also Fedič 2001) and Papín. The initial relocation of the settlements forged an important context for the post-war efforts to remove them altogether.

It was the settlements in Papín and Slovenská Volová that, along with Podskalka, had been the focus of attention of the regional authorities since at least the late 1950s. In its plans, the District National Committee in Humenné had, since 1958 at the latest, been repeatedly underlining the necessity of moving both settlements to their original location in the village. For example, a 1958 resolution sent by the Department of Construction and Water Management to the Department for Internal Affairs (both at the ONV in Humenné) spoke of the necessity of relocating "citizens of G*psy origin from the settlements near Papín and Slovenská Volová to the built-up area of the village". It was apparently approved by the respective councils of the Local National Committees.[138]

Despite the agreement reached by the ONV in Humenné and the MNVs, the subsequent fate of the two settlements and their inhabitants took radically different directions. In the case of Slovenská Volová, the relocation of the residents of the settlement to the built-up area of the village was accomplished as early as May 1959, when the first family signed a sale and purchase agreement for a plot of land in the village.[139] The settlement in Slovenská Volová was listed as completely liquidated in a statement referring to Humenné in 1962,[140] though it figured yet again amongst the liquidated settlements in 1966 (perhaps more as an attempt on the part of the ONV to juke the stats after the new government resolution 502/1965 took effect).[141]

The settlement in Papín was also demolished, though its fate was far closer to that of Ľubiša (see Chapter One for a description of the Papín settlement). The Roma from the Papín settlement regularly travelled to Czechia in search of work and the centralised settlement liquidation policy did not lead to their being resituated in the village, but to their being definitively evicted from it. The differences between Slovenská Volová and Papín were made clear to me during my visit to the villages in 2021.

138 ŠOkA Humenné, f. MNV Humenné, kart. 23, sp. 12, "Premiestnenie cigánskych osád", 30 December 1958.
139 ŠOkA Humenné, f. MNV Humenné, kart. 23, sp. 26, Rada MNV v Slov. Volovej, 28 May 1958.
140 ŠAKE Košice, f. Komisia Vsl. KNV pre cigánske obyvateľstvo, kart. 1, sp. 21, "Zpráva na úseku riešenia otázok občanov cigánskeho povodu v okrese Humenné", 22 May 1962.
141 ŠAKE Košice, f. Komisia Vsl. KNV pre cigánske obyvateľstvo, kart. 11, sp. 120, "Hodnotenie výsledkov za I. Polrok", undated.

An employee of the municipal authorities in Papín told me with a degree of pride and perhaps even relief that "no G*psies live in our village", whereas in Slovenská Volová several Romani families lived in the village itself (albeit in some cases on its outskirts).

As in Ľubiša, a key role was played in Papín by what were basically the explicitly anti-Roma attitudes not only of the local residents, but more importantly of representatives of the Municipal National Committee, who opposed the presence of Roma in the village. Such attitudes rose to the surface all the more since Papín was at the time designated an administrative centre to which building restrictions did not apply, a relatively common argument resorted to by the local authorities in other "non-administrative" villages when refusing to allocate land to Roma from the settlement (see Guy 1977, 454). Moreover, as well as the Roma being refused planning permission, there is evidence that building permits were allocated to non-Romani villagers in the case of Papín during the period under consideration.[142]

The issue of the relocation of the settlement was addressed by the municipality as early as 1956, when it initially granted its consent to the district's attempts to move it back to the built-up area of the village. On 16 June of that year, the MNV issued a resolution according to which "citizens of G*psy origin will be moved from their present location to the original place where they lived during the First Czechoslovak Republic and whence they were evicted during the period of the Slovak State."[143] The situation remained the same for the next two years, with the MNV repeating its positive stance regarding the relocation of the settlement in 1958[144] and 1959.[145] In 1960, according to the records of the MNV, twelve families were living in the settlement under unsatisfactory hygienic conditions, of which eight families were at that time working in Czechia. Bearing this in mind, the construction of new housing was envisaged for only the four remaining families.[146] However, in 1962, representatives of the G*psy Commission at the ONV, in their report to the meeting of the presidium of the District Committee of the Communist Party of Slovakia,

---

142 ŠOkA Humenné, f. MNV Papín, kart. 12.
143 ŠOkA Humenné, f. MNV Papín, kart. 1, sp. 2, "Zápisnica", 16 July 1956.
144 ŠOkA Humenné, f. MNV Humenné, kart. 23, sp. 12, "Presťahovanie cigánov", 16 October 1958.
145 ŠOkA Humenné, f. MNV Humenné, kart. 23, sp. 12, "Sťahovanie cigánov v obci Papín", 14 May 1959.
146 ŠAPO Nižná Šebastová, f. KNV Prešov, odbor pre vnútornéveci, kart. 222, inv. č. 53, "Úradný záznam z príležitosti riešenia likvidácií cigánskej osady", 24 March 1960.

stated that "[in] the Papín settlement, which is perhaps in the worst location, nothing has been done".[147] It was for this reason that attention was drawn to the Papín settlement in what otherwise was a numerically classified plan for the liquidation of the settlements in the district by 1970 (see above),[148] while according to the regional report of May 1965, the removal of the Papín settlement was to take place in the same year (Jurová 2008, 998). While work on relocation of the settlement stagnated, perhaps due to the lax approach of the local authorities, in documents from that time one can follow the explicitly formulated approach of individual actors.

In June 1966, an event was at a district level involving officials of the MNVs, trade unionists and economic workers, and including the participation of the Roma, which addressed the situation of the "G*psy population in the district". One of the speakers, the secretary of the MNV Papín, complained of the lack of discipline and fluctuation of Papín's G*psies. He also emphasised that "unless every G*psy works hard, no improvement in the situation in this area can be expected, since only the work of every person can educate". With a view to resolving the situation in Papín, he proposed "putting all the old people / pensioners from the settlement into a retirement home, integrating the young into the workforce, and **driving back those who deliberately return to the settlement from Czechia**" [emphasis J. O.].[149] In addition to the undisguised attempts of the secretary of the MNV to prevent the return of migrating Roma, another document from the same year captures the anti-Roma attitudes of non-Romani villagers in an ongoing discussion regarding the possible provision of housing in the village for families from the settlement:

When discussing the issue of withdrawal [of the Roma] to the village with the citizens at a public meeting, the citizens concerned said they did not agree with it and that if it is enacted, they will kill them.[150]

Perhaps aware of such attitudes, the MNV proposed the removal of the settlement through the relocation of all affected families to Czechia.

---

147 ŠAKE Košice, f. Komisia Vsl. KNV pre cigánske obyvatelstvo, kart. 3, sp. 55, "Komplexný plán na riešenia cig. ot. do r. 1970", 2 March 1963.
148 ŠAKE Košice, f. Komisia Vsl. KNV pre cigánske obyvatelstvo, kart. 3, sp. 26, "Situáčna zpráva na úseku riešenia osôb cigánskeho pôvodu", 16 November 1962.
149 ŠAKE Košice, f. Komisia Vsl. KNV pre cigánske obyvatelstvo, kart. 10, sp. 104, "Zápisnica", 23 June 1966.
150 ŠOkA Humenné, f. MNV Papín, fond MNV Papín, kart. 2, sp. 13, "Návrh na likvidáciu cigánskej osady v Papíne" 1966.

To begin with it conducted a valuation of all the shacks in the settlement as preparation for their purchase. It also planned to visit all those families living in Czechia in order to conclude an agreement on the sale of their property. Additionally, it announced its intention to assist these families in finding permanent housing in the "vicinity of their workplace" in Czechia in cooperation with the local authorities. The resettlement of the remaining families to Czechia was supported by those who had drawn up the proposal with arguments that placed them in ideological conformity with the official policy towards the Roma. The text claims that it would be inappropriate for the Roma to remain in the village in Slovakia because of the lack of employment opportunities, which were to be the "basis for the re-education of the G*psy population". In contrast, they were convinced that resettlement in Czechia would open up improved opportunities for educating young people and leading them away from a life of begging. Finally, mobilising the dominant logic of dispersion, the proposal envisages that "by relocating them to different parts of the republic, [the Roma] would not be able to cluster together, and this would definitively assist in civilising them."[151] The approved plan to relocate all families from the settlement to Czechia was successfully realised over the next few years. Individual buildings were valued between 1967 and 1970, and although the final confirmation of their purchase is dated 1970 and 1971, as early as May 1969, in an application for a valuation of the remaining buildings, the MNV in Papín stated that "at present, there is not so much as one person or family living in the settlement anymore: only one family lives near the village, since they have built a shack there. As a result, the problem can be dealt with easily".[152]

For the families from Papín this did not involve an "organised transfer" to partner districts, and even in the case of the remaining families there was continuity with their migration trajectories. Nevertheless, a focus on the perspective of the local authority reveals that the ideological underpinning of the resettlement policy became a tool helping to justify the shift of emphasis away from the previously planned (in the case of the local authorities only performatively, it would seem) return of the families from the settlement to the built-up area of the village over to their definitive resettlement in Czechia (which, on the contrary, took place relatively quickly). My point here is not to shift all our attention to

151 Ibid.
152 ŠOkA Humenné, f. Finančný odbor ONV Humenné, kart. 17, sp. 145, "S. Ján". [unprocessed].

the attitudes and agency of the Municipal National Committees. However, even given how these attitudes might have been explicitly racist, they form an important backdrop to post-war Romani migration, which in turn was a key context for the practice of the centrally defined effort to remove the settlements. At the same time, it should not be forgotten that, although the Roma had only very limited room for manoeuvre in the situations outlined above, the actions of the local authorities cannot be understood as the sole determinant of the movement of individual Romani families (regarding the agency of the Roma of Papín, see Chapter Four). Moreover, the approaches taken by individual authorities and the situation in individual villages also differed (see the comparative example of the municipality of Slovenská Volová; see also Chapter Two), with the authorities able to take a more nuanced approach in relation to the Roma in their municipality (see the Introduction and the situation in Kapišová, also Chapter Two and the situation in Brekov and Hostovice).

3.4 Podskalka: Between Marginalisation and Autonomy

When Davidová criticised the "incorrect" practice of "permitting the new construction of detached houses for families in close proximity to the old settlements" (which was supposedly at odds with the endeavour to liquidate them), she cited as an example the newly built part of the settlement in Humenné–Podskalka (Davidová 1965, 107). However, she herself, as an employee of the Regional National Committee, had two years earlier linked this construction work to the improved situation in the same settlement in her report:

> A short inspection was carried out in the G*psy settlement at Podskalka, where the situation has improved greatly, especially as regards solutions for the gradual liquidation of the G*psy settlement. Credit for this is due to the deputy of the MNV, the representative of the settlement, Mr Gorol, as well as to the other G*psy citizens who are doing good work among their fellow G*psies. The number of new family houses in the settlement has increased, as well as the number of families who have been allocated flats in the town among the rest of the population. (Jurová 2008, 950)

Two different declarations by the same person in the span of just two years illustrate certain tensions and contradictions in the policy being advocated and the change in emphasis over time. Such tensions are also well illustrated by other sources dealing with the settlement in Podskalka. The locally implemented policy, at least that in place since the 1950s, was balanced between new construction work and the removal of the settlement as a "G*psy concentration", though at some point the status of Podskalka as an independent municipality also came into play. However, what was important, as Davidová herself had already indicated in the report cited above, was that such policies cannot be understood independently of the agency of the Roma from Podskalka, who themselves shaped their settlement as a locus in its own right, and who sought to improve their living conditions while also being an integral part of local political structures. In order to capture the diversity of their life trajectories and the complexity of the practice of the liquidation programme within the framework of the resettlement policy, I will focus on the stories of specific families after summarising the dynamics of the development of the politics of place. Since I was only able to conduct a limited number of interviews in Podskalka itself, I will have to rely heavily on the sometimes fragmentary archival sources or already published interviews, which were recorded within the context of other research projects focusing on different areas.

3.4.1 Relocate, build or liquidate?

Chronologically speaking, the first more complete record from the post--war period of the Podskalka settlement, which according to the records of the Town National Committee (MsNV) numbered 405 inhabitants,[153] is a request for the relocation of the settlement submitted by a resident, Andrej M, at a meeting of the local authorities in 1950. From 1945 to 1950, Andrej M himself was to perform the role of *vajda*, which here refers to an officially charged administrator and representative of the settlement, for which he received financial remuneration approved by the local councillors and paid retrospectively.[154] His request is summarised in the minutes as follows:

---

153 ŠOkA Humenné, f. Odbor vnutorných vecí ONV Humenné, kart. 21, sp. 104, "Cigáni v obci Humnné". 24 September 1951.
154 ŠOkA Humenné, f. MNV Humenné, kart. 4, "Zápisnica", 4 April 1950.

Andrej M, within the context of freely submitted motions, presented a complaint from the inhabitants of the Podskalka settlement, in which he states, inter alia, that the conditions are unsustainable, since it is not rare for 14–15 [persons] to be living in one unsuitable small building with only one room. So far his requests that the municipality should make the entire settlement more decent have fallen on deaf ears. It is spring and warmer weather is on its way, during which there is a real danger that the settlement will become a breeding ground for various bugs. He therefore believes that it would be advisable to relocate the entire settlement and at the very least provisionally secure building plots for 80 detached family houses. The inhabitants of the settlement cannot wait any longer, and if their request is not granted, they will be forced to take their grievances to a higher level.[155]

This application captures the dismal living conditions in the settlement and confirms the image of such enclaves in the war-torn region of eastern Slovakia (see for example Ort 2022a,b). However, it can also be understood as a reversal of perspective in respect of the monitoring of post-war (local) policies towards Romani settlements. Andrej M makes his appeal not as an individual, but as a representative of the entire settlement, reflecting the inaction of the authorities up till then. He expresses a determination to submit his request to higher authorities in the event of continued inaction. And so inasmuch as I intend to discuss specific policies intended to lead to improvements in the living conditions of the residents of Podskalka, these must also be understood as a response to similar – to all intents and purposes ongoing – demands and pressure exerted by the residents themselves.

In response to this specific complaint, the local councillors passed a resolution expressing the need to buy up land from particular village residents, and in the event of resistance, to proceed to compulsory expropriation.[156] Although I was unable to find other sources continuing the discussion on the acquisition of land for the relocation of the settlement, it is clear that over the next few years the situation in Podskalka did not improve. At a public meeting attended by around 900 people in March 1954 at the Partizan cinema in Humenné, Pavel M from Podskalka submitted another request for the relocation of the settlement. He argued that its location was unsuitable, above all in view of the spring and

---

155 Ibid.
156 Ibid.

autumn floods which were destroying the existing dwellings. According to the minutes of the meeting, he asked that the MNV allocate building plots "where [the citizens of Podskalka] would then build their own homes". On the basis of a condemnation of the "dilapidated" (*dezolátny*) and "life-threatening" (*život ohrozujúci*) state of the settlement by the MNV,[157] a commission comprising representatives of the District and Regional National Committees met in April of that year in the presence of the "chairman of the settlement", Andrej M. The commission confirmed the unsatisfactory state of the housing (500 persons living in a total of 104 wooden shacks spread over a surface of 1,000 m²) and health (the spread of tuberculosis). Given the urgency of the situation, the commission recommended that the council of the MNV contact their superiors, including the Central Committee of the Communist Party of Slovakia, the Ministry of the Interior, the Ministry of Health, and the Ministry of Local Commerce, and declare bluntly that the public reportedly held a very poor opinion of the state of the settlement at Podskalka throughout the entire region.[158] Unfortunately, the available archival materials say nothing regarding the results of the (proposed) transfer of the problem to a higher level in the hierarchy of the state apparat. In contrast, another request was submitted by Andrej M at the meeting of the MNV in July of the following year (1955), this time not calling for the relocation of the settlement, but for the allocation of thirty-nine building plots in its grounds. Without offering further details, the minutes of the meeting state that the MNV granted this request.[159]

At a meeting held in May 1956 and attended by representatives of the Municipal National Committee, the District Committee of the Communist Party, the District National Committee and the inhabitants of Podskalka, it was decided that what was needed was not relocation, but the overall transformation of the existing settlement grounds. It was agreed that a building plan was essential (to be drawn up by the Design Institute in Prešov under the aegis of the Construction Department of the District National Committee in Humenné), which would include a school with three classrooms, a nursery, a house of culture and a shop as part of the capital investment. Two alternatives were outlined for residential construction in the settlement. The first involved individual housing construction, for which the working population would receive

---

157 ŠOkA Humenné, f. MNV Humenné, kart. 5, "Zápisnica", 5 April 1954.
158 ŠOkA Humenné, f. MNV Humenné, kart. 4, "Zápisnica", 4 June 1954.
159 ŠOkA Humenné, f. MNV Humenné, kart. 4, "Zápisnica", 6 June 1955.

a building loan of up to 25,000 crowns and an exceptional allocation of building materials. The alternative ("which the commission recognised as quicker and more suitable given the circumstances of the settlement") would involve the state construction of detached houses for families, which would be paid for in the form of rent.[160]

Michal Goroľ, himself from the Podskalka settlement and chairman of the district G*psy Commission, participated in the meeting as a representative of the District Committee of the Communist Party of Slovakia. In the report cited above, it is he whom Davidová identifies as an important agent who was eventually to push for the construction of detached houses in the settlement. However, this did not involve construction on the basis of an overall development plan, as had been envisaged in the outcomes of previous negotiations, but the construction of nineteen detached houses for selected families. The entire project began to take shape after the meeting of the council of the MNV in July 1957. As well as the necessity of conducting awareness-raising activities and various activities in the settlement (e.g. literacy and cookery classes), the resolution passed by this meeting issued an instruction to "identify and hold discussions with applications for land allocation". Goroľ had already observed that he would only allocate land to those "who are expected to build".

A total of nineteen detached houses were later built on the land of the existing settlement. During discussions at the 1957 meeting, one of the councillors, Dr. Némethy, questioned this procedure. According to the minutes, however, his question – "why could citizens of G*psy origin not live in Humenné, which would be more advantageous in respect of hygiene and moral education" – remained unanswered.[161] However, a clear departure from the possibility of continued construction in the land of the settlement is evident in the following years. In September 1958, the district G*psy Commission proposed an inspection of the building work taking place in Podskalka, "since the commission has found that other huts are being built without permission".[162] The proposal for a complete ban on independent construction work in the settlement was put forward at a meeting of the MNV in Humenné in June 1959, which

---

160 ŠOkA Humenné, f. MNV Humenné, kart. 23, sp. 12, "Previerka osady", 30 May 1956.
161 ŠOkA Humenné, f. MNV Humenné, kart. 7, "Informatívná zpráva k riešenie cigánskej otázky", 25 June 1957.
162 ŠOkA Humenné, f. Odbor vnútorných vecí ONV Humenné, kart. 22, sp. 122, "Zápisnica", 24 September 1958.

was also attended by representatives of selected divisions of the ONV. This special meeting, devoted to "the matter of the relocation of the Podskalka G*psy settlement", saw a longer-term plan for dealing with its gradual liquidation formulated for the first time. Under this plan, the MNV was to provide building plots in parts of Humenné included in the land registry for fifteen people interested in individual construction work (4–5 building plots per year) by 1962, and replacement apartments for forty-eight families (4–5 apartments a year) by 1968. In the case of permanently employed Roma the situation was to be resolved by means of corporate housing.[163] The move away from building work in the grounds of the settlement to its removal through the relocation of individual families (mainly to the town of Humenné) may also have been related to the government resolution on Work amongst the G*psy Population of April 1958, in which an emphasis was placed on the disposal of the settlements.

3.4.2 Self-governing Podskalka?

Prior to the move toward prioritising the complete removal of the settlement, it was mooted as to whether Podskalka would be recognised as an independent municipality. The town was assisted in this respect by the continued presence of its own school, the roots of which dated back to the First Republic. A development plan was also proposed, which envisaged the construction of a community centre (see above).

The first mention of the independence of Podskalka appears in the material of the Regional National Committee in Prešov, specifically in the report of a survey conducted in the settlements dated 1956. The authors of this report write, inter alia, that "the settlement [in Podskalka] has all the prerequisites that would allow it to be recognised as a political community in its own right, something the inhabitants of the settlement are requesting".[164] In the same department's materials of April 1957, the independence of Podskalka as of 1 January 1958 was already envisaged.[165] This was also discussed at a meeting of the MNV in Humen-

---

163 ŠOkA Humenné, f. MNV Humenné, kart. 23, sp. 26, "Premistenie cigánskej osady Podskalka v Humennom", 2 June 1959.
164 ŠAPO Nižná Šebastová, f. Odbor vnutorných vecí KNV Prešov, kart. 219, sp. 53, "Zpráva zo služobnej cesty konanej v dňoch od 8 do 12 júna 1956", 1956.
165 ŠAPO Nižná Šebastová, f. Odbor vnutorných vecí KNV Prešov, kart. 219, sp. 53, "Reflexia uznesenie 301/1956", 26 April 1957.

né in June 1957 (i.e. the meeting at which the plan for the allocation of building plots in the settlement was mooted, see above). Referring to the inadequate conditions in the settlement, the representative of the ONV expressed concern as to whether the "prerequisites exist for independent management, when even now the difficulties cannot be resolved". Goroľ, who did not wish the settlement to become independent, responded by confirming in a somewhat paternalistic spirit that the preconditions for independence were "not yet in place".[166] It is not certain to what extent this exchange influenced subsequent developments. Whatever the case, Podskalka did not achieve independence on 1 January of the following year. Plans for independence appeared again in March 1958 in the KNV report.[167] However, the May report on the survey of the settlement carried out by representatives of ONV Humenné (i.e. after the government resolution of April, see above) stated that "the independence of the settlement is not necessary, since construction plans for Humenné and the settlement are such that they will very soon be linked"[168] (even though the plan had been to liquidate the settlement in the same year and not connect it, see above). In the spirit of the assimilationist logic advocated, the question of Podskalka becoming independent was also raised by Vasiľ Biľak, Commissioner for Education and Culture, in his final speech at the nationwide meeting in January 1959. Complying with the dominant understanding of "G*psy concentration", Biľak rejected such plans out of hand, expressing his fear that Podskalka would become a kind of centre for a "primitive way of life":

The comrades in Humenné, in the Podskalka settlement, want to acquire the status of municipality. How will they manage it? A municipality must have the right economic base, but what will Podskalka have? The reality would be that in a few years many who do not want to fit in with the population and would prefer to maintain their primitive way of life would relocate to Podskalka and the "village" would grow to a settlement numbering five thousand. How would this be dealt with then? Where would they work? (Jurová 2008, 761–763)

---

166 ŠOkA Humenné, f. MNV Humenné, kart. 7, "Informatívná zpráva k riešenie cigánskej otázky", 25 June 1957.
167 ŠAPO Nižná Šebastová, f. Odbor vnutorných vecí KNV Prešov, kart. 220, sp. 53, "Informatívna zpráva o plnení uznesenia rady KNV 301/1956", 31 March 1958.
168 ŠOkA Humenné, f. Odbor vnutorných vecí ONV Humenné, kart. 22, sp. 122, "Záznam z prieskumu na Podskalke", 8 May 1958.

The exploration of various ways of resolving the unsatisfactory situation in the Podskalka settlement, including acceding to the demand for independence, fits to some extent into the broader picture of centralised policy towards the Roma in the first half of the 1950s. During that period, various approaches were considered and combined before the definitive shift to an assimilationist policy in 1958 (see Donert 2008, Spurný 2011). For Podskalka, this shift meant an emphasis on gradual removal, culminating in the resettlement policy of the 1960s.

3.4.3 The position of the Roma

On the basis of the previous subsection, two important aspects can be identified in respect of the perspective of the Roma of Podskalka. Firstly, there is the fact that the Roma were not merely passive recipients, but through their representatives exerted pressure aimed at improving the conditions of their housing and lives in general. Secondly, the situation in Podskalka is another example of the disruption of a simple opposition between the state and the Roma as its marginalised inhabitants, in this case through Goroľ's involvement in local political structures. As chairman of the district G*psy Commission, Goroľ was in a position to promote concrete measures aimed at improving the situation in the settlement. Among the people I interviewed in Podskalka in 2019 and 2021, the building work carried out in the late 1950s was associated with his name, as Davidová had earlier pointed out (see above). However, it is also clear from the material cited above that Goroľ himself adopted a somewhat paternalistic attitude towards the Romani people in Podskalka, no doubt in part because he was one of the Roma who already had his own housing in the town of Humenné.

In an interview with Hübschmannová, who regularly visited Podskalka and had close friends there, Michal Kašo and Olga Tokárová, both originally from Podskalka, recalled that the local Roma used to live in the town of Humenné itself, in a place called in Romani *pro Riňos*, before being relocated to Podskalka, i.e. several kilometres outside the town, during the First Republic. According to them, at the time the interview was conducted in 2000, none of the Roma had any direct recollection of the original location of the settlement. However, these Roma had up till then referred to themselves as "urban Roma" (*foroskere Roma*; Hübschmannová [forthcoming]). This is very important in respect of the theme under discussion, since it means that the designation of Podskalka as a "G*psy space" was not a given, but was itself the result of the terri-torialisation, or rather the displacement, of the Roma. At the same time, the Roma themselves perceived the unsatisfactory situation in Podskalka as the outcome of sluggishness on the part of the local authorities (see the request submitted by Andrej M at a meeting of the MNV discussed above), which may have been in contrast with the overall post-war devel-opment of the town.

In addition to collective demands for the relocation of the settlement and the resolution of the inadequate housing situation, other reactions on the part of the Roma to their marginalised status can be traced back to the post-war period. As in other settlements (see Ort 2022b), this was primarily about spatial mobility, i.e. (temporary) escape from the set-tlement. Inasmuch as the MNV planned to resolve the removal of the settlement by relocating its population to the area forming the town of Humenné, it should be remembered that in the case of individual fam-ilies such movement had been taking place since at least the immediate post-war period. This is evidenced not only by the testimony of witnesses I interviewed during my visits to Podskalka,[169] but also by archival mate-rials from the MNV fonds, which contain approved applications for the allocation of building land going back to 1949.[170]

The second form of mobility was migration to Czechia, a strategy that a relatively large number of families from Podskalka resorted to in the immediate post-war period. Among them was the family of Michal Kašo, who was born in Podskalka in 1939, but left for Czechia with his parents and other relatives shortly after the war and spent his childhood in sever-al different locations there. However, as he states in his autobiographical piece included in the book devoted to the recollections of Humenné natives (Mišková 2016, 78–106), his family returned to Podskalka around the mid-1950s. With his wealth of detail regarding life in the settlement, Kašo provides a valuable counterbalance to the official surveys, typically conducted by representatives of the local and district authorities (see Chapter One). Although he describes his initial shock as a child upon returning from a city in Czechia to the east Slovakian settlement, he goes on to provide a vivid and slightly nostalgic description of the way that holidays were celebrated, the life of a professional musician, his

---

169 For example, interviews with Štefan K (b. 1960) and Jolana K (b. 1961), recorded by the author in May 2019 and June 2021 in Podskalka in Romani (recordings in the possession of the author).
170 ŠOkA Humenné, f. MNV Humenné, kart. 4, 5, 6, 7.

own schooling, and the generally rich life of Podskalka, which had its own football team, fire brigade, and its own dance troupe, in addition to a school. It is often impossible to deduce which period of time Kašo is referring to. He seems to refer to the period of his own adulthood, when he began working at Podskalka as a teacher, following which he moved directly from Podskalka to Humenné. However, the particular cultural and social activities by means of which the Roma of Podskalka were granted wider social participation are also present in archival materials from the late 1950s. I shall leave to one side for a moment the fact that some of these activities were imposed from outside as part of educational projects (such as sewing courses, also referred to by Kašo), which meant they partly recapitulated the idea of the settlement as a site of cultural backwardness. I am more interested here in the fact that Podskalka was conceived of as a distinct space (with the inclusion of certain activities from outside), which means it is not necessary to view it only within the logic of a marginalised place from which people would try to escape. This is backed up not only by the collectively articulated requests discussed above, which envisage the preservation of the common space, but also by the demand for self-government, which, according to one of the documents cited above, allegedly came from the residents of Podskalka themselves.[171]

Let us return for a moment to the introduction to this chapter and the letter written by Mr Tokár sent to the editors at Czechoslovak Television. He, too, counted on remaining in "his village" and only left for Ostrava because he did not qualify for new housing and could not find decent working conditions in the region. Moreover, as Hübschmannová points out, notwithstanding its dismal conditions, the settlement may still have represented a safe space for the Roma of Podskalka, (see Skupnik 2007; also Guy 1977, 486):

> In the 1950s, the large family moved from České Budějovice [Czechia] back to the settlement at Podskalka, because several family members were sentenced to long prison terms following a fight. In Budějovice they had apartments and well-paid jobs, yet they returned to the far worse housing conditions of the

---

171 In the end, even though thoughts of granting autonomy to Podskalka were short-lived, the inhabitants nevertheless elected their own "settlement committee", as evidenced in one of the archival sources (ŠOkA Humenné, f. odbor vnutorných vecí ONV Humenné, kart. 22, sp. 122, "Záznam z prieskumu na Podskalke", 8 May 1958).

settlement, where they felt safe and protected by relatives. (Hübschmannová 1999b, 125)

One more aspect of the Romani identification with Podskalka deserves a mention. The settlement did not have to be understood only in terms of, say, its socio-cultural profile, but also in purely material terms. This is also evident to an extent in the testimony provided by Kašo, who mentions that he was shocked by the living conditions of the settlement after returning from Czechia, but that he loved the surrounding landscape. Another person with a close relationship with the physical space of Podskalka was Aladár Kurej, a naive painter of the village, who, according to his own recollections, had a strong relationship with the environment and local wildlife. This was reflected in paintings depicting Podskalka. Later, when he moved to a city apartment, he said that he could never get used to the urban environment (e.g. Kurej 1996). The cemetery above the settlement with its own bell tower undoubtedly helped cement the idea of Podskalka as an independent space. Kašo refers to this, and during my own visits the local Roma spoke with pride of these features and how they contributed to the specificity of the place. This character of the location is of course difficult to reconstruct for the period of the 1950s and 1960s. Moreover, the sources make it impossible to relate it to the removal of the shacks. It must therefore be approached with some caution, though I believe it should not be completely overlooked. I am reminded here of the case of "old Pompa" referred to by Davidová, who spent the night on the site of the demolished settlement in Miklušovce, though the author uses the story to reveal the necessity of severing ties to the settlement as a physical space (see above).

3.4.4 Buying up the shacks

Apart from the fact that Podskalka was listed in the records of the district and regional authorities since the 1950s as the largest settlement in the district, and as such received a lot of attention, the actual buying out of the shacks as recorded in the archive fonds specified above is exceptional in terms of the sheer variety of solutions found to the problem of providing their original owners with housing (a total of eleven shacks that were bought up in this way are listed in the archive). Most of the families moved to the county seat, though the Roma of Podskalka were among the few who participated in the "organised transfer" to partner districts in Czechia, with three families moving to the village of Nové Lublice in the Opava district (see Chapter Four). Only one case involved the retroactive "liquidation of a shack" caused by previous migration to Czechia, which is clearly the file that Mr Tokár, author of the letter to the television cited in the introduction, touches upon.

In the context of Podskalka, far more ambitious plans for the removal of the shacks were formulated in the documents of the District National Committee, and the final numbers are a rather weak outcome from this perspective. Neither did the figures reflect the priority given the settlement in the resolution of the district G*psy Commission in March 1967. In that resolution, it was to be exclusively G*psies from Humenné (i.e. from Podskalka) that were to be resettled to the partner districts of Opava and Bruntál.[172]

The 1966 report by the G*psy Commission in Humenné offers concrete figures. The authors of the report state that in 1966 not a single "buy-out of shacks" took place, although all of the "dilapidated buildings" were valued and new records drawn up. With the following year already in mind, an ambitious plan was drawn up (which, as we have seen, remained unmet), under which a total of twenty-six families were to be relocated to partner districts, sixteen families were to build their own accommodation, and five families would purchase "old detached houses".[173] And so the eleven purchases of shacks listed in the records of the Finance Department covering the entire period up to 1970 represents failure to carry out these plans, above all given that only three families were resettled in Czechia.

3.4.5 Elemír T.: From Podskalka to the town

On my first visit to Podskalka I met the married couple Štefan and Jolana, who were born in the village in the early 1960s. Their two sons ran the civic association, and the elder, Peter, was conducting his own research into the history of the neighbourhood, recording interviews with witnesses and using old photographs he had collected from local families to organise a public exhibition about the history of the Roma in Podskalka

---

172 ŠAKE Košice, f. Komisia Vsl. KNV pre cigánske obyvatelstvo, kart. 15, sp. 71, "Uznesenie", 22 March 1967.
173 ŠAKE Košice, f. Komisia Vsl. KNV pre cigánske obyvatelstvo, kart. 15, sp. 96, "Zpráva o práci cigánskej komísie", 24 May 1967.

(see Chapter One). During our conversation about the names mentioned in the archives in connection with the purchase of the shacks in the village, Štefan and Jolana confirmed that, with one exception, the former owners of these buildings were now deceased.

The only person still alive was Elemír T, born in 1940. In his brief and somewhat sketchy recollections, Elemír T described the selling off of his own shack as pretty much a done deal that made sense from the perspective of all the actors involved:

> The shacks were being sold off. The state took them and offered us money for them. They gave me money too, I received money for the shack I had [...] That's when a *goro* [non-Rom] from Humenné came from the social services. He said that we had to surrender the house so that it wouldn't fall down. And then I got an apartment in town. Otherwise it would have fallen down and could have killed my children. We had five kids; four girls and one boy. [...] We had to sell it, otherwise it would have fallen on the children. I worked in construction, so they gave me a house in the city, where I lived for twenty-eight years. [...] It was a better environment, know what I mean? And it was closer to work, too. We were better off there. [...] The sold shacks were dismantled by the Roma who had remained there [in the settlement], they did it for the wood. [...] I received [for the shack] some money for furniture, around ten thousand crowns. I had a paper [voucher], and I was able to use it in shops. But we could also always reach an agreement with the manager along the lines of "Give me money for that" [...] He would write out "For furniture" and give you some money.[174]

The fact that it did not even occur to Elemír T to question the significance of the entire project and his own motives for moving to the town can be read in two ways. Firstly, there were the dismal living conditions that he believed represented a threat to his children's lives. From this perspective the purchase of the shacks can be interpreted as a response to ongoing demands for a solution to the dismal living conditions in Podskalka, and was in line with the movement of the Roma from Podskalka to the town. However, the second important point is the later development and overall context of the situation in which Elemír T recalled the events of the 1960s. He stated that other families moved to

---

174 Interview with Elemír T (b. 1940), *op. cit.*

Humenné from Podskalka in the later period. However, after the Velvet Revolution of 1989 and the privatisation of housing, a large number of these families, including Elemír T, were tagged collectively as "non-payers" and forced to move back to Podskalka, where apartment blocks were being built for them. It was in front of one of these blocks that I recorded an interview with him, during which he informed me, with a tinge of nostalgia, that he had lived in his allocated apartment in the town for twenty-eight years.

Elemír T did not elaborate on the course and specific circumstances of the sale of his own shack. Nevertheless, his testimony reveals that the state's purchase became part of other economic transactions between various local actors. However sketchy, the remark about vouchers being issued "for furniture", i.e. for fitting out new apartments, is particularly interesting in this respect. According to the documents accompanying the implementation of the resettlement policy, funds were to be set aside for new housing and/or its fittings and fixtures (Guy 1977, 282). Yet Elemír T.'s remark is somewhat obscure when compared with the contents of the relevant file in the archive of the finance department.[175] The document pertaining to the repossession of Elemír T's shack states that he had secured alternative accommodation in the city in the apartment of his father, Andrej T, who had also sold off his shack and bought an apartment in the town from a certain Marie M. The Finance Department of the Humenné ONV wrote to its budgetary division that the purchase price of the repossessed shack should be assigned to Elemír T so that he might secure alternative housing. After Elemír T had proved to the department of internal affairs that he had indeed secured alternative housing, approval was given to the sum involved to be paid into a "free account". It is therefore not entirely clear what voucher Elemír T was referring to in our interview or how the money was eventually paid to him. What his testimony does suggest, however, is that in the disbursement of funds, certain Romani people may have been able to circumvent centrally determined measures with the help of local non-Romani actors. However delicate the situation, it is a reminder that it is not possible to think of Romani agency in isolation from local networks of socio-economic relations. Despite its spatial separation and the debate around the possibility of its acquiring autonomy, not even Podskalka was isolated,

---

175 ŠOkA Humenné, f. Finanční odbor ONV Humenné, kart. 16, sp. 57, "T. Elemír, Podskalka" [unprocessed].

and its inhabitants were embedded in socio-economic networks that necessarily transcended it. In addition to the convergence of interests of central policy and of the Roma themselves (Guy 1977, 329; Sadílková 2017), there was room for manoeuvre in which the latter, with the help of other local actors, were able to further reshape these policies to their own benefit.

3.4.6 František B: A shack to be liquidated?

The records of the Finance Department indicate that it oversaw the first repossession of a shack belonging to František B of Podskalka in 1966. This case is a good example of the sheer variety of constructions that could be deemed a "G*psy shack". Clearly not all the buildings involved were in a "life threatening" state, as Elemír T had described them in an interview with me. The case of František B also problematises that part of the central policy promoting liquidation, since not all of the repossessed buildings were physically demolished. In addition to demonstrating the room for manoeuvre in which individual actors were able to reshape central policy to their own benefit, the case of František B also highlights a certain tension between cultivation of Podskalka as a distinct space and the liquidation of the settlement as exemplifying a "backward way of life".

At odds with the notion of a substandard and dilapidated building, the document containing a valuation of František B's home states that it was a brick "newbuild" constructed in 1958[176] on a concrete foundation with electrical wiring beneath the plaster, albeit without water and sewage, with a total living area of 44 m². The building was valued at 41,600 crowns in total, and after a fifteen percent deduction due to its being incomplete, the owner received a one-off sum of 35,360 crowns. However, the case of this detached house now becomes even more interesting, since instead of being demolished, the building served as a replacement for the substandard premises of the Podskalka Nursery School. The archived documentation of the ONV in Humenné reveals that the real reason for the repossession of this building, which was discussed with its owner even prior to the government resolution of

---

176 The question is whether the construction of this building was part of the construction of nineteen detached family houses in Podskalka in the same year (see above).

October 1965 coming into force, was the need to increase the capacity of the local kindergarten. In the 1965 district plan, approved in February of that year, the following targets were set in the sphere of school education:

The Humenné-Podskalka Nursery School [is planned] to be expanded by one classroom on 1 September 1965 and to include a further 25 children of G*psy origin of pre-school age, but under such circumstances that the owner of the building where the nursery school is located will receive a family apartment in a state or cooperative building in Humenné. The owner agrees to vacate the building for the purpose of the nursery school.[177]

It is likely that this entry refers to František B, who again expressed an interest in selling the building in January 1966 on the grounds that "he wanted to bring up his children in a completely different environment to the one they are living in at present."[178] The sale of František B's house was completed in the same year, as was the acquisition of a new apartment, which he and his wife bought in the town of Humenné.

Looking at other examples of the repossession of shacks in the district, it becomes clear that the utilisation of such expropriated properties for other purposes was not unique. Two buildings in the village of Kamenice nad Cirochou, one in the built-up area of the municipality and the other outside it, received a similar valuation to František B's house. One included a fenced garden with seven fruit trees. The records indicate that the owners of these houses were amongst the few people to be part of an organised transfer between partner districts upon being allocated housing in the county seat of Opava. And yet there is no evidence that any of these buildings were actually demolished. In the case of Ján B, one of the owners, there is a sale and purchase agreement under which the MNV in Kamenice is responsible for demolition. However, another contract from the same year (1967) sets forth the terms of the sale of the building to one Július B.[179] In addition, two other families were resettled from Kamenice to Opava, and their houses were bought by the former Romani owners of officially "liquidated shacks" in other municipalities

177 ŠAKE Košice, f. f. Komisia Vsl. KNV pre cigánske obyvatelstvo, kart. 6, sp. 25, "Plán na úseku riešenia otázok občanov cigánskeho pôvodu", 3 February 1965.
178 ŠOkA Humenné, f. Finanční odbor ONV Humenné, kart. 15, sp. 1, "B. František" [unprocessed].
179 ŠOkA Humenné, f. Finanční odbor ONV Humenné, kart. 16, sp. 91, "B. Ján" [unprocessed].

in the district (Kamienka and Veľopolie).[180] What is remarkable about such a resale is the fact that both parties, the seller and the buyer, were officially reported to be on schedule with the resettlement policy. That such a situation could have proved advantageous during the compilation of progress reports on the implementation of the central policy in a given district can be seen in the way things were dealt with in Podskalka. In the 1967 district report on "resolving the housing problem [and] repossessing shacks", a financial exemption was granted Michal D, the breadwinner of a family of seven, who planned to purchase a detached house for his family from Štefan G in the town of Humenné itself. Štefan G, on the other hand, was planning to move his family of eleven to the Louny district in Bohemia, where he had arranged to buy another detached house. State support of 17,000 crowns, i.e. the value of Štefan G's house, was to be transferred to Michal D in a move that was justified as follows: "The building that the citizen Michal D wishes to buy is inhabitable. The situation of two G*psy families would thus be resolved."[181]

Examples of the owners of demolished shacks receiving new housing by purchasing it from other Romani families who had relocated (usually to Czechia) were far from unique, perhaps in view of the unavailability of new housing and the reluctance of non-Romani residents to allow the Roma into their territory (see Guy 1977, 308). In addition to the files held in the archive of the Financial Department, where such practices are recorded, something of the kind cropped up in an interview I conducted with a married couple, Štefan and Jolana K from Humenné, both of whom were natives of Podskalka: "The Roma sold the buildings amongst themselves. This one went and sold it to another, because the other one wanted to stay [in the settlement]."[182] Štefan and Jolana were born in 1960, and so it is not entirely clear whether they are referring to the latter half of the 1960s or to a later practice. However, taken in conjunction with the archival materials referred to above, it becomes clear that the implementation of the resettlement project as a whole was an intra-Romani matter and part of their economic transactions.

---

180 ŠOkA Humenné, f. Finanční odbor ONV Humenné, kart. 15, sp. 89, "F. Alexander" and sp. 90 "G. Vojtěch" [unprocessed].
181 ŠOkA Humenné, f. Finanční odbor ONV Humenné, kart. 15, "Materiály komisie pre riešenie otázok cig. obyvateľstva, roky 1966–1971" [unprocessed].
182 Interview with Štefan K (b. 1960) and Jolana K (b. 1961), *op. cit.*

3.4.7 Who benefitted from the "G*psy policy"?

On the basis of what has been said so far, it is worth repeating the argument formulated in Chapter One and examined in more detail in Chapter Two, to wit, that the resettlement programme did not affect only Romani people, but entered into locally specific, historically shaped relationships, where details of its implementation – who would be affected and how, and who would benefit from it – were decided. Up till now I have acquiesced to the claim that the targeting of the settlement *liquidation* policy may have converged with the interests of the Roma. However, it is now time to reveal the heterogenous agency of the Roma and to look at which Roma may actually have managed to reap benefits from the centrally formulated policy. This depended on their position in the hierarchy of locally negotiated relations, in this case not necessarily according to the logic of G*psyness (see Chapter Two), but the accumulation of social and economic capital.

During the planning stage of the construction of single-family houses in 1958, Mr Goroľ of Podskalka, in his capacity as representative of the District Committee of the Communist Party and chairman of the district G*psy Commission, proposed the allocation of land only to those "who can be expected to use it for building purposes" (see above). The method of selecting those families who could build homes was criticised by Mr Tokár in his letter (see the letter to Czechoslovak TV in the introduction to this chapter), who pointed out the importance of social relations: "And so only a few houses were built, and only by those with family contacts to the district authorities. Those who had the bad quality houses remained."[183] I have noticed similar criticisms of the way that shacks were repossessed in the latter half of the 1960s in the village of Stakčín. Just as Mr Goroľ of Podskalka was chairman of the district G*psy Commission in the 1950s, Ján Oláh from Stakčín was secretary of the successor Commission responsible for the implementation of the resettlement programme in the 1960s. And just as Mr Tokár recalled the importance of connections with officials when it came to receiving new housing in the settlement (and perhaps he had in mind Mr Goroľ), so contemporary witnesses in the Romani community in Stakčín have reported to me

---

183 NA Prague, KSČ-ÚV-05/3, f. KSČ – Ústřední výbor 1945–1989, Praha – oddělení – oddělení ideologické, sv. 37, č. j. 299.

that Mr Oláh favoured his relatives when it came to repossession of the shacks in his home village.[184]

Although there is no such explicit criticism of the repossession of shacks in Podskalka, it is clear that being in a position to benefit from the central policy did not depend on a person's readiness to quit the settlement (as assumed by the categorisation of G*psies according to the degree of social assimilation, see Chapter Two), but on their ability to secure new housing, which, especially given the anti-Roma discrimination of the authorities and local residents, was by no means a simple matter. From this perspective, it is significant that in the vast majority of cases, not only in Podskalka but throughout the region, the Roma arranged for alternative housing themselves, sometimes even by buying apartments from other Roma who had left for Czechia. The absolute minimum number of cases was resolved by resettlement to partner districts, which meant disappointment for most of the twenty-six people who applied to be resettled from Podskalka.

3.4.8 The reproduction of territorialisation

As in the case of Ľubiša and Papín, in Podsalka the "liquidation of the settlements" campaign largely involved a continuation of existing processes. However, while in Ľubiša and Papín it allowed for the complete eviction of the local Roma, in Podskalka the repossession of the shacks meant the continuation of two interlinked phenomena. The ongoing relocation of the Roma from Podskalka to the centre of Humenné was accompanied by the reproduction of a logic under which the "G*psy way of life" was to remain enclosed within the settlement since its manifestation in the town was deemed undesirable. This is indicated by the attitude of one of the two residents (a non-Rom), who, like Mr Tokár, responded to the TV broadcast of 1966. In her letter, she writes:

> You cannot compare Podskalka to the worst G*psy settlements. Ok, there are some nice new houses with comfortable furnishings. But there are also those in which ten or twelve people are crowded into one room. Unfortunately, this is not only the case in Podskalka, but in the town itself. As soon as someone moves into an apartment building, the flat is occupied by G*psies, with

---

184 For example, the interview with Mária K (b. 1950), *op. cit.*

whom you can't get along merely using nice words or even threats. As you walk past such houses you wrinkle your nose. If only it were a question of housing! But it is also a question of behaviour. Why do they never have anything to do but sit in the city park in winter or summer and hurl comments in "their vernacular" at passers-by? Their kids don't go to school, and by the age of five or six they are already smoking and testing the limits of what they can get up to.[185]

While the central policy anticipated the assimilation of the Roma, which in turn was intended to lead to an outcome in which they were no longer considered G*psies (see Chapter Two), it seems that in Humenné itself there was more of a tendency to push those leading a "G*psy way of life" into the settlement as its supposedly natural location. It was also in 1966 that Pavel M, a resident of Podskalka, submitted a complaint to the district authorities regarding the existing practice whereby the "SNB [National Security Corps, i.e. the police] expelled all G*psies from the town regardless of whether they were guilty of a crime or not."[186] A representative of the SNB Humenné responded, explaining that "the Public Security services do not expel G*psy citizens from the town because they have no right to live there, but because they should be doing work at home, the laundry etc., rather than idling away their time in the town."[187] He was in essence admitting not only that the Roma were being expelled, but that this was taking place purely on the basis of their presence in the town and the sense there was a need to discipline them as G*psies. The assimilationist policy coincided with the local practice of territorialising Roma in the sense that its logic reproduced G*psyness as a category of social deviance and an understanding of the settlements as the natural home for the expression of such deviance. The emphasis placed on the liquidation of the settlements did not contradict this logic, but its implementation in practice offered an opportunity for individual families to transcend the practice of territorialisation and achieve a certain socio-economic mobility.

185 NA Prague, KSČ-ÚV-05/3, f. KSČ – Ústřední výbor 1945–1989, Praha – oddělení – oddělení ideologické, sv. 37, č. j. 299.
186 ŠAKE Košice, f. Komisia Vsl. KNV pre cigánske obyvatelstvo Košice, kart. 10, sp. 104, "Zápisnica", 23 June 1966.
187 Ibid.

3.5 Conclusion

In this chapter I have shown how settlements are specific sites that are co-created through the complex actions of diverse actors and associated accordingly with different meanings. I have shown that the settlements in the form they took in the period under discussion were the result of a historically unbroken local practice of territorialising the Roma as G*psies. In this respect, the settlements cannot be regarded as naturally segregated spaces that stand apart from local socio-economic systems, but as spaces that are part of said systems and constructed as a distinct place within them. State policy, however much it sought to disrupt the territorialisation of the Roma, reproduced the separation of these places as spaces of social deviance and backward ways of life. However, the logic of the settlements as separate places was also reproduced to some extent by criticism at the time and subsequently, which regarded them as distinct socio-cultural systems, however connected to their surroundings.

The view of the settlements as places of cultural backwardness is significant in that it may have been shared to some extent by the Roma themselves. This does not only apply to Mr Goroľ, who as a local official living in the town reproduced a paternalistic discourse in relation to the inhabitants of Podskalka, or Mr Kašo, who as a child was shocked by the environment of a settlement after returning from an urban environment in Czechia. It also applies to František B, who when confirming the sale of his own home, stated that he wanted to bring up his children "in a different environment to that in which they have lived up till now". The ongoing movement of the Roma out of the settlement, which has been described in broader terms for other places (Grill 2015b; Hübschmannová 1999b; Ort 2021, 2022b; Sadílková 2017) can thus be understood not only as an effort to achieve more dignified housing, but also in terms of broader socio-economic mobility and social belonging (see especially Ort 2022b). On the other hand, even Hübschmannová's culturally relativist understanding of settlements, which distinguishes them from artificially created ghettos (1993, 23; 1999a, 31), or an emphasis on the emotional attachment of the physical space of settlements, cannot be dismissed as the romanticisation of the social exclusion of the Roma. I have shown that many of the Roma's requests for improvements to their living conditions were formulated collectively and did not always represent an attempt at individual mobility ("escape") from the settlement. I also hinted at the possibility of tracing links to the physical space of the settlement, which the Roma themselves actively shaped. In their recollections, the Roma from Podskalka related to the place in this way. We might also recall the words of Pavlína B, originally from Papín, whose colourful language was in strong contrast with the recollections of a non-Romani villager, but also with the focus of debates held by the local authorities (see Chapter One).

However, Hübschmannová did not criticise the central policy merely for its emphasis on the liquidation of what she understood as distinct socio-cultural units. She also condemned the social engineering inherent in its intervention in existing natural processes, especially the socio-economic mobility strategies of the Roma themselves, typically those who wanted to move out of the settlement (see Hübschmannová 1999b). From this perspective, Hübschmannová criticised restrictions on freedom of movement deriving from the government resolution discussed, the purpose of which was to specify where Roma could relocate to and where not. The situation in Humenné shows that the designation of the partner districts to which the Roma were permitted to move did not in fact constitute a fundamental restriction on movement. The vast majority of the Roma who left for Czechia secured their housing on the basis of their own socio-economic contacts, or had been living in Czechia for a long time. From this perspective it would appear that, rather than a newly established central policy, the room for manoeuvre for individual families was defined by continuous processes of territorialisation led by the anti-Roma attitudes of the local authorities and non-Romani residents. With a defined understanding of the settlements as part (and product) of local socio-economic systems, it is important to recall that the ongoing processes that could have been affected by central policy include not only the economic strategies of the Roma themselves (as Hübschmannová observes), but also this practice of territorialisation. And just as the resettlement policy basically failed to direct the migratory movement of the Roma into defined partner districts (see Chapter Four below), it was also unable to change the entrenched practices of the local authorities.

As a policy, the liquidation of the settlements entered into locally embedded socio-economic relations where the form it would take, by no means a settled matter, was negotiated. This depended on locally specific conditions, the sheer diversity of which is represented by the case studies presented so far, whether this be the overturning of the decision to demolish the settlement in Kapišová, the solidification of the status of the Roma in Brekov, the resolution of the conflict in Vlachovo and Hostovice, the definitive eviction of the Roma from Ľubiša, or the reversal of the emphasis on the resettlement of Romani families back to the village in Papín. In Podskalka it eventually led to a rebalancing of existing policies away from granting autonomy to the settlement and towards emphasising the need to remove it.

These examples illustrate the fact that, however much central policy liked to speak of overcoming anti-Roma attitudes, depending on the place and context it became a tool using which the local authorities might affirm the continuity of their own efforts to keep the Roma out of the non-Romani part of a municipality, given they could eventually evict them entirely from the settlement itself. On the other hand, the central policy came up against the desire of many Roma to resolve their own dismal living conditions, even if for many of them this meant a definitive uprooting from their home village. Based on the material presented it would be worth wondering whether the central policy itself, by targeting "citizens of G*psy origin" who were determined to break out of what was deemed from the dominant perspective an unhealthy environment, was successful in furnishing the Roma with sufficient tools to overcome existing barriers, rather than representing a violent intervention in their strategies of socio-economic mobility. In addition to the ongoing segregation processes, such barriers included a housing crisis, in which state construction came nowhere near to meeting the needs of the Czechoslovak population (Guy 1977, 298–308), while the newly emerging cooperative housing was often denied to the Roma, not only due to their lack of funds, but the unwillingness of the other inhabitants to accept Roma into the cooperatives (ibid.). In this situation, the main beneficiaries of the central policy were those Roma who were in some way situated in socio-economic relations, usually with higher social (and economic) capital.

Tracking the trajectories of individual Romani families is methodologically somewhat questionable. Given the lack of sources and the very few oral history interviews available, it is clear when looking at the situation in Podskalka how limited the possibilities are of piecing together the period structure of local relations, and interrogating – or at least examining more critically – the constructed image of Romani families who were sympathetic to central policy and were waiting for the opportunity to move from the settlement to the town. Inasmuch as my focus here was on the repossession of the shacks, I inevitably ended up charting the stories of those families for whom such a buyout did actually take place. In the case of the archive materials, this is the paradox I outlined in the first chapter, namely, that the traces left behind in the archives are mainly of this visible agency. On the other hand, those waiting in vain to be included in the resettlement programme (as indicated by the initial number of twenty-six interested families), or those implacably against inclusion, are generally speaking not represented in the archived materials. Such research might even end up overlooking those Roma who were prevented from moving outside the settlement by the restrictions imposed by the resettlement policy (see Hübschmannová 1967, 1999b). The research presented here goes some way to reproducing the dominant logic of agency and tracks the story of those Roma whose actions were deemed relevant and recorded by the local authorities. While I have attempted in part to reverse this focus, in failing to conduct oral historical interviews I have again relied on the narratives of those Roma who were situated in a particular way, which to a large extent contributed to their narratives being immortalised (such as the testimony of Kašo, a teacher at Podskalka, and that of Kurej, the painter, both of whom had gradually moved to the city). I will attempt to remedy this situation in the final chapter, in which I shift my focus from the liquidation of the settlements to the experiences of the Roma in the resettlement process itself and its logic of dispersion.

4. CHAPTER FOUR
Resettlement, Migration, Dispersion: Movement Control and Agentive Strategies

Milena Hübschmannová: When you came to Spyšová [Czechia], were the *gadje* nice to you?

MŠ: All the *gadje* were nice to us. (XXX – request to evict them – [*note by MH*]). I went to the cinema and they gave the children clothes, chocolates, sweets. There were really nice people there.

MH: And why did you leave?

MŠ: Because we didn't have our own house. They wanted to take the house, they said it wasn't ours. The authorities wanted to give us another house, so they placed us here.

MH: What did they do with the house?

MŠ: They took it apart.[188]

This is an excerpt from an interview conducted in April 1977 with Mrs Helena Š (born 1941) at her family's new home in Ústí u Staré Paky [Czechia]. The family was relocated to the district of Jičín in north-eastern Bohemia in 1967 and, together with other Roma from the village of Šemetkovce in what was then the district of Bardejov in north-eastern

---

188 Archive of MRK, Brno, f. Pozůstalost Mileny Hübschmannové, kart. 9_ET, sp. Transkripty_ MH, č. 110.

Slovakia, became part of the "organised transfer" (*organizovaný přesun*) of Romani people from (eastern) Slovakia to Czechia. The short passage above touches on several topics connected with the wider practice of the resettlement programme and the relocation of Roma. Firstly, though the entire project represented continuity in respect of efforts to control and restrict the movement of Roma, in practice it had exactly the opposite effect, i.e. it actually provoked yet more movement. In this respect, two factors played an important role, which were later described in the literature as significant reasons for the failure of the entire programme. The first factor was how the non-Romani population felt about the Roma, and the second was the housing conditions in those locations where the Roma from Slovakia were resettled, in this particular instance in a house that was to be demolished after the family had moved out. However, the testimony always contains a degree of ambivalence as regards attempts to grasp the position of the Roma. Although Helena Š speaks of receiving a warm welcome from the local non-Roma and thus reflects the broader Romani migration narrative of Czechia as a country of egalitarian relations (see Hübschmannová 1993; Ort and Dobruská 2023; Sadílková 2016; Synková 2006), at another point in the interview she discusses the anti-Roma prejudices the family had to face, including the requests of their neighbours that they be evicted. I deliberately chose a passage in which Hübschmannová herself points this out in her marginalia. It reminds the reader of her role as interviewer and the need for a cautious approach when reading the transcripts of the interviews, of which no original recording has survived and regarding which no other circumstances are known. At the same time, however, it underlines Hübschmannová's role as a central figure in the criticism aimed at the resettlement policy, which, even after 1989, largely predetermined the way in which this policy was understood in scholarly literature. In the dominant narrative of Romani studies, not only was the assimilationist policy of the communist regime criticised primarily for its disregard for the interests of the Roma themselves, but in an attempt to take these interests into account individual scholars have accepted at face value what Hübschmannová wrote or said in her lectures. Paradoxically, her work – albeit extensive, complex and admirable – appears to have partly prevented the possibility of a more rigorous examination of the experiences, attitudes and actions, i.e. the agency, of the Roma themselves. In this chapter, I find myself in a rather ambivalent position. On the one hand, I draw extensively on the unique sources archived in Hübschmannová's estate. On the other, when interpreting said sources,

I feel it incumbent upon me to point out some of the limitations of her interpretations.

Subsequent to the removal of the settlements, the central policy envisaged an "organised transfer" of the Roma from Slovakia to Czechia, which was at the same time to be subject to the logic of their "dispersion" (*rozptyl*) in the dominant society. When examining the agency of the Roma in this chapter, I will look at how this was reflected in their economic strategies and broader strategies of sociability. I will show that the resettlement programme, in practice, was inseparable from migration as an agentive economic strategy in its own right, and that this in turn created a long-term need for the authorities to control the movement of what they termed G*psies. In the first part of the chapter, I will discuss the discourses of that time surrounding the "dispersion" of the Roma and the way their movement was interpreted. In the second part, I will examine the practice of the government resolution in the district of Humenné. In light of the cross-border character of the resettlement, in the third part of the chapter I will shift my attention from Slovakia to Czechia. In doing so, I will at least in part attempt to provide a counterbalance to the focus on the situation in eastern Slovakia as the overarching framework of the entire book. Taking the border region as an example, I will show both the practice of resettlement within the context of the migratory movements of the Roma, and the continuity of the policy towards the G*psies from the perspective of the situation in border regions in Czechia. In the fourth section of this chapter, which focuses on the relocation of the Roma from what was then the district of Bardejov to Jičín, I again move beyond the district of Humenné that forms the basis of this study. I opted for this strategy because of the uniqueness of the source base referred to above, namely, the interviews conducted by Hübschmannová at the end of the 1970s. This section allows me to highlight the plurality of the positions, attitudes and experiences of individual interviewees. In addition to interviews with representatives of the regional authorities, the interviews with Romani women are well worth noting here, as they allow for the inclusion of a gender-based perspective on the topic in question, which adds depth to the analysis "from the margins" (see Chapter One).

In this chapter I pick up the threads of the previous chapter regarding the removal of the settlements. Inasmuch as Hübschmannová understood the settlements as independently functioning socio-cultural units, she viewed the migratory movement of the Roma from rural Slovakia to urban Czechia as a kind of uprooting, a loss of natural social ties and a decline in cultural values. This is also the lens through which she evaluated the central resettlement programme, which, she claimed, distorted traditional migratory patterns based primarily on kinship networks. In this somewhat complex chapter, I will attempt to revise the view of the Roma as "uprooted migrants" by taking into account their different types of agency. In doing so I will show that even the logic of dispersion may have intersected with the Roma's economic strategies and broader strategies of sociability.

4.1 Genesis of the Resettlement Policy

Although texts written at that time and later often refer to a "policy of dispersion" (*politiky rozptylu*) or a "dispersional policy" (*rozptylová politika*), it is important to distinguish between two different concepts and emphases contained in the central policy that converge under this label. Firstly, there is the logic of "dispersion", which in the official ideological discourse was based on the assumption that the "backward way of life" was a product of the historically entrenched isolation of the Roma population and that only by systematically disrupting this isolation could such a way of life be eliminated in a socialist society (see Chapter Two). But then there is the resettlement itself (also referred to "transfer" in officialese), which I use here both as an umbrella term for the entire policy aimed at the relocation of the Roma from place to place, but also as a term referring to the relocation of the Roma from Slovakia to Czechia. The interconnectedness of terms and emphases resides in the fact that this transfer was also to be carried out according to the principles of dispersion. However, the two terms must continue to be analytically separated.

In addition to longer-term efforts to remove the settlements, the resettlement policy also represented the continuation of policies aimed at controlling the movement of the Roma. This was especially true of that part of the government resolution that spoke of an "organised transfer". It was this organised character that was contrasted with the "spontaneous migration" (*živelná migrace*) between Slovakia and Czechia and the consequent labour "fluctuation" (*fluktuace*). Resettlement was therefore intended to meet the needs of the modern state's supervision of its inhabitants by eliminating chaotic concentrations on the one hand, and restricting their mobility on the other (see Scott 1998).

The part of the government resolution that spoke of an organised transfer not only related to organised labour recruitment, but to earlier, more systematic plans to resettle the Roma from Slovakia to Czechia (e.g. Hübschmannová 1999a). For example, the "liquidation of G*psy settlements" as set forth in Regional Resolution No. 39/1956 was to be undertaken in what was then the region of Prešov by means of, inter alia, "borderland settlements" and "recruitment in mines". In April 1958, the Central Committee of the Communist Party of Czechoslovakia passed a resolution in which the necessity of "preventing the undesirable movement of G*psies" and "liquidating undesirable concentrations of G*psy streets, quarters and settlements" was formulated. As a result, the need for a more systematic approach to the resettlement of G*psies from the region of eastern Slovakia began to be discussed in the early 1960s, with local voices stating that the "G*psy question" could not be resolved on a purely regional basis (Haišman 1999). Haišman sees this as linked to the restructuring of regions and districts in 1960, when two smaller regions (Košice and Prešov) were merged into one large eastern Slovak region. This increased the need to resolve the situation of the Romani settlements (ibid.). On the other hand, as I will show in more detail in the third section of this chapter, a more systematic centralised policy towards the Roma was also responding to demands being made by the authorities in those regions in Czechia to which the Roma had been moving since shortly after the war. Here, the policy of dispersion displayed a certain continuity, since it belonged to a broader arsenal of strategies targeted on what were more generally referred to as "undesirable" groups of the population (see Hajská 2020, 344; Spurný 2011).

In the case of Government Resolution No. 502/1965, the need to control movement was based on the entrenched idea of the Roma as naturally mobile, and of "fluctuation" and local volatility as an inherent feature of the "G*psy way of life". In the document Main Directions for Resolving the Question of the G*psy Population of 18 December 1965, the existing controls were deemed insufficient. Compared to the 1958 resolution, there was a shift in the classification of G*psies based on nomadism to one based on social assimilation (see Chapter One). However, as Guy points out, the abandonment of the old terminology did not necessarily mean the removal of the association of Roma with a particular type of "uncontrolled" movement, said to find its roots in a "backward" way of life. Moreover, the earlier classification had not completely disappeared by the mid-1960s. In line with the 1958 government resolution, Davidová and Nováček continued to divide G*psies into "settled", "semi-settled/semi-nomadic" and "nomadic" in the mid-1960s, and according to this logic even those who were deemed to be settled were assumed to have previously led a nomadic life. Nomadism thus functions as an inherent feature of G*psyness, while "settling down" is a sign of its eradication and accompanying social assimilation (Davidová 1965; Nováček 1968).

In this respect, one can observe a clear continuity with the practice of the First Republic Act 117/1927 on "itinerant G*psies". As historian Pavel Baloun has shown, the category of "itinerant G*psy" (*potulní c*káni*), which according to the legal wording was to include "G*psies wandering from place to place and other work-avoiding vagrants who live like G*psies", was strongly racialised when it came to implementation of the law (Baloun 2022). With the extermination of the majority of the pre-Second World War Romani population living in the territory of Czechia, in the immediate post-war period the term "G*psy nomad" (*C*kán – kočovník*) was applied to Romani migrants from Slovakia (see also Hajská 2020, 348). Notwithstanding the narrative, widespread amongst the Roma, of Czechia as the "promised land" (Hübschmannová 1993, 31), in this new environment the Roma were seen mainly as foreign elements, both as orientalised immigrants from Slovakia, but also specifically as G*psies, whose movement was understood as qualitatively distinct (Sokolová 2008; Spurný 2011).

Control over the movement of these Roma was to be enshrined in Act 74/1958 on the Permanent Settlement of Nomadic Persons. The lawmakers, who drew on the wording of a similar regulation in the Soviet Union that came into force in 1956, had one key problem. Explicitly targeting Roma would have been not only contrary to the constitution, but at odds with the established ideology of the Central Committee of the Communist Party of Czechoslovakia, which rejected discrimination of any sort on the basis of ethnicity or race. It was for this reason that all references to G*psies were removed from the final text of the law during its committee stage (Zapletal 2012). However, the insistent targeting of Roma was revealed not only in the earlier wording of the law, but also in the accompanying documentation, communications with local authorities, and its application in practice (see e.g. Ort 2022a). Nevertheless, ideologues of the central policy towards the Roma continued to insist that while the 1927 law was a manifestation of the racial persecution of the Roma during the First Republic, the 1958 law was intended to contribute to their social integration, primarily through the provision of housing and employment by the local authorities (Guy 1977, 193–197).

Implementation of the 1958 government resolution on Work amongst the G*psy Population was half-hearted and the Act on the Permanent

Settlement of Nomadic Persons of the same year achieved only the elimination of "traditional forms of nomadism" (Jurová 2008, 1019–1026; regarding the stories of specific families and the lived experience of "settling down" see above all Hajská 2020, 2024).[189] In recognition of these weaknesses, Resolution No. 502/1965 was intended to allow for greater control to be exerted over the movement of the G*psy population. The restrictions placed on movement were intended to apply to G*psies across all of the categories. The plan was to make it impossible to move to places with already higher concentrations of G*psies, and to prevent migration from taking place outside the resettlement timetable, i.e. outside the designated partner districts.

There was one major change on the 1958 law, namely, the specification of the G*psies as the target group of the government resolution, even though this category had been redefined in the official discourse in social terms, i.e. as representing a "way of life" (see Chapter Two). However, as such measures could not be supported by existing legislation, since they were at odds with the freedom of movement guaranteed under the constitution. A newly appointed Government Committee therefore proposed amending the 1958 Act so as to explicitly target G*psies so that the management and control of their movements could be legalised. The discriminatory nature of the amendment was circumvented by the Government Committee's by now familiar emphasis on the purpose of such a measure, which, it was claimed, was not to discriminate against G*psies but rather to assist them in achieving a "higher standard of living" (Guy 1977, 272). Such an explanation, however, did not pass muster with other branches of the state apparatus, and this part of the government resolution thus failed to find firm legal anchorage (ibid., 272–273). As Guy concludes: "in inducing local authorities to resist any unplanned movement of G*psy residents and to return such migrants to their homes at their own expense, the government committee apparently incited them to break the law" (ibid., 273). Moreover, the absence of a legislative

---

189 Hajská casts considerable doubt on the entire narrative of the successful "elimination of traditional forms of nomadism". Taking the situation in several Bohemian districts as an example, she demonstrates the continuity of anti-Roma measures aimed at controlling movement. Although the very practice of holding lists of "nomadic persons" and their "settlement" could be presented by many authorities as a relatively smooth process, the Vlax Roma recalled it as a brutal policy intervention involving the confiscation of their horses (see Sokolová 2008, 98). At the same time, the Roma who were "settled" in this way found themselves in a position of even greater social marginalisation and pauperisation when, contrary to the inventory guidelines, they were not provided with adequate housing (Hajská 2020).

framework offered the local authorities and others, including the Roma themselves, significant room for manoeuvre as regards the practice of the government resolution.

4.2 The Discourse of "Dispersion"

It is clear from materials dating back to that time that the officially enforced resettlement policy did not find favour among the non-Romani population, mainly due to its emphasis on the logic of what it called "dispersion". The public were overwhelmingly in favour of restrictive measures in relation to the Roma and perceived their relocation as a moral threat to society rather than a form of re-education (see Chapter Two). The opinions of those who wrote letters in response to the state policy as presented on television are well illustrated by the repeated call for "civil servants to take them [the G*psies] into their own home" (see Chapter Two). In their own letters (roughly a quarter of the 100 letters received), the Roma emphasised the need for a restrictive policy of "re-education" applied to the "less respectable" members of their community. However, unlike the non-Romani viewers, many of them supported the official emphasis on resettlement. For example, Mr Jozef S of Prague wrote:

> Comrades, I believe that as long as you isolate them [the backward G*psies] from your people, the worse things will be, because it will create greater possibilities for them to visit each other since they will be grouped together. I think it would be better to distribute them amongst your people or to select a few respectable families and offer them as a model to other G*psies.[190]

Mr Rudolf K of Vítkovice (Silesia) took a similar stance when he argued that it was not right that "comrades of G*psy origin work together" in factories.[191] In his opinion, "they make work unpleasant for each other" and "moreover, they should be amongst mature people who would guide them down a constructive path".[192] For his part, Gustav Karika (see Donert 2017, 77) expressed the need to address the issue of

---

190 NA Prague, KSČ-ÚV-05/3, f. KSČ – Ústřední výbor 1945–1989, Praha – oddělení – oddělení ideologické, sv. 37, č. j. 299.
191 Ibid.
192 Ibid.

"G*psy settlements" in particular, since "these are the cause of that old way of life". Mr Ladislav suggested "distributing the G*psies throughout the republic, so that two families live in each village, and to put the worst ones on the border".[193] Unlike the letters from the non-Romani viewers, in these cases there is no criticism of the "civil servants", i.e. the central policy itself, but rather of the local authorities tasked with its implementation.

However, it is apparent that these are the opinions of Roma who enjoy a higher social status and who refer to what they call "respectable/ integrated G*psies" (see Chapter Two). More or less explicitly present in their endorsement of the central policy is the assumption that it should affect not the letter writers themselves, but the "backward G*psies" (associated mainly with the settlements of eastern Slovakia). Those Romani voices that recount their personal experience with the central policy show that it could, on the contrary, very easily diverge from their particular interests.

4.2.1 Complaints regarding restrictions on movement

One of the television viewers, Marie V from Ústí nad Labem in northern Bohemia, reflected upon the course of her life. The impossibility of registering for accommodation in a village in Slovakia – though it is unclear who or what was preventing her – led her to a somewhat contradictory assessment of the central policy.

> Comrades, I have been living in Czechia for eighteen years and I wanted to travel to Slovakia, but they told me that they would not register me. And I'd like to know why not. On the one hand it is right and proper that they can't travel in that way [the G*psies? – J. O.], but on the other hand it is wrong.[194]

This excerpt from the letter reveals a certain conflict of interests. Marie V endorses the policy towards the G*psies, whom she refers to in the third person. At the same time, she questions the legitimacy of the policy inasmuch as it affects her as a "respectable G*psy woman". Although somewhat confused, Marie V highlights a key feature that was

193 Ibid.
194 Ibid.

at the heart of the criticism levelled against the central policy on the part of certain other Roma and already formulated in personal complaints. Criticism of the basic assumptions of the resettlement policy was formulated in a letter addressed to the Central Committee of the Communist Party of Czechoslovakia on 6 July 1967 by Mr Zikmund Vágai, a "G*psy citizen" and, in his own words, an active civil servant:

> This means that I, as a citizen of our republic, cannot travel from our district to another to live or work because I am a G*psy, even if it improves my working conditions. It is symbolically phrased, but this is its outcome. So why, then, must we, as citizens of our state, fulfil all our obligations to society when, on the other hand, such discrimination is displayed against us? [...] There are many questions that I cannot understand regarding this matter and which trouble me and lead me to various thoughts. When this government decree [Decree No. 502/1965] was published, there was no way that comrades thought that they would always recognise on the National Committees who is a G*psy and who not. In what way will the NV [National Committees] deal with this and meet the terms of the resolution? Perhaps some 'designation' for these citizens would be a good idea. After all, the comrades who decide on this matter will already have thought of 'some way' of avoiding writing about it as a restriction of personal freedom. We are only permitted to write in this way about black people in Western countries. (Sadílková et al. 2018, 160–161)

In openly pointing to the discriminatory nature of the government resolution that applied restrictions on freedom of movement to a specific group of people, Mr Vágai is taking aim at a previously discussed contradiction in the way the category of G*psyness was understood. Inasmuch as some of the Roma endorsed the central policy and anticipated its application to a socially defined group of "backward G*psies", Mr Vágai frames this as an ongoing ethno-racial conception of this category that cannot be detached from the context and implementation of restrictions on movement ensuing from the central policy.

Ondrej G, one of the Roma expelled from the village of Vlachovo in the district of Rožňava (see Chapter Two), addressed a similarly phrased complaint to the presidium of the government of the Czechoslovak Socialist Republic. He stated that he had decided to return to his home town in Slovakia, where he had purchased a house, but that the local authority refused to issue him a residence permit, stating that "a foreign G*psy cannot move to Rožňava, since they have enough citizens of

G*psy origin from Rožňava for whom they need apartments." Ondrej G adds the following:

> We are of the opinion that every citizen of the Czechoslovak Republic can decide for himself where he wants to live and, if he has the money to do so, he may buy a house anywhere that suits him. [...] We are of the opinion that not even the MsNV [Town National Committee] in Rožňava can tell a house owner whom he is to sell his house to and under what conditions, nor can it prevent us from moving to Rožňava [...] The MsNV is acting against me for discriminatory reasons, because I am a person of G*psy origin.[195]

Although Ondrej G does not name the government resolution in force at that time, it is clear that, as in the case of Zikmund Vágai, his criticism is directed at the fundamental assumptions of the resettlement policy and shows how, in specific cases, it could become a tool wielded by the local authorities in a bid to resist the arrival of "foreign G*psies" (see Chapter Two) in a village (even though such a practice had no legal basis, see above).

Amongst the observations made by the Roma regarding the practice of the resettlement policy, this in-depth criticism of its assumptions and discriminatory nature is unique. As I will show below, even in the many complaints that have survived, the Roma did not reject the policy in principle, but pointed to problems in practice, above all to the continuity of precarious conditions in their new place of residence. As in the case of the disposal of the settlements, the Roma's desire to harmonise the implementation of the central policy with their own strategies of socio-economic mobility was evident.

4.2.2 Criticism of resettlement at the time

Not even the public criticism voiced of the resettlement programme was completely consistent. An open critique of the central policy was formulated in 1966 by Davidová (see Sadílková et al. 2018, 150–155). However, it should be remembered that in her monograph of the previous year, Davidová herself had supported the necessity of implementing

---

195 ŠAKE Košice, f. Komisia Vsl. KNV pre cigánske obyvatelstvo, kart. 19, sp. 100, Complaint – Ondrej G., 14 November 1968.

"dispersion" and – as an employee of the Regional National Committee in Košice – had featured in the media campaign that accompanied the implementation of the policy (see Chapter Two). Not even Davidová takes aim at the basic premises of the resettlement policy, but rather at the overall lack of preparation and communication and the mismanagement of its implementation (ibid.).

A similarly ambiguous attitude towards resettlement policy is evident in texts published in the journal *Demografie* in 1969 by Miroslav Holomek and Tomáš Holomek, both publicly active Roma (from families of the original Moravian Roma, see, for example Horváthová 1994), who were present at the launch of the Union of Gypsies-Roma (Donert 2017, 189–193; Lhotka et al. 2009; Sadílková et al. 2018). Holomek, for instance, states that "it is impossible [...] to agree with the extent and above all the manner in which the so-called dispersion of the G*psies has been carried out" (Holomek, M. 1969, 206), and offers eight reasons for his assertion. In the sixth point especially, Holomek's thoughts already anticipate the later criticism (formulated in her time by Hübschmannová), according to which the "dispersion" destroyed established social bonds and socio-cultural structures (by dispersion, Holomek is probably also referring to the resettlement from Slovakia to Czechia):

> The psychological aspects of the dispersion were completely neglected: the G*psy, by moving to a completely new environment to which he was unused, was left to his own devices and his family found itself isolated. (ibid., 207)

Even this, however, is more a critique of the problematic practice of state policy than a fundamental interrogation of its premises. For example, in point four Holomek concludes that, in addition to specific people, the "problem" to be resolved had now been "dispersed" and was no longer concentrated in eastern Slovakia as previously, but was present in new locations. This conclusion resonates, paradoxically, with the attitudes of those television viewers who resisted dispersion because of the potential creation of new breeding grounds for "problematic coexistence", although Holomek's position was nuanced differently: he was aware of racial prejudice in society and feared it would be exacerbated. Even in this respect, Holomek assesses the policy as "ineffective", the main criterion for evaluation in his critique. In this respect, too, he is partly on the side of those television viewers who complained about the resources being wasted on the "re-education" of "irredeemable G*psies" (see Chapter Two). Similarly, Tomáš Holomek summed up the situation thus:

With the passage of time, questions have been asked as to whether and to what extent dispersion is contributing to the attainment of the purported purpose of re-educating persons of G*psy origin. It turned out that dispersion itself, with rare exceptions, did not contribute to this objective and that the relatively generous funds made available by the state for these purposes were far from profitable. This was one of the main reasons why dispersion has recently been abandoned *via facti* [by way of deed]. (Holomek, T. 1969, 212–213)

In the same issue of *Demografie*, however, criticism of the basic principles of the central policy is finally voiced in an edited interview with Anton Facuna (see Donert 2017, 135–138), chairman of the newly formed Union of Gypsies-Roma in Slovakia (see Lužica 2021). Facuna concludes as follows:

Article 31 of our constitution, for instance, states that the inviolability of the home as well as freedom of residence are guaranteed. How does this fit in with Government Resolution No. 502 of 1965? [...] It is inconceivable that the state authorities should plan where G*psies should live, how many of them, where they should work and where they should settle down permanently. [...] Of course, we are against the nomadic way of life. However, every G*psy, just like any other citizen, has the right to live where he wants, work where he wants, and move to where he wants. This freedom cannot be restricted in any way. (Facuna 1969, 215)

It is worth noting at this point that even Facuna's unequivocal criticism of the unconstitutionality of restrictions on the free movement of G*psies includes a partial acquiescence to the central policy where it speaks of the necessity of ending the "nomadic way of life". This was, in fact, the position taken by virtually all publicly active Roma on this issue (see Donert 2017, 137), and illustrates the various forms and degrees of distance that the Roma themselves exhibited towards the "cultural backwardness of the G*psies", thus to a certain extent reproducing the official discourse of the "G*psy way of life". Such a definition sits alongside to the category of "respectable G*psies" (see Chapter Two) and is at least implicit in the work of Miroslav and Tomáš Holomek. Depending on the context, the term "problematic G*psies" could be aimed at those situated in "G*psy settlements" in orientalised eastern Slovakia (as in the case of Gustav Karika's letter, see above). However, this particular category could also intersect with sub-ethnic divisions, i.e. the relationship with the Vlax Roma, or the relationship of Czech/Moravian Roma to Romani immigrants from Slovakia. However, among the politically active Roma, who had been striving to form an official Romani organisation since at least the 1950s (see Donert 2017, 135–138; Sadílková et al. 2018), one can also sense a partial acquiescence to existing policies (in particular the need to crack down on the nomadic way of life) as a pragmatic approach aimed at strengthening their position as full partners in discussions with the central state authorities.

In addition to the reservations voiced by Anton Facuna in his capacity as representative of the Union of Gypsies-Roma in Slovakia, direct criticism of the government resolution can be read in the Memorandum of the Union of Gypsies-Roma in Czechia. In line with the criticism articulated by Davidová and referred to above, the authors first remind the reader that the section of the government resolution that envisaged "evidence-based scientific research" being carried out had not been fulfilled. A fundamental criticism of the government resolution is contained in the section seeking recognition of Romani ethnicity:

> We believe that the recognition of Romani ethnicity in the formal sense of the word, i.e. granting them the status of an ethnic group, would create better conditions within which the Roma could participate in the resolution of their social situation such that they would feel themselves to be truly equal citizens of the Czechoslovak Socialist Republic. (**As we have seen, article 20 of the 1960 constitution did not ensure equality, otherwise Assimilation Resolution No. 502/1965 could not have been passed.**) (Memorandum SCR 1970; emphasis J. O.)

Although it is listed as the work of a collective of authors, the initiation and authorship of the text is attributed to Hübschmannová (Pavelčíková 2006, 194–195; Donert 2017, 193–194). Its assessment of contemporary politics and the clarity of the demands formulated are in line with Hübschmannová's other texts from that period (e.g. 1967, 1968, 1970) and contrast with the more hesitant evaluation of the government resolution by the Union's co-founders, Miroslav and Tomáš Holomek. The criticism voiced by Hübschmannová and referred to above, which in essence targeted the discriminatory character of the government resolution, was followed up in the latter half of the 1970s by those who drafted Charter 77 (Charta 77 1999, 4–7) and by Guy in his dissertation, which was, however, defended at Bristol University in Great Britain (1977).

Thus, although such opinions have become part of the post-revolutionary history of the Roma, or rather the history of anti-G*psyism (to draw on the distinction made by Baloun; Baloun 2022, 15–24), the criticism of that time was more restrained. In addition to isolated voices expressing open scepticism, reactions tend to be in line with the official discourse surrounding the G*psies (though said discourse is assessed and applied differently to diversely defined groups of the population, see Chapter Two). This can be partly explained by the pragmatism of the critics, who may have appropriated the official discourse in order to advance their own interests or those of the Roma as a group. It is, however, significant that the most strident voices denouncing the state's policies were raised by the non-Roma, even though in their struggle for equality they highlighted not so much discrimination against the Roma as the alleged "inviolability of the G*psies" as a "privileged" social stratum ("caste") and, in accordance with this assumption, demanded the application of highly restrictive policies against them.

4.3 Resettlement from Humenné

From the perspective of the state policy, the implementation of resettlement from the district of Humenné is a story of failure (see Chapter Three). On the one hand, the target numbers of families and individuals to be resettled was not met; and on the other hand, the numbers involved in the "controlled resettlement" were nothing compared to those of "spontaneous migration" (see Guy 1977, 333–338).

According to the plan drawn up by the Party's district committee in Humenné in April 1966, a total of eighty-five families were to be resettled in Czechia by 1970: ten in 1966, fifteen in 1967, and twenty families per annum in 1968–1970.[196] Just a month before, a representative of the district G*psy Commission in Humenné confirmed the interest shown in the resettlement on the part of the Roma themselves, from whom she had received a total of thirty applications.[197] But the minutes from the following meeting note that representatives of the assigned partner districts of Opava and Bruntál (Silesia) "have not yet [...] responded to

196 ŠAKE Košice, f. Komisia Vsl. KNV pre cigánske obyvatelstvo, kart. 10, sp. 66, "Kontrolná zpráva o riešení otázok cigánskych obyvateľov", 14 April 1966.
197 ŠAKE Košice, f. Komisia Vsl. KNV pre cigánske obyvatelstvo, kart. 9, sp. 56, "Zápisnica ze zasadnutie", 29 March 1966.

written requests from the Department of Employment",[198] a foretaste of the chronologically linked source documents on the poor quality communication and cooperation between the districts.

Having been postponed several times, the first visit to partner districts only took place in June 1967. Representatives of the District National Committee in Humenné reported that officials in the districts of Czechia "show reluctance in accepting G*psy families and allocating apartments [...] although our findings show there are enough apartments, but not for G*psies".[199] On the other hand, according to the minutes of a meeting of the district Commission of the ONV in Opava from July of the same year, "the main obstacle to the planned transfer of G*psy families from the Humenné district [...] was the lack of suitable apartments, both in towns and villages".[200] In addition, the minutes of the November meeting of the Opava district Commission speak of resistance on the part of the Municipal National Committee (MNV) and United Agricultural Cooperative (JZD) in individual municipalities, which declared that they were already using vacant buildings for their own purposes and would prevent them from being "taken over by G*psy families".[201] However, it does not appear from the minutes themselves that the district Commission appealed for the participation of the municipalities in the implementation of the resettlement programme. On the contrary, in the November minutes, attention turned to the complications that had accompanied the relocation of four families up till now, which had apparently been "influenced to no small extent by the way their houses in Slovakia had been sold off". These houses had allegedly been "sold to persons of G*psy origin" who, however, "had not managed to find the financial means to pay the stipulated purchase price".[202] According to the earlier minutes of the July meeting, representatives of the district Commission in Opava had already concluded that "[b]ased on an analysis of the options, it will be possible this year to relocate a maximum of three families from the Humenné district, while in following years four families can be relocated

198 ŠAKE Košice, f. Komisia Vsl. KNV pre cigánske obyvateľstvo, kart. 7, sp. 57, "Zápisnica zo zasadnutie", 7 May 1966.
199 ŠOkA Humenné, f. finanční odbor ONV Humenné, kart. 15, "Materiály komisie pre riešenie otázok cig. obyvateľstva, roky 1966–1971" [unprocessed].
200 ZAO, Opava f. ONV Opava, kart. 260. inv. č. 116. "Zápis ze schůze okresní komise pro řešení cikánské otázky", 10 July 1967.
201 ZAO, Opava, f. ONV Opava, kart. 260. inv. č. 116. "Zápis ze schůze okresní komise pro řešení cikánské otázky", 13 November 1967.
202 Ibid.

outside the towns, so that only persons who would be involved in agriculture could be moved".[203]

The implementation of resettlement was suspended in autumn 1968, though in Humenné itself the buying up of Romani dwellings, as well as the relocation of the families involved to Czechia (as well as within the district), continued at least for as long as the government resolution remained valid in Slovakia, i.e. until 1972 (Guy 1977, 273). The total number of families resettled according to the schedule was in single figures,[204] notwithstanding the fact that the original plan was to resettle eighty-five families, and thirty applications were received (see above).

It is clear that the archival sources fail to convey the perspective of the Roma themselves, a fact that remains true even after research has been scaled down and targeting made more localised. Even these materials for the most part reproduce the dominant perspective of the authorities. In September 1967, the ONV in Opava communicated with its counterpart in Humenné regarding the disbursement of funds to three resettled families, those of Ján D, Josef G Sr. and Josef G Jr. (all from Podskalka), for the purpose of buying houses in the village of Nové Lublice in the Opava district. The archives contain only the sale and purchase agreements and some basic bureaucratic formalities. The Nové Lublice chronicle recounts the arrival of these families and states that in September 1967, "four families comprising citizens of G*psy nationality [národnost] settled in the local village with the consent of the ONV in Opava", and that they were employed in the local United Agricultural Cooperative (JZD). The chronicle also mentions the subsequent arrival of other relatives of the families in question, which apparently led to "outrage amongst the inhabitants of the village", with some of the "older residents" threatening to "move away in such a situation".[205] Other sources reveal what the local authority had to say regarding the plight of the two families. In the minutes of one of its meetings, the MNV addressed the plight of Ján D, recently widowed and father of seven dependent

203 ZAO, Opava, f. ONV Opava, kart. 260. inv. č. 116. "Zápis ze schůze okresní komise pro řešení cikánské otázky", 10 July 1967.
204 ŠAKE Košice, f. Komisia Vsl. KNV pre cigánske obyvateľstvo, kart. 13, sp. 1, "Vyhodnotenie výsledkov práce", 1966; ŠAKE Košice, f. Komisia Vsl. KNV pre cigánske obyvateľstvo, kart. 14, sp. 53, "Súčasný stav riešenia", 23 February 1967; ŠAKE Košice, f. Komisia Vsl. KNV pre cigánske obyvateľstvo, kart. 17, sp. 201, "Zpráva o plnení", 1967; ŠAKE Košice, f. Komisia Vsl. KNV pre cigánske obyvateľstvo, kart. 16, sp. 163, "Výkazy plnenia niektorých vybraných úloh", 30 September 1967.
205 Kronika obce Nové Lublice (Chronicle of Nové Lublice municipality), p. 116.

children, who was himself semi-retired.[206] The municipal chronicle also tells of the situation of Mrs S, whose five children were taken into care after their father abandoned the family. He was apparently sacked from the United Agricultural Cooperative, where he had worked until then, for "repeated drunkenness".[207]

All of this fits snugly into Hübschmannová's view of the communist regime's assimilationist policy, which led to the disruption of Romani socio-cultural links and solidarity networks, and ultimately to the break-up of individual families. At the same time, the arrival of other relatives in the village supports her thesis regarding the importance of kinship networks in migration strategies, including the formation of socio-economic and broader solidarity and emotional networks in the new environment. However, both the migratory preferences of the Roma and the impact of central communist policies on their lives need further critical evaluation drawing on more comprehensive data.

4.4 The Post-War Migration of the Roma to the Borderlands

In order to examine the life trajectories of those Roma who moved from Humenné to Czechia, we must shift our attention away from the organised transfer to what in official documents was called "arbitrary" relocation, which was embedded in the broader phenomenon of the post-war migration of the Roma from Slovakia. This move makes sense, in part because migration as a distinct strategy of socio-economic mobility was significantly more prevalent in Humenné and beyond than controlled resettlement, and is inseparable from the implementation of the planned timetable. At the same time it allows for the contextualisation of the resettlement policy within the broader movement of the population, its control by the state, and the overall building of a socialist society in post-war Czechoslovakia.

The nature of the post-war migration of the Roma from Humenné to Czechia is in many ways comparable to the situation I described in the village of Kapišová (the district of Bardejov, later Svidník; see the Introduction). Migration, which often began in the first years after the

---

206 ZAO, Opava f. ONV Opava, kart. 181, "Zápis ze zasedání NV v Nových Lublicích", 26. 3. 1969.
207 *Kronika obce Nové Lublice*, p. 117.

war, was a response to the demand for labour and the need to populate the borderlands in Czechia, as well as to the dismal economic situation in the rural areas of eastern Slovakia. Moreover, in an already marginalised region, the Roma, often found themselves in a subordinate position in the racialised hierarchy of socio-economic relations, which was in many places compounded by the still traumatic experience of racial persecution during the Second World War (Sadílková 2020). Migration also took place on the basis of organised labour recruitment, though at the same time it depended on the initiative of particular families (ibid.). Existing kinship ties then led to the movement of other families between Czechia and Slovakia (as well as within Czechia itself), a movement which, in the newly established "transnational" networks, was bidirectional (ibid., see also Ort and Dobruská 2023). The duration of a stay in Czechia, on the part of either entire families or individual members (usually male workers), varied considerably, from long-term continuity of residence in specific locations, to short-term work trips with regular visits back to Slovakia. This entailed varying degrees of embeddedness in socio-economic structures situated in their home village. As I have already shown, while the Roma in Kapišová managed to maintain a sense of local belonging despite efforts to liquidate the local settlement (Ort 2022a), in many villages of the Humenné district the policy of liquidating settlements led to Romani families being cut off entirely from the village in Slovakia, i.e. the complete erasure of the Roma from local socio-economic structures (see Chapter Three, also below).

The recollections of Romani migrants from individual municipalities in the Humenné district have been saved for posterity in books (Kramářová 2005; Sidiropolu Janků 2015; individually in the journal *Romano Džaniben*), as well as video vignettes as part of the *Paměť Romů* project (Memory of the Roma: www.pametromu.cz).[208] Worthy of a spe-

---

208 Along with the anthology *(Ne)bolí. Vzpomínky Romů na válku a život po válce* (It Does (not) Hurt: Recollections of the Roma of the War and Life after the War, Kramářová 2005), these are the memories of Michal and Juliána Demeter, from the villages of Borov and Volica respectively, in both cases now part of the Medzilaborce district) and Vojtěch Demeter (from Veľopolie in the district of Humenné). From the publication Nikdy jsem nebyl podceňovanej (I have never been underestimated, Sidiropolu Janků 2015), which is based on the project Leperiben. Paměť romských dělníků (Leperiben: The Recollections of Romani Workers). This is the story of Ladislav Dudi-Koťo from Snina, now a county seat. The project *Paměť Romů* recounts the story of Ján Surmaj and Olga Fečová of Kochanovce (district of Humenné), Ladislav Dudi-Koťo of Snina (district of Snina) and Michal Hučko and Margita Hlaváčová of Hostovice (district of Snina). For a more detailed analysis of the recollections of Romani migrants, see above all Sadílková (2016, 2020).

cial mention here is the testimony of Olga Fečová, which she herself transformed into a published autobiography (Fečová 2022). The story of Fečová, who was born in 1942 in Kochanovce (a few kilometres from Humenné) and moved with her parents to Prague in 1947, is one of many examples attesting to the fact that relocation to Czechia by no means meant being uprooted and losing existing social ties. Fečová describes both the maintenance of strong relationships with that part of the family that remained in Slovakia,[209] and the establishment of relationships with the other Roma living in her new home and, indeed, with non-Romani people. While proud of being a Romani woman[210], Fečová questions the idea that cultural assimilation will be the inevitable consequence of the transition from a Romani settlement to the more anonymous non-Romani environment of a Czech city, which was one of the aims of the resettlement policy. At the same time, she throws doubt on the stubbornly held idea that socio-cultural values will be fatally sabotaged due to urbanisation and the assimilationist policy of the communist regime.[211] Fečová's story serves as a warning to be cautious when dealing with other entrenched narratives of the migration of the Roma from Slovakia to Czechia. Above all, the socio-economic status of the family on her mother's side, who owned a farm in the village of Dedačov, undermines the homogenised image of the poor eastern Slovak Roma as inhabitants of segregated enclaves. Similarly, the story of Fečová's relative from this branch of the family who had already emigrated to America in the interwar period (and subsequently returned) illustrates the otherwise unrecorded[212] participation of the Roma within the broader phenomenon of overseas migration from central and eastern Europe in the early 20th century (see, for example, Zahra 2016).

It was in the Czech metropolis where Fečová moved that one of the surveys was conducted that attempted to examine the post-war migration of the Roma from Slovakia not only on the basis of individual accounts of witnesses, but by defining the specific place to which the Romani

---

209 It should be added here that in Kochanovce itself, where Fečová lived until her family departed for Prague, no Roma had lived since the 1970s, partly as a result of the targeted "liquidation" of the settlement (see Chapter Three).

210 Fečová, for example, describes how she forced her husband, a renowned Romani musician, to learn Romani, since he had not acquired the language from his own family.

211 Such a narrative is reproduced somewhat uncritically in the light of the entire story in an editorial (Jandáková and Habrovcová 2022).

212 Hübschmannová refers to the socio-economically well situated Romani families of the pre-war eastern Slovak countryside, as well as the migration of several Roma to the US, only in passing (perhaps on the basis of her interviews with Fečová?; Hübschmannová 1993, 36; 1999b, 132).

people travelled (Hudousková et al. [unpublished]).[213] The testimony of Romani women who were part of the second generation of migrants travelling to Prague during the first few years following the war, mainly from the village of Ľubiša (see Chapter Three), correspond to a significant degree to Fečová's autobiographical narrative in these respects. Contrary to the idea of a cultural and social uprooting, their recollections reveal the maintenance of social networks, regardless of the way their realisation in space may have changed. Although the physical removal of the settlement in Slovakia and the relocation of individual Romani families to the city largely corresponded to the logic of dispersion, even in the new environment the Roma maintained their meeting places. In the absence of the environment of the Romani settlement in Slovakia, such a function could now be met by public spaces (witnesses spoke of Arbesovo náměstí in Prague's Smíchov district) and specific pubs. Like Fečová, these Romani witnesses also pointed to the continuity of musicianship as a way of generating income. Romani musicians from Ľubiša (exclusively male, unlike the musicians from Kochanovce) used to play in Prague cafés (ibid.).[214] Unlike Fečová, at least part of whose family enjoyed high socio-economic status in Slovakia, the story of the Romani migrant families from Ľubiša is an example of significant upward mobility from the starting point of a highly marginalised status in their home village in Slovakia (see Chapter Three).

4.4.1 From Papín to North Bohemia

In Papín, as in Ľubiša, the resettlement programme led to the removal of the local Romani settlement and the definitive severing of the Roma from the local structure of socio-economic relations (Chapter Three). One of the buildings demolished in the Papín settlement was that belonging to Michal B (born 1919). It had already been described at the time of its valuation as "dilapidated and run down" due to the fact that "the person in question moved to Czechia and nobody took care of its

---

213 For an overview of regionally defined work on the post-war migration of the Roma from Slovakia to Czechia see Sadílková (2016).
214 Thanks to the contacts they struck up with Czech actors and directors, the musicians from Ľubiša later featured in the popular Czech TV series *Sanitka* (Ambulance) and had even had a walk-on role in the Czech "comedy of the century" "S tebou mě baví svět" (I Enjoy the World with You/You Take the KIDS!).

maintenance".[215] The village of Horní Podluží in the border region of north Bohemia in the district of Děčín was listed as Michal B's new place of residence. The sisters Monika H (born 1971) and Marcela S (born 1977) spoke of their paternal grandfather in an interview with me. The house in Horní Podluží, in which they and their families were still living at the time of my research, had already been bought by their father Michal S (born 1946) in 1975 (he died in 1980). However, in the early 1960s, long before the liquidation of the Papín settlement, the entire family had apparently been living in another house in Horní Podluží. As regards the other families from Papín, the documentation from the late 1960s lists places of residence in various districts spread around Czechia (Prague, Louny, Hradec Králové and Rychnov), as well as in another village in the district of Humenné. It must be stressed, however, that the maintenance of vibrant socio-economic ties among the Roma themselves transcended the logic of specific place. For one thing, the testimony of both sisters points to ongoing links across individual locations in Czechia that were maintained even with the knowledge of a common place of origin in Slovakia at the time of my research. On the other hand, in the borderland regions of Liberec and Děčín, the Papín Roma met up with acquaintances and relatives originally from other villages in the district of Humenné. This was especially true of Hostovice (see Chapter Two),[216] whence hailed the mother of the two sisters Marcela S and Monika H. It seems that the mother had moved with her parents to the region in 1963. The transfer of existing social networks from Humenné to the Czech border region is evident in the marriage of the two sisters' parents: though both families knew each other in Slovakia, they only became acquainted in Czechia (see below).

In my interview with them, the two sisters also spoke of the strategies and methods of settling down in the region upon the arrival of larger numbers of Romani families. In the following story, the trajectories of their father's and mother's families were intertwined.

MH: [Granddad on the father's side] when he came to Czechia he arranged for housing and moved to somewhere in the region around Pilsen and then to somewhere in the area around Liberec. Some of the family, the aunts, remained in Liberec, granddad's daughters. And then granddad settled here

---

215 ŠOkA Humenné, f. Finanční odbor ONV Humenné, kart. 17, sp. 138, "B. Michal, Papín" [unprocessed].

216 See the recollections of Margita Hlaváčová and Michal Hučko (*Paměť Romů* [online]).

in Horní Podluží sometime in the sixties. [...] There was a public announce-
ment saying that they needed people to work here in the borderlands, especially on the farm, and they were offered both accommodation and work.

MS: But they didn't leave Slovakia together, my mum and dad's family. They
left in such a way that they met here in Czechia, probably somewhere in
Liberec.

MH: But Andrej [their maternal grandfather] had four younger siblings. And
they actually followed him with their families, and so they remained together.
There was perhaps a year separating their arrival as they gradually left Slovakia. But they still knew of each other, and it was like, hey, Andrej has gone to
Doubice, so we'll go too. He's doing well for himself there, so we'll go there
too. He's got a job so we're going to follow him. So in the end they were all
in the same place here.

MS: But I know that they didn't want to live here together any longer. Because
our grandfather – our mother's father – he said he didn't want to live with
them anymore, that he wanted to live somewhere by himself, and that they
should find their own place, that they needed to become independent. But
it's just as Monika describes it, they were here in the Hook [the Šluknov Hook
or Spur on the border with Germany] but everyone had their own place. They
didn't live on top of one another in a ghetto.

MH: Depending on housing possibilities.

MS: There were one or two in Rybniště, some in Doubice, some in Krásná
Lípa, some in Varnsdorf, but all within the Šluknov Hook. But they kept in
contact and visited each other regularly as a family. It just meant they didn't
all live in the same house.[217]

This passage illustrates well the broader dynamics of the migratory
patterns of particular families and the socio-economic strategies open
to them. At the same time it confronts the assumptions underlying the
resettlement programme itself. Firstly, the movement of the Roma from
Slovakia to the Czech borderlands described here corresponds to the
migration patterns of the Roma and others in the period and region

---

217 Interview with Monika H (b. 1971) and Marcela S (b. 1980), op. cit.

under consideration.[218] In particular it highlights the key role played by typically male labour migrants, followed by their families and subsequently, on the basis of existing kinship networks, other families, something that ensured the continuity of solidarity networks. On the other hand, it is the example of the Romani families from Papín, as well as the overall practice of the "organised transfer" from the Humenné district, that shows that, notwithstanding official restrictions, movement from Slovakia continued to take place primarily on the basis of these ties. Above all, the entire quotation reveals the method and preferences of the distribution of this social organisation in space. In this case, too, one can observe a replication of strategies from Slovakia, with women remaining in the place of residence of their new partners (the principle of virilocal post-marital residence – see the example of Michal S's sisters who remained with their partners in Liberec), and entire families relocating to new residences. As historically was the case in rural eastern Slovakia, the presence of the Roma in new locations was largely determined by the demand for labour.[219] To these economic factors must be added the "housing opportunities" to which Monika H refers. However, when her sister Marcela S says that "my grandfather wanted to live somewhere by himself!", she is perhaps also referring to a desire to break out of the stigmatised Romani environment and a broader effort to achieve a degree of autonomy.[220] In our second interview, for example, Monika H said that the house that their parents moved into in 1975, now situated in Horní Podluží, was already "slated for demolition, but mum simply wanted to live alone, she wanted to break away from my father's family so that we could live alone".[221] These reflections upon similar strategies, including the specificity of gender positions, foreshadow what I will describe in the next part of this chapter, which looks at more detailed

---

218 For more on Romani migration, see Dobruská 2018; Hübschmannová 1993, 31; 1999b, 127; Ort and Dobruská 2023; Sadílková 2016, 166–177; 2020.

219 In the region of eastern Slovakia, this movement has been described in terms of the generational transmission of the profession of blacksmith in Romani families, when a new generation of metalworkers had to find employment in other villages (e.g. Hübschmannová 1998). It is the arrival of a Romani blacksmith that dates the establishment of many east Slovak settlements (see Ort 2021).

220 Of course, it must be borne in mind that the two women may have been influenced by what they had heard from their parents regarding the period under study. This might account for the observation that the families in question did not form "ghettoes": Marcela S may well be putting a distance between herself and the stigmatised Romani ghettoes that were part of the image of the Šluknov Hook as a socio-economic periphery in the era of neoliberal capitalism at the beginning of the new millennium (e.g. Hajská et al. 2013).

221 Interview with Monika H (b. 1971) and Marcela S (b. 1977), *op. cit.*

empirical material relating to the resettlement of the Roma from the village of Šemetkovce. Even the testimony of my interviewees, however, points to possible intersections between the targeting of central policy to "disperse the G*psies" and the socio-economic mobility strategies of the Roma themselves.

4.4.2 Immigrants in the borderlands

Perhaps the strategy of achieving autonomy may also have contributed to the family's embeddedness in Horní Podluží. Both sisters told me that their grandfather Michal B, and later on their father Michal S especially, were highly regarded by the local population. The sisters explained this by pointing to both men's work ethic, which earned them the status of trusted and sought-after workers. Both worked on a local farm, where the sisters' father, after completing his education, had worked as a vocational training teacher.

The position of the Roma as newcomers within the Czech border region was relativised by the fact that most of the local population shared the experience of immigration after the war. After the expulsion of the originally German population, the area was repopulated both by Czechs from the interior and by those who formed the Czech emigration colonies abroad. However, Romani and non-Romani migrants from Slovakia also travelled here (see especially Spurný 2011). It seems that only three German families remained in Horní Podluží itself (formerly German Obergrund) after the war.[222] For Romani families, the shared experience of immigration may have meant on the one hand a relative attenuation of their position as outsiders, while on the other it also created the possibility of replicating broader socio-economic networks. In addition to the links between individual Romani families within the region (see the quotations above), this may also have involved relations with the non-Roma from Slovakia – one female resident of Horní Podluží was said to have arrived directly from Humenné, and a Catholic priest who had studied theology in Litoměřice and had been active in the region in the early 1970s also came from Humenné.[223] In their interviews, both sisters said that in Horní Podluží in 1980,

---

222 Ibid.
223 Ibid.

the priest officiated at the lavish funeral of their grandfather Michal B, a fact which, as well as highlighting regional affinities, demonstrated not only their grandfather's embeddedness in locally formed socio-economic networks, but also, given the presence of mourners from Slovakia, the continuity of transnational social ties.

4.4.3 Policy toward the Roma in the borderlands

On the basis of very sketchy data, which I have been unable to supplement with direct testimony (either from Romani or non-Romani sources) from Horní Podluží and its surroundings, and in the absence of more detailed archival materials, it is not possible to undertake a major reconstruction of the position of the Roma in the locally formed hierarchy of socio-economic relations. On the other hand, it is clear from district archives (the ONV fonds in Děčín) and from earlier historical studies that the image of equal status in the new environment, which was a component of the migration narratives of the Roma arriving after the war from Slovakia (see, for example, Hübschmannová 1993; Synková 2006), had its limits even in the newly populated border region. Indeed, as Spurný shows, with the post-war emphasis on "cleansing" the borderland of "unreliable elements" (Spurný 2011, 244) as part of the process of building a nationally homogenous society, the "G*psy question from the Czech perspective was often linked to the question of the borderland" and the "[s]ettling of the borderland by the G*psies was described in this context as 'Beelzebub driving out the devil'" (ibid., 240).[224] This perception of the borderland as a strategic territory in terms of state security saw the image of the G*psy as an "unemployed criminal" characterised by "filth" and a lack of hygiene become the natural antithesis of "good workers and reliable citizen-borders people" (ibid., 246), though it should not be forgotten that other groups of new arrivals also found themselves labelled in this way, such as ethnic Slovaks or Czechs repatriates (ibid., 242).

As early as November 1946, the Provincial National Committee in Prague noted the increasingly frequent appearance of "G*psy clans", "especially in the border districts". A decree was passed aimed at "curbing

---

224 For the citation in Spurný's text, see Náš starý vlastenecký boj o dnešek (Dr. Hubáček), *Náš hraničář,* I/8, 27 November 1946, 6–12.

the public nuisance of vagrancy and the increasing criminality of the G*p-sies".[225] In this respect, however, the authorities distinguished between working G*psies with Czechoslovak citizenship who had already moved "away from a nomadic way of life to a form of residence in one place", and "G*psy-foreigners", who were to be expelled across the border.[226] The decree and commentaries upon its implementation point to an interest in controlling the movement of G*psies in the borderlands and other locations from the very first post-war years (or rather the re-commencement of a pre-war practice, see also Hajská 2020). They are also an early pre-echo of the unclear definition of G*psies at the borderline of social and ethno-racial categories so characteristic of the period to come (see Chapter Two). The fluidity of the definition, which left room for manoeuvre on the part of the local authorities, became apparent the very same year, when, with reference to the still valid Act No. 117/1927, a nationwide census of "all nomadic G*psies and other vagabonds shunning work who live in the G*psy fashion" was carried out in August 1947. As other authors have noted, the resulting figure of 17,000 persons clearly included mainly newly arrived Romani immigrants from Slovakia (e.g. Pavelčíková 2004, 29–31). Spurný highlights a paradox, to wit, that "of the adult men included in the census, almost 80% were (according to the classification of the census organisers) working men". He also points out that, though the new regime had been promoting the patient "re-education" of the G*psies as "victims of the capitalist order" since the early 1950s, in the border regions there was an ongoing, increasing demand for restrictive measures to be applied towards a specific group of the population.

In Děčín itself, the District Labour Protection Office complained in March 1948 that "as a result of preventive measures against the influx and settlement of G*psies in the surrounding districts, applications from newly arriving G*psies to the local authority are multiplying at an unprecedented rate". For this reason, the office demanded both "the prevention of the influx of G*psies" and the expulsion of those without employment.[227] This is an example of the vicious circle of control over the movement of the Roma on the part of local officials: on the one hand, the encouragement of movement on the basis of restrictive

225 SOkA Děčín, f. ONV Děčín, inv. č. 391, ev. č. 74, "Oběžník – zemský národní výbor v Praze: Opatření proti cikánům pokyny", 1 November 1946.
226 Ibid.
227 SOkA Děčín, f. ONV Děčín, kart. 74 inv. č. 391, "Žádost o zamezení přílivu cikánů do zdejšího okresu", 18 March 1948.

measures in other districts; and on the other, the demand for further restrictions in their own district. However, these officials still attribute this movement to the way of life of the G*psies themselves. This is illustrated well in a letter sent in 1952 by the KNV in Ústí nad Labem (which included the district of Děčín) to all districts in the region. Although the writers speak of the successful "re-education of persons of G*psy origin", they nevertheless claim that their movements must continue to be controlled. They complain that their work in this sphere "is hampered by the influx of nomadic persons of G*psy origin from neighbouring regions and by the fact that the G*psies already settled in our region have been seduced by the nomadic G*psies, either directly or indirectly, into a nomadic way of life."[228] This is further evidence of the way that nomadism was regarded as an inherent feature of G*psyness in the policies of the time (see Nováček 1968, see Chapter Two). In September 1955, a meeting of representatives of the G*psy Commission of the Děčín ONV discussed the continued movement of the G*psies as representing a major obstacle to the implementation of control measures and the labour inclusion of a specific segment of the population. When articulating the problem of the ongoing arrival of G*psies from Slovakia, those present called for a more systematic solution from the higher levels of the state apparat. Dr. Chalupa observed that this was a "nationwide problem", and proposed that "towns be allocated a certain quota of G*psies", which he said would "protect both the town and the G*psies themselves". Commission member Švábová summed things up when she said that "it would be without doubt better if the government were to deal with the G*psy question, because Slovakia wants to get rid of them."[229]

4.4.4 The Act on the Permanent Settlement of Nomadic Persons

As Spurný argues, similar demands from regions in Czechia formed an important context for a definitive move toward a restrictive and assimilationist approach to the Roma at the central level. It was against this

---

228 SOkA Děčín, f. ONV Děčín, kart. 74, inv. č. 391, "Pohyb osob cikánského původu", 16 May 1952.

229 SOkA Děčín, f. ONV Děčín, kart. 74, inv. č. 391, "Zápis ze schůzce komise ONV Děčín pro cikánské otázky", 26 September 1955.

backdrop that Act 74/1958 on the Permanent Settlement of Nomadic Persons was passed. Uncertainty regarding what exactly constituted a nomadic person meant the legislation impacted the Roma in particular, not only itinerant Vlax Roma (see Hajská 2020, 2024), but also Romani labour migrants (e.g. Donert 2017; Ort 2022a, Pavelčíková 2004; Sokolová 2008; Spurný 2011, see the Introduction and the situation in Kapišová, also Chapter Two and the situation in Brekov). Spurný notes that "in the border region of north Bohemia, the majority of the G*psies who resided in the region were probably included in the census", and that "the Regional National Committee in Ústí nad Labem saw the entire project as a long-awaited chance to gain control over that which had been hitherto uncontrollable, namely, the ongoing migration, fluctuation and nomadism of part of the population that has been causing problems for the authorities in the border region for years" (Spurný 2011, 269). The application of the new law led, on the one hand, to a deepening of the pauperisation and social marginalisation of specific Romani families (see Hajská 2020), and, on the other, to greater movement (see Ort 2022a), since it often failed to prevent even the continued movement of persons included in the census (see also Pavelčíková 1999, 89). The regional report on the situation in the Děčín district cited above also reflects upon the fact that those recorded in the census were changing their residence and that the directives of the Ministry of the Interior were not being followed during this process.[230]

However, as well as tracking the continuity of control over the movement of the Roma, the reason I would like to examine the implementation of Act 54/1958 here is because of the "fundamental and often overlooked fact" that the law targeted not only those who "settled down permanently" but also the "dispersion" of the people recorded (Spurný 2011, 279). Earlier in his text, Spurný illustrates this by citing a directive for the implementation of the Act under which "part of the 'settlement' [...] should include measures to ensure that 'groups of nomadic persons are dispersed as far apart as is possible', i.e. that group, kinship or family ties should be sundered" (ibid., 269). Yet if the implementation of these central measures failed to bring a halt to the ongoing "undesirable movement" and "fluctuation of G*psies", still less did it lead to the desired "dispersion of G*psy concentrations". Under the Act, it was the

---

230 SOkA Děčín, f. ONV Děčín, kart. 759, inv. č. 1372, "Zpráva pro evidenci býv. Kočujících osob /cik. původu/", 28 October 1960.

Municipal National Committees that were tasked with overseeing the allocation of appropriate housing and job placements. However, in practice they were not equipped with the tools and means to do so. As regards Slovakia, this is again well illustrated by the situation in Kapišová, where the practice of "settling down" led to an intensification of the housing crisis in the local settlement (Ort 2022a). Moreover, as Hajská shows, even in the case of the "successful elimination of traditional forms of nomadism", new concentrations of Romani families were created in significantly substandard housing (Hajská 2020, 355; Hajská is describing the situation in districts in Czechia).

4.4.5 Continuity of dispersion in the border region

The ineffectiveness of legal practice in this sphere can be observed in Děčín itself, where during the first half of the 1960s documents repeatedly appear in which the local officials call for the implementation of "dispersion" throughout the district. Spurný notes that dispersion took its place alongside practices such as expulsion, internment and re-education, a combination that characterised official policy towards the Roma in the first five years after the war. He adds that "perhaps with the exception of re-education", these were also "characteristic practices that were applied at that time even to other undesirable group of the population, first and foremost, of course, to the German minority" (Spurný 2011, 243). When contextualising dispersion as a broader, longer-term practice, he later turns his attention to its utilisation in relation to the Roma in the border regions. For it was here, he writes, that dispersion was "one of the standard instruments of state policy", where "the need for the directive deployment of labour was felt most intensively". However, when simultaneously examining the targeted "concentration of G*psies" that frequently appeared in diverse post-war proposals[231] (and was still clearly preferred to dispersion in the popular discourse of the 1960s; see Chapter Two), the "central authorities began to incline towards dispersion as a tool to facilitate the adaptation of G*psies to life as 'ordinary' citizens and to ensure that they were uprooted from 'their often primitive habits, needs and demands'" (ibid., 279). Taking the Ústí region as an example, Spurný illustrates a well-known dilemma associated with

---

231 Berkyová, R. 2018 [online]. Accessed 22 July 2023.

dispersion, quoting a document from 1953. Although it acknowledges the undeniably discriminatory nature of the practice, its very purpose is to legitimise it: "the needs and interests of society demand it [dispersion] of necessity, and so even from the point of view of anti-discrimination policy it can be justified. This solution is rationalised from the point of view of social, health and moral concerns, the raising of children and improving the work ethic".[232]

As the previous documents I have cited show, representatives of the district G*psy Commission were considering a kind of dispersion in the Děčín district: Dr. Chalupa proposed setting "quotas" for the placement of "G*psies" (see above). In December 1960 (i.e. when the resolution and the 1958 Act were already in force), the district G*psy Commission issued a resolution on "voluntary resettlement" from villages with higher numbers of G*psies to villages "in which either there are no G*psies or they are only present in insignificant numbers". The archives do not include any commentary on the implementation of this measure. At a meeting of the same commission in November 1963, one of its members recommended "insisting on a resettlement policy that must be strictly observed and must be understood first and foremost by the governing body". In this respect, said member made reference to a well-known problem, namely, that "there is dislike on the part of the citizens towards the G*psies, they do not want to take them in and there are a lot of difficulties and complaints around this".[233]

The perpetuation of enforced dispersion (even though individual resolutions had been shown to be ineffective in the light of the attitudes of the local inhabitants) shows that the adoption of Government Resolution 502/1965 on "dispersion" and "organised transfer" was a response not only to growing pressure for a solution to the situation in eastern Slovakia, but also to that in the borderlands in Czechia, where demands for a central solution had been voiced since at least the early 1950s. This is all the more important because in the post-war period it was the situation in the (border) regions in Czechia that was crucial in the formulation of a policy towards the Roma, while the region of eastern Slovakia was seen as a bigger security risk more in light of its socio-economic

232 NA Prague, f. 850/3 (AMV-D), k. 1283, Cikánská otázka v kraji ústeckém, 18 September 1953 (see Spurný 2011, 279).
233 SOkA Děčín, f. ONV Děčín, kart. 759, inv. č. 1372, "Komise pro převýchovu osob cikánského původu v Děčíně", 13 November 1963.

marginalisation, ethnic and religious heterogeneity, and the historical instability of the state border (Donert 2017, 89). Although the Ústí region offers a possible case study for monitoring the processes outlined above, the entire region of north Bohemia is exceptional in that it was excluded from the timetable for resettlement from Slovakia to Czechia due to the high number of Roma living there. It is not entirely clear on the basis of what criteria this decision was reached, since, as Pavelčíková (2004, 95) points out, the same could be said of other regions, specifically north Moravia (see Pavelčíková 1999), where the Roma from Humenné were to be moved to the districts of Opava and Bruntál. What is certain, however, is that only part of the policy under consideration was to relate to north Bohemia, specifically, the section that spoke of the "dispersion of undesirable G*psy concentrations" (Pavelčíková 2004, 92).

In the Děčín district, the plan was to apply dispersion in several larger villages. However, even here the practice was to come up against "staunch resistance from the National Committees in the district", which could not be persuaded to find places for "G*psy families".[234] On the other hand, smaller villages, including Horní Podluží, had already encountered the logic of dispersion and funds were being directed more towards the resolution of sanitary problems in the existing dwellings of individual families. Romani families were thus hemmed in from two sides by the resettlement policy: firstly, through the liquidation of their homes (often already abandoned) in settlements in eastern Slovakia; and secondly, through the related housing policy in Czechia.

Tracking the situation in the border region allows us to observe the continuity of policies directed at "undesirable" groups of the population, a category that was applied within the context of the post-war building of a socialist society in this region in particular to the G*psies, above all the newly arriving Romani migrants from Slovakia. Given that the "organised transfer" was only carried out to a limited extent in the case of Humenné, the study presented here offers important insights into the prevailing experience of Romani families who came to Czechia from this region. It shows that their social position was co-shaped by local histories, not only in the region of eastern Slovakia, but also in regions in Czechia, including locally contingent histories of the way the category

---

234 SOkA Děčín, f. ONV Děčín, kart. 759, inv. č. 1372, "Zpráva o činnosti komise pro řešení otázek cikánského obyvatelstva", 1 March 1968.

of G*psyness targeting these people was understood. The resettlement policy affected the Roma not only as the (marginalised) inhabitants of the eastern Slovakian countryside, but also as agents who were part of the newly formed post-war society, in which they found themselves in the ambivalent position of both much needed and welcome workers and "undesirable G*psies" (see Sadílková 2018).

4.5 The Resettlement of the Roma in the Jičín Region

From the late 1970s onwards, Milena Hübschmannová and her husband Josef Melč had been in close contact with the family of Vasiľ and Helena Š, who were both originally from the eastern Slovakian village of Šemetkovce in the district of Svidník. In the mid-1960s, Vasiľ and Helena were part of the organised transfer from what was at that time the district of Bardejov in Slovakia to the district of Jičín in northeastern Bohemia. In the latter half of the 1970s, in interviews with Hübshmannnová and Melč, the couple described their departure from Slovakia, the subsequent movement between different villages in the Jičín district caused both by inadequate housing, discrimination and even physical assaults on the part of the locals, and the relationships pertaining between resettled Romani families. However, the key issue was of a highly personal nature, since Vasiľ Š served ten months in prison in 1977 for social parasitism. Upon his release, the authorities placed the couple's children into institutional care. It would appear that four of the seven children were minors and three were already living independent lives by that time.

Helena and Vasiľ Š attributed their family's plight primarily to external factors. After their arrival in the Jičín district from Slovakia, they were forced to move several times within a short period of time. To begin with they lived in Radkyně, whence they were hounded out by Vasil's brother, with whom they shared a house. After a short period with another brother in the village of Mlázovice, they were assigned a house in the village of Spyšová (in the municipality of Sobotka). However, the local non-Roma were having none of it, and so Vasiľ and Helena moved once more, this time to Ústí u Staré Paky. Even here, however, they were the target of hateful anti-Roma attitudes. In an interview conducted in 1977, their adult daughter Božena Š recalled how once, while in the waiting room at the train station in Nová Paka in the winter, they heard a man calling out to his young daughter: "Don't go in there, there are G*psies, they stink. Why are you going there?"[235] Helena Š told how, while Vasiľ was still in prison, some men smashed the window of their house on their way home from the pub.[236] In an interview given in 1979, Vasiľ Š said that their son was too scared to go to school, because the teachers there had threatened to send him to an institution, and a somewhat vague passage suggests that some of the locals tried to attack his children and actually managed to beat one of them up.[237] As regards school attendance, Vasiľ Š said the situation was complicated by the fact that his children had to travel 16 kilometres to school, while he and his wife had to commute to work every day. He swore that he had not wanted to create any further problems upon returning from prison and that he had given up alcohol. He spoke of poor relations with his siblings, several of whom had been resettled with their families in the same district. He said he preferred not to see them anymore.[238] During the first interview, his wife Helena said that while her husband was in prison, his siblings had basically deserted her and left her on her own.[239] Vasiľ himself also reflected upon the strained relationship he had with his son-in-law, the husband of his daughter Božena, who, he claimed, was partly responsible for him being imprisoned.[240] Upon his release, Vasiľ refused to be part of the same household, and so Božena, his son-in-law, and their three children moved to a company apartment in Hořice.[241]

In an attempt to pin down more precisely the situation of this family, its history and its position within the wider networks of socio-economic relations, Hübschmannová and Melč interviewed other relevant parties. Rather than expressing anti-Roma sentiments or referencing broader structural conditions, these highlighted the individual failings of Vasiľ Š, whom they portrayed as a deeply troubled individual. They described his wife as a hard-working woman nevertheless unable to manage everything on her own, while at the same time – and in accordance with the logic of gender relations – as someone unable to "straighten out" her

235 Archive of MRK, Brno, f. Pozůstalost Mileny Hübschmannové, kart. 9_ET, sp. Transkripty_MH, č. 110.
236 Ibid.
237 Archive of MRK, Brno, f. Pozůstalost Mileny Hübschmannové, kart. 11_ET, sp. Transkripty 77-83_MH, č. 38.
238 Ibid.
239 Archive of MRK, Brno, f. Pozůstalost Mileny Hübschmannové, kart. 9_ET, sp. Transkripty_MH, č. 110.
240 Archive of MRK, Brno, f. Pozůstalost Mileny Hübschmannové, kart. 11_ET, sp. Transkripty 77-83_MH, č. 38.
241 Ibid.

husband.[242] The family's non-Romani neighbour stated, contrary to what Vasiľ Š himself claimed, that after being released from prison and returning home, Vasiľ was permanently drunk. She even went so far as to state that the children who had been taken into care would be definitely better off in an institution.[243] The director of the company Velveta in Stará Paka testified that he had employed members of the family on the basis of his positive experience with Helena Š (Vasiľ's wife), who worked there as a cleaner. However, speaking of her husband and their adult son Ján Š, he complained of poor work.[244] The harshest words were those spoken by Vasiľ's brother, Michal Š, illustrating the strained sibling relationships. According to Michal, Vasiľ's work morale was bad enough in Slovakia, but after his arrival in the region of Jičín things went from bad to worse.[245] Peter M, another of the Roma who travelled with his family from Šemetkovce to Jičín, added his voice to the claim that the children were better off in institutional care. He saw the problem as residing in the fact that after arriving in Czechia, the children were left with only one adult male role model in the form of their troubled father, having lost any natural daily contact with other ("decent, hard-working") adult Roma.[246]

It is clear from the interviews that Hübschmannová and Melč were primarily concerned with helping this family and did not approve of the children being taken into institutional care. Other documents in the same archive show that they personally campaigned for the children to be returned to their parents. On the other hand, it is clear from the interviews and notes in the margins of the transcript that they, too, saw the situation as resulting from failure on the part of the father. For example, Hübschmannová asks Michal Š in an interview whether "something could be done with him [Vasiľ Š]", and then wonders out loud how it was possible that "one brother could be good [lačho] and the other [not]".[247] It is irrelevant to the issue at hand that Hübschmannová and Melč to a large extent shared the majority opinion of Vasiľ Š, and it is certainly

---

242 E.g. Archive of MRK, Brno, f. Pozůstalost Mileny Hübschmannové, kart. 14_ET, sp. Transkripty 70_MH, č. III/4.
243 Archive of MRK, Brno, f. Pozůstalost Mileny Hübschmannové, kart. 11_ET, č. 63.
244 Archive of MRK, Brno, f. Pozůstalost Mileny Hübschmannové, kart. 11_ET, sp. Transkripty 77-83_MH, č. 37.
245 Archive of MRK, Brno, f. Pozůstalost Mileny Hübschmannové, kart. 14_ET, sp. Transkripty 77_MH, č. III/4.
246 Archive of MRK, Brno, f. Pozůstalost Mileny Hübschmannové, kart. 14_ET, sp. Transkripty 70_MH, č. III/7.
247 Archive of MRK, Brno, f. Pozůstalost Mileny Hübschmannové, kart. 14_ET, sp. Transkripty 70_MH, č. III/4.

not appropriate to inquire into the "real" nature of Vasiľ Š's behaviour and the circumstances surrounding the removal of his children. On the contrary, it is interesting to note that Hübschmannová (with the acquiescence of her husband/collaborator) essentially linked the plight of this family to the social engineering of the resettlement policy and regarded the family as one of its victims. Melč reflected upon the effects that implementation of the policy had in an interview with Mr Janeček, then head of the HR department of the ONV in Jičín: "I believe that you did it out of the goodness of your heart. One wants to offer help... we know [Vasiľ] Š and during that time [after the resettlement], he was a demoralised person." Hübschmannová herself, in the same, surprisingly frank interview, highlights the paradox at the heart of the dominant logic of dispersion, which, in her view, instead of re-education, led to the disruption of natural mechanisms of social control.[248] It was with this in mind that she interpreted the disintegration of the Š family, while in another interview, she expressed her agreement with Peter M regarding the absence of natural Romani role models for the children of the family.[249] Hübschmannová's opinion of the case is in line with the criticism of the resettlement policy as engendering a fatal disruption of the socio-cultural and broader value systems of Romani communities and representing the wilful social engineering of their natural socio-economic strategies.

In the context of my research, during which I often relied on isolated archival sources and sometimes fragmentary, mediated recollections, the interviews thus framed represent unique material that captures the position, attitudes and experiences of individual parties, above all the resettled Roma themselves, but also representatives of the local authorities and businesses in Slovakia and Czechia. Transcripts of the recordings of the original interviews have survived, which were probably edited or had marginalia added by Hübschmannová herself. The material held in the archive of Hübschmannová's estate provide valuable insight into what she herself thought of the resettlement policy. These interviews also form an important part of the broader empirical materials on which she based her critique of the impact of this policy on the Roma. I supplement this material with related sources from regional archives in Slovakia, though sadly I have been unable to find relevant materials pertaining to the

---

248 Archive of MRK, Brno, f. Pozůstalost Mileny Hübschmannové, kart. 14_ET, sp. Transkripty 70_MH, č. III/3.
249 Archive of MRK, Brno, f. Pozůstalost Mileny Hübschmannové, kart. 14_ET, sp. Transkripty 70_MH, č. III/7.

district of Jičín itself. On the other hand, I did manage to contact one of the descendants of the participants of the interviews conducted by Hübschmannová. However, he was not over-enthused by the thought of a personal meeting and follow-up interview, and in the end declined my request completely.

4.5.1 Initial conditions of resettlement

The village of Šemetkovce, from which Vasiľ Š hailed, is located only a few kilometres from Kapišová, and the Roma from both villages were linked by kinship and other social ties that, according to some indications,[250] remained in place even after the resettlement/migration of individual families from both villages to Czechia. Beginning in 2014, I conducted ethnographic field research in another village in the Svidník district and heard that Šemetkovce and Kapišová were villages from which all the Roma had been resettled. The situation in Šemetkovce was similar to that in Kapišová in terms of the position of the Roma in local socio-economic relations. Here, too, the Roma were supposed to have lived "since time immemorial" (Jurová 2002, 19–20), while according to Vasiľ Š, during the pre-war period they were still making a living by lining the ovens of their non-Romani neighbours and breaking stones on paths. His father had been a blacksmith and musician (see Hübschmannová 1998).[251] Like other villages in the district (see Ort 2022a,b), Šemetkovce had been virtually razed to the ground during Second World War and according to Vasiľ Š, both the Roma and *gadje* built improvised dwellings upon their return to the village.[252] In the case of the settlement at the bottom of the slope, the dismal conditions were exacerbated during the early 1960s by heavy rain and the threat of landslide, which Hübschmannová's interviewees cited as a key factor in the resettlement of its inhabitants.

The second factor cited by several witnesses involved the deteriorating relations between Romani and non-Romani villagers. Marika M (born in 1944 in Kružlová) articulated her disillusionment with the

---

250 When I put out a call to Romani Facebook groups asking if anyone knew of any Roma from Kapišová living in Czechia, I was contacted by Ladislav C from Šemetkovce, who was able to name some of the places where descendants of the Kapišová Roma were living at that time. Ladislav C himself had left Slovakia when he was four years old.

251 Archive of MRK, Brno, f. Pozůstalost Mileny Hübschmannové, kart. 11_ET, sp. Transkripty 77-83_MH, č. 38.

252 Ibid.

behaviour of the non-Romani villagers from the position of a woman who had moved to Šemetkovce from another village in the district where, according to her, the Roma enjoyed higher socio-economic status and a more egalitarian position in local relations. In her interview, she said that "they [the *gadje*] really humiliated the G*psies, who they felt had no value whatsoever", though she also believes that a particular conflict that escalated played an important role in the implementation of the resettlement. According to Marika M's account, one of the *gadje* had a shed in close proximity with the settlement containing a canister of petrol, which the Romani children punctured while playing. The owner of the shed went to sort things out with the father of one of the children and slapped him across the face. When Marika's husband found out, he "went to stand up for the G*psy [...] [and] slapped the *gadjo* back". As a result, the Roma in the settlement had all of the windows "smashed by the *gadje* by morning".[253] Marika M went on to describe the entire conflict in terms of a generational change in the way that the Roma responded to their own oppression:

MH: You weren't afraid?
The older ones were really scared of the *gadje*: "Don't do that, don't do it! Christ, the *gadje* will kill us all!" [...] [B]ut the younger ones, once they began to understand that a great injustice was being perpetrated, they became angry and wanted to do something. And so the *gadje* agreed that the G*psies should move away from them.[254]

Although the statement that "the *gadje* agreed that the G*psies should move away from them" sounds somewhat unclear, what was said about the attack on the settlement as a whole following a conflict between two individuals is fully in line with similarly described situations in other eastern Slovak villages (see Chapter Two). However, in terms of the intergenerational transformation of the reaction to oppression, i.e., from fearfulness to an unwillingness to accept the established order, it can be seen as a strategy of escape from these unequal conditions.

A similar development of the position of the Roma in the local community was voiced from the other side by Mr Železniak, then chairman of the MNV in Šemetkovce, with whom Hübschmannová recorded an

---

253 Archive of MRK, Brno, f. Pozůstalost Mileny Hübschmannové, kart. 14_ET, sp. Transkripty 70_MH, č. III/3.
254 Ibid.

interview in October 1979. Železniak said that in Šemetkovce there lived "around 98 G*psies", who before the war had lived in extreme poverty, but who after the war were "better dressed and didn't wander around the village [...] begging".[255] However, a certain social mobility led, in his words, to an unwanted disruption of the established order:

> MH: How did they [the Roma] get along with the locals?
> To begin with it was as I described. But then they started going to the shop, and when no one wanted to serve them, they started to get angry with the locals, that they were bigger, that they had more power than we had. [...] They'd become too big for their boots.[256]

Železniak's testimony sits well not only alongside the intergenerational shift to be seen in the words of Marika M, but also the broader popular discourse of the G*psies as a "privileged caste" in socialist society (see Chapter Two). From this perspective it would appear that the departure of the Roma of Šemetkovce for Czechia was the logical outcome of a situation in which increased social mobility in a Slovak village might have come up against the boundaries of a historically shaped dominant order and ideas regarding the strictly defined position of the Roma in the local socio-economic system.

4.5.2 Regional policies in Šemetkovce

In the case of Šemetkovce, too, resettlement itself was linked to the (short-term) labour migration of the Roma on the one hand, and to policies implemented on a local level in respect of the "G*psy settlements" on the other. A longer-term experience of migration, especially amongst the Romani men, was evident from the references made by individual witnesses to work stays in various parts of Czechia. A certain form of movement based around the idea that the "G*psy way of life" is rootless is then indicated, as in the case of Kapišová, by the census of "nomadic persons" taken in Šemetkovce in February 1959. The total of nineteen such persons recorded is likely to include five family units, most of whose representatives, including Vasiľ Š, expressed a wish to remain in their

---

255 Archive of MRK, Brno, f. Pozůstalost Mileny Hübschmannové, kart. 11_ET, sp. Transkripty 77-83_MH, č. 28.
256 Ibid.

home village and work in Svidník (the county seat at that time). Ignác C was the only person to state that he did not own any property in Šemetkovce and that he wanted to be accommodated in Czechia, where he was "ready and willing to take on any kind of work".[257]

The only other mention of similar preferences amongst the Roma is contained in a complaint dated 25 June 1963 and addressed by representatives of the district G*psy Commission in Bardejov to the Czechoslovak prime minister Viliam Široký. The complaint concerns the unrealised relocation of the Roma from Šemetkovce to the district of Cheb in western Bohemia, allegedly initiated by the Roma themselves. They (i.e. "citizens of G*psy origin") apparently requested the relevant district commission "to provide them with assistance in moving their entire families to Czechia permanently". According to those who drafted the complaint, the district of Cheb at first confirmed its interest in the workforce, including the possibility of accommodation, but after an agreement had been entered into by both districts, its representatives allegedly remained silent for an entire month, after which they expressed their concerns as to "whether these citizens will work honestly and not destroy [...] national property". They then stopped communicating altogether. The letter writers concluded that, if there hadn't been these unnecessary delays, they would have already found work and accommodation elsewhere in the region of west Bohemia for these citizens, and that in improperly implementing the resolution of April 1958, "the comrades from the ONV in Cheb" had done a disservice to "the citizens of G*psy origin themselves".[258]

Given that the planned relocation of families from the Šemetkovce settlement to western Bohemia failed to materialise, this and other settlements were still in October 1963 slated for liquidation. However, this time round the plan was to build new housing in the village itself, something that had been called for by representatives of the G*psy Commissions of eastern Slovak KNV in Košice and the ONV in Bardejov.[259] I have not found any further details of this plan, also unrealised, in the relevant archives. However, in an interview with Hübschmannová, the then secretary of the MNV, in office at the time of the interview in

257 ŠOkA Svidník, f. ONV vo Svidníku I. (1945-1960), kart. 322, sp. 2, "Súpis kočujúcich a polokočujúcich osôb v okrese (cigáňov)", 1959.
258 ŠAKE Košice, f. Komisia Vsl. KNV pre cigánske obyvateľstvo, kart. 3, sp. 83. "Stížnost na plnení usnesení ÚV KSČ", 25 June 1963.
259 ŠAKE Košice, f. Komisia Vsl. KNV pre cigánske obyvateľstvo, kart. 3, sp. 138. "Zápisnica", 1 October 1963.

October 1979, discussed retrospectively the potential possibilities.[260] He pointed to the absence of land on which to build houses, something that applied to the village as a whole. To illustrate this fact, he noted that he himself had been able to build a house in 1970, but that by 1972 another inhabitant had been refused planning permission. The clear contradiction contained in his statement given that the Roma had already left the village in 1966–1967, i.e. before the building restrictions took effect, is pointed out by Hübschmannová in the margins of the transcript.[261] Without a knowledge of the other circumstances surrounding the building options and a more detailed insight into the preferences of the inhabitants of the settlement themselves, it may be concluded that this contradiction may be yet another example of the unequal status of the Roma in respect of building land and the opportunity to acquire planning permission in specific villages in this and other districts, and thus an important structural condition of resettlement itself (see Ort 2022a,b).

In documents dating from 1966, i.e. when Government Resolution 502/1965 was already in force, Šemetkovce was no longer listed amongst the settlements earmarked for liquidation. On the contrary, the settlement was to be upgraded through the construction of a well and the purchase of two sitting toilets.[262] In light of these facts, the Commission's 1966 progress report, according to which Šemetkovce was one of the first villages to have overseen the liquidation of the settlement and the transfer of its population to Czechia, is somewhat surprising. The "G*psies of Šemetkovce" are mentioned as an example of those resettled people who "bought detached houses in Czechia [in this case in the Jičín district] immediately after the redemption of their shacks".[263]

4.5.3 The partner district of Jičín

The most detailed insight into the preparation and implementation of the resettlement programme from the perspective of the authorities was provided by Janeček, then head of HR at the ONV in Jičín. From the

---

260 Archive of MRK, Brno, f. Pozůstalost Mileny Hübschmannové, kart. 11_ET, sp. Transkripty 77-83_MH, č. 28.
261 Ibid.
262 ŠOkA Bardejov, f. ONV Bardejov, Komisia pre cigánske otázky, sp. 196, "Zpráva o koncepčnom riešení otázok cigánskeho obyvateľstva v okrese Bardejov za rok 1966", 1966.
263 Ibid.

interview with Hübschmannová it seems that he himself viewed the resettlement of Romani families from Slovakia as a highly important task that was accomplished only thanks to the personal commitment of the parties involved, i.e. the "officials, National Committees [and] the Women's Union".[264] When asked about the criteria used when allocating partner districts, Janeček replied that this had been a central decision based on the options open to individual regions. He noted that within the entire region of north-eastern Bohemia, Jičín was *not* among the districts "with a high percentage of G*psies". In comparison with Opava and Bruntál, the partner districts for the Slovak district of Humenné, or Děčín, referred to above, the starting point was different. Unlike Opava, which focused on the existing situation of the Roma in the district (see, for example Pavelčíková 1999) and where representatives of the G*psy Commission of the ONV were lukewarm when it came to accepting more families (see above), the image conjured up by Janeček regarding Jičín was of determined officials who were committed to fulfilling the central task to the best of their abilities. Nevertheless, even Janeček was forced to concede that they had only been able to find housing for a total of nine families in villages spread around the district, i.e. all the families affected by the move from Šemetkovce. From the interview it seems that the transfer of families from Šemetkovce was the only such transfer in the entire district. The number of resettled families was therefore ultimately comparable to the relocation of families to the Opava district. Janeček offers a depressingly predictable explanation of the difficulty in finding greater accommodation capacities, namely, resistance on the part of the local authorities and residents in the villages concerned.[265]

4.5.4 Categorisation of resettled families

Prior to the implementation of the resettlement policy, there were reciprocal visits between the two districts. The inspection of the situation in individual villages in the Jičín district, which was attended by male representatives of the families selected for resettlement (see below), was preceded by a visit by representatives of the ONV Jičín to Šemetkovce itself. Describing the visit, Janeček wrote that the Czech representatives

---

264 Archive of MRK, Brno, f. Pozůstalost Mileny Hübschmannové, kart. 14_ET, sp. Transkripty 70_MH, č. III/3.
265 Ibid.

were surprised by the "extremely bad" situation in the settlement, which was under immediate threat of a landslide. Even in the wake of this, the "officials [of Šemetkovce] literally begged on the spot" for representatives of the Jičín district to "expedite" matters for them, because "it was in any case necessary to clear out the population".[266] Železniak, chairman of the Šemetkovce MNV, admitted that some of the Roma were not enthused by the offer of leaving for the Czech borderlands since they did not want to leave "their village".[267] A key role, according to him, was to be played by two Romani men who had participated in visits to the Jičín district and "held conversations with the other citizens of G*psy origin such that they were able to be persuaded." However, representatives of the local authorities also played their part: "we also motivated them to move out of our village".[268]

Although Železniak was able to draw a distinction between the interests of individual Romani families (whose opinions are outlined below), for him they represented a homogenised group of residents whom under the circumstances (unsuitable housing and a disruption of the established hierarchy of relationships) it was both possible and desirable to evict. From this perspective, such a homogenised group of the population was characterised by the inherent passivity of the individuals intended for resettlement. And so even from the perspective of the authorities, participation in the project was not the outcome of carefully arrived at decisions taken by the residents themselves, but primarily a sign of successful education and persuasion. In the end, the secretary of the MNV in Šemetkovce, who was in office at the time of the interview with Hübschmannová, summed up the solution to the problem as follows:

MH: What was it brought you to Šemetkovce?
It had been discussed all around the country. And those [G*psies] who allowed themselves to be persuaded, they left [for Czechia].[269]

As he continued, it became clear that he perceived the participation of the Roma in the central policy as a litmus test of their willingness and ability to "integrate" into society:

266 Ibid.
267 Archive of MRK, Brno, f. Pozůstalost Mileny Hübschmannové, kart. 11_ET, sp. Transkripty 77-83_MH, č. 28.
268 Ibid.
269 Ibid.

So when you say that they are well off there, that they are now citizens of the republic, that means that anyone who wants to be, can be, and nothing will help those who do not want to be.[270]

And so while the Roma are placed in the position of passive, "evictable" objects (van Baar 2016) on the one hand, the possibility of their full inclusion in society depends solely on their own resolve on the other. In this context, it was the attitudes and conduct of other parties that were muted, in this case the representatives of the National Committees and the local population, whose resistance to the relocation of the Roma was mentioned by Janeček and on which the public enlightenment campaign in the Jičín district itself had been targeted. It is not clear to what claim by Hübschmannová the secretary of the MNV is reacting when he says: "So when you say that they are well off there…". However, it is evident from other interviews, not only with Janeček, but above all with the Roma themselves, that this "social inclusivity" had clear limits, not least in the form of continuing marginalisation even in Czechia (see below).

The division of the Roma into those who "can be persuaded" and "manage to fit in" and those who "cannot be helped" is fully in line with the logic of the central administrative classification that distinguished between G*psies prepared to relinquish the "backward way of life" (category II) and pathological cases against whom restrictive measures were to be taken (category III, see Chapter Two). It is clear from Hübschmannová's interviews that these categories were rigorously applied by representatives of the ONV in Jičín, who, in Janeček's words and on the basis of in-depth interviews with individual family members, "verified that the ONV Bardejov had no intention of getting rid of those who would cause us much inconvenience here [i.e. in the Jičín district]":[271] Elsewhere in the interview, Janeček, again conforming to the logic of the central categories, speaks of G*psies being "suitable" (*vhodní*) or "unsuitable" (*nevhodní*) for resettlement, taking as his criteria children's school attendance, the work ethic of the adults, etc.[272]

The district of Jičín is referred to in a letter that illustrates well how the resettlement project was viewed at the official level. According to the header and signature, the letter was written by Karel Šoltys, chairman of

---

270 Ibid.
271 Archive of MRK, Brno, f. Pozůstalost Mileny Hübschmannové, kart. 14_ET, sp. Transkripty 70_MH, č. III/3.
272 Ibid.

the ONV in Jičín, while the addressee according to the address and its place in the fonds of the G*psy Commission of the east Slovakia KNV was its secretary Juraj Špiner. The letter, dated 15 June 1966, is worth reproducing in full:

Dear Jirka [Czech informal version of Juraj],
I apologise for the delay in responding to your message, but I would like to link it to a request I have. Thank you for your greeting. I'm sorry I wasn't in attendance, but hopefully you will get back to us again sometime or I will get back to you.
This year we have been tasked with settling five families of G*psy origin. We have everything ready, we have discussed the matter at the MNV and there are vacant apartments. We just **need more settled families.** We are aware of the fact that **this won't be easy, something I know from settlements in the borderlands.** Comrades will travel from here to the district of Bardejov and arrange things on the spot. It would be great if you could have a quiet word with the employees of the ONV Bardejov, **so that they are people who are a little more settled in their ways.**
Otherwise there is plenty of work here now the tourist season is starting. We managed the beet harvest on time and without work brigades, and at present we are harvesting hay. It has rained heavily several times, and that has been a lifesaver for everything.
I'm done now, please send my regards to your family and colleagues.
Šoltys [handwritten signature][273]

The first thing to say is that Janeček's definition of "suitable" versus "unsuitable" for resettlement is understood here via the logic of sedentism, and the demands thus formulated are a good illustration of the persistent association of the "G*psy way of life" with "undesirable movement" and "fluctuation" (if not directly with nomadism). This makes clear the long-term perspective of the authorities in Czechia (see part three of this chapter). Secondly, the friendly tone of the letter and the request that extra care be taken when selecting the "right" families points to unexpected relationships between the various parties involved, who may have ultimately influenced who would or could be included in the resettlement project and who not. Finally, the brevity of the letter, in

---

273 ŠAKE Košice, f. Komisia Vsl. KNV pre cigánske obyvatelstvo, kart. 11, sp. 112, "Dopis", 15 June 1966; emphasis J. O.

which a friendly tone is combined with officialese and the "five families of G*psy origin" appear alongside details of the harvesting of beet and hay, underlines both the social engineering of the policy and the dehumanisation of those identified as G*psies. In this respect the letter is reminiscent of Facuna's ironic comment regarding the resettlement policy: "[t]hey decide how many horses, cows and G*psies there should be in each village." (Hübschmannová 1968, 37).

4.5.5 Attitudes of the Roma from a gender perspective

The Roma interviewed by Hübschmannová did not in hindsight question the necessity of their own resettlement in the district of Jičín, but placed it within the context of the critical situation in the settlement in Šemetkovce. When asked by Hübschmannová whether they had wanted to move to Czechia, Helena Š was very clear:

> We wanted to because the land was sliding down upon us. On our homes. The mud slid onto the road and we had our houses next to it, so the district [ONV] offered us housing here in Czechia. It was what we wanted.[274]

Marika M saw things similarly:

> The buildings were located beneath a slope. There was this high hill, and when it rained, the water simply flowed down off the hill and onto the buildings. So the entire community of G*psies had to move here to Czechia.[275]

Even given the fact that the then chairman Železniak claimed that many of the Roma did not wish to leave, it is worth noting that in their interviews with Hübschmannová, none of the Roma even mentioned the possibility of an alternative solution to the situation, such as newbuilds, either in the village itself or elsewhere in the surrounding district. Perhaps this was because such a vision was scarcely to be imagined under the circumstances and so they were simply resigned to the inevitability of resettlement. Financial considerations may have played a role too, given

---

274 Archive of MRK, Brno, f. Pozůstalost Mileny Hübschmannové, kart. 9_ET, sp. Transkripty_ MH, č. 110.
275 Archive of MRK, Brno, f. Pozůstalost Mileny Hübschmannové, kart. 14_ET, sp. Transkripty 70_MH, č. III/7.

the desperate situation of some of the families. However, this was only mentioned by representatives of the authorities involved. Janeček stated in an interview that the value of the houses of individual families was perhaps deliberately exaggerated by the authorities,[276] and Železniak added that the Roma were "very happy" when they learned that they would receive around 9,500 crowns for the properties (only to be disappointed when they found out that this money had been transferred directly to the ONV in Jičín and earmarked for new housing).[277] The financial aspect in the form of better remunerated work was also present in the statement given by the oldest of the Roma, Anna C (born 1905), regarding her own reasons for leaving the settlement:

MH: Why did you move to Czechia?
One Romani man wanted to leave, and my husband too. He said there were better jobs here [in Czechia]. The pay there [in Slovakia] was poor. So my son came and all three of us signed up.[278]

Anna C's testimony is reminiscent of the statement of the then chairman of the MNV cited above, according to whom the decision reached by a few individuals was crucial in respect of the implementation of resettlement as a whole, since they were able to entice others. At the same time, this also reveals a gendered element to the policy in practice. Anna C mentioned this in passing when, referring to the attitudes and actions of the men as the natural representatives of individual families, she affirmed the normality of the patriarchal order. However, other women interviewed by Hübschmannová had spoken of their own interests and experiences in greater detail.

Mária Š (born 1937), wife of Michal Š, the brother of Vasiľ Š, agreed with the others that the settlement in Šemetkovce was threatened by landslides during the rainy season and stated that "that's **probably** why we moved here [to Czechia]" (emphasis J. O.). Though she claims to have had some information at her disposal, overall Mária Š describes the decision to go along with resettlement as the result of external pressures.

---

276 Archive of MRK, Brno, f. Pozůstalost Mileny Hübschmannové, kart. 14_ET, sp. Transkripty 70_MH, č. III/3.
277 Archive of MRK, Brno, f. Pozůstalost Mileny Hübschmannové, kart. 11_ET, sp. Transkripty 77-83_MH, č. 28.
278 Archive of MRK, Brno, f. Pozůstalost Mileny Hübschmannové, kart. 14_ET, sp. Transkripty 70_MH, č. III/5.

When reflecting upon the uncertain future that the resettled Roma faced, she also hinted at a gendered difference in approach:

MH: Did you want to leave or stay?
Well, we didn't know what it was going to be like here.
MH: Nobody knew?
They came to look around, but they didn't live here, they just reconnoitred things.[279]

In addition to the fact that they only had the opportunity to "reconnoitre" the new environment but not to live there directly, it is worth pointing out that it was the men who paid visits to the Jičín district, as confirmed by Michal Š (husband of Mária Š).[280] Further on in her interview, Mária Š suggests that people's different expectations may have been related to their diverse experiences of residence in Czechia in the past. Although entire families sometimes decamped to Czechia in order to work, this often involved more a seasonal labour migration usually undertaken by male work groups, while the women stayed at home in the role of housewives and caregivers. Reflecting upon the uncertainty and disappointment of conditions in the new environment, Mária Š referred to the compulsory military service that men from Slovakia undertook in Czechia:

We came here completely goggle-eyed. We'd never been to Czechia before, or rather I hadn't. My husband had at least been in the army.[281]

The most open, concrete description of gendered experiences and expectations was that of Marika M:

MH: Did you want to move to Czechia or remain in Slovakia?

---

279 Archive of MRK, Brno, f. Pozůstalost Mileny Hübschmannové, kart. 14_ET, sp. Transkripty 70_MH, č. III/4.
280 Ibid. It is known from other places that men and women's expectations may have differed in this respect. For example, Július Ž, according to his own complaint, agreed to the "liquidation" of his own "shack" in the village of Jarovnice (district of Prešov) and to being relocated to Chrudim in eastern Bohemia, a place he had visited in the past. However, his wife was dissatisfied with the new accommodation and so the couple and their children returned to Slovakia, where Július Ž applied unsuccessfully for a resident permit. ŠAKE Košice, f. Komisia Vsl. KNV pre cigánske obyvatelstvo, kart. 20, sp. 93/68. "Ž. Július", 8 October 1968.
281 Archive of MRK, Brno, f. Pozůstalost Mileny Hübschmannové, kart. 14_ET, sp. Transkripty 70_MH, č. III/4.

I didn't want to come here. My parents didn't want me to leave because they live like the gentry in Kružlová in Slovakia. But I had got married to a man from another village [Šemetkovce], so I simply had to go with them. My parents didn't want to see me leave, my husband was on national service, and you know how it is with the G*psies – if I hadn't gone with them that means I was unfaithful. I simply had to go and leave my family [parents and siblings] behind.[282]

The quandary Marika M found herself in was mainly due to the fact that she had moved to Šemetkovce from Kružlová, another village in the district of Svidník (at that time Bardejov), where, according to Marika, her parents "lived like the gentry". Such a practice was in accordance with the dominant patriarchal and patrilocal model, typical of rural areas in Slovakia (see, for example, Kandert 2004; Kobes 2009), according to which a woman moved, if not directly into the household, then at the very least into the village of her new husband or partner, thus essentially becoming part of his extended family. While this position had previously permitted Marika M to reveal and articulate the everyday oppression of the Roma of Šemetkovce by their non-Romani neighbours (see above), in the context of resettlement it meant the necessity of submitting to the decisions of her husband or his extended family, and consequently to the decisions of other Romani families living in Šemetkovce. The situation described is at the same time another important reminder of the diverse positions of the Roma in individual municipalities, and ultimately points to the fact that kinship and other social and economic relations cannot be defined by village boundaries, much as one might be tempted down that path not only by the perspective of the local authorities, but also my own delineation of individual case studies (see also the migration of the Roma to the borderlands, see the third part of this chapter). This gendered perspective serves as a reminder that a sense of belonging to locally defined Romani communities is a matter of dynamic negotiation within broader socio-economic networks and is largely subject to a patrilocal model (see Ort 2022b).

Marika M not only implied that downward socio-economic mobility, including a deterioration in the quality of her overall living conditions, had resulted from her marriage, but also said that the relocation of the

---

282 Archive of MRK, Brno, f. Pozůstalost Mileny Hübschmannové, kart. 14_ET, sp. Transkripty 70_MH, č. III/7.

Roma from Šemetkovce to the Jičín district ultimately meant a severing of contact with her own parents and siblings. When asked by Hübschmannová whether her parents did not want to move in with her, Marika M offered an eloquent response that hinted at the relativity of the socio-economic mobility achieved.

No way, each of them has their own villa, car, garden, they have a wonderful life. Nobody here in the village or in Jičín has it as good as they do.[283]

What for many Romani families from Slovakia would have been a welcome improvement in living standards would for others, in this particular instance, have represented a step backwards in material terms, not to speak of the uncertainty provoked by the new environment.

4.5.6 Resettlement and the production of movement

In the interviews with those Romani people who experienced the resettlement programme, descriptions of its implementation tend to be brief. Perhaps only Marika M offers a more detailed account, when she describes how they took only blankets, dishes and food from Šemetkovce and that they were taken to Jičín on several buses, where they waited for the next stage of "allocation".[284] This lack of detail makes the insights of Janeček, who was in charge of moving some of the families, all the more valuable. Because this is a unique description of the conditions under which the "organised transfer" took place, I am offering an abbreviated though nonetheless relatively long passage:

[W]hen we brought them [the resettled families] here to the courtyard of the ONV and then delivered each one in the evening, I was put in charge of one bus. [...] I personally transported the five families allocated to me like a cat carrying kittens all around the district... The fact that this took place at night meant that they couldn't see much of their surroundings, and so, for example, one family refused to get off the bus for the cottage they had been allocated in a remote part of Uhlíře in the Peckov region, saying that they would live like rabbits on that hillside. [...] At one point, three families expressed a desire

283 Ibid.
284 Ibid.

to move into one building, and we had to insist that each family had to live separately. [...] I was on the verge of despair. I still had two large families on the bus and I took them to a building that had not yet been bought up but was still in negotiations and I said: you'll like this, and they said they would. So I had to convince the owner [...] and when he saw the situation and was interested in selling his house [...] he agreed to our proposal. So we unloaded the luggage being carried by the relocated G*psies and loaded up his stuff. They helped us load up and I moved the guy from Tetín from the settlement of Vlkánov.[285]

A detail that stands out in what can only be described as a process of ongoing improvisation is the fact that the delivery of families to their "new" homes (often apparently quite isolated buildings that no one else was interested in) took place in the middle of the night. At that point, the parents and children were at the end of a long journey from the northeastern tip of Slovakia, a journey that Janeček says lasted two days due to frequent stops, with overnight stays on the bus itself. In response to a comment by Melč that it was "tough luck that they arrived late evening", Janeček claimed that "to leave them on the buses was unacceptable for health reasons".[286] Tellingly, he highlights the work of the truck drivers, who "after two days of arduous driving were still moving families in the district".[287] The undignified conditions faced by the families during the implementation of resettlement are illustrated by an observation in which Janeček relegates the families to the role of "kittens", as he puts it, that he, as the "cat", was to distribute around the district.[288]

According to Janeček, the first phase of resettlement was followed by a long period in which he personally dealt with requests from representatives of individual families and attempted to resolve problems with existing accommodation or find new housing. He said that "for a month [...] I did nothing else but [...] arrange things" (i.e. he found furniture, fixed stoves, moved families, etc.).[289] His experience led him to question the stereotypical view of the Roma as destroying their assigned apartments (see Hübschmannová 1999b, 135), as well as the thesis formulated.

285 Archive of MRK, Brno, f. Pozůstalost Mileny Hübschmannové, kart. 14_ET, sp. Transkripty 70_MH, č. III/3.
286 Ibid.
287 Ibid.
288 Ibid.
289 Ibid.

by Hübschmannová that the Roma from the settlements were not used to using the facilities located in urban apartments (see Hübschmannová 1993, 43):

> They receive a lot of abuse, but in practice it didn't seem to us that they were deliberately damaging anything [...] ripping up floors for lack of fuel or anything... there were other concerns, we tried to buy a washing machine, an electric oven, but the buildings weren't set up for them. So he [one of the Roma] said he wanted an electric oven, but it wasn't possible to plug it in with just one fuse.[290]

Although his description of the relationship he had with the Roma was extremely paternalistic, even Janeček portrayed them as agents who refused to live "like rabbits on a hillside" and actively articulated their own preferences in dealings with the authorities.

The unsatisfactory conditions of the new housing, including its distance from any employment opportunities, were recalled by the Roma in their interviews with Hübschmannová. In this respect, it is worth highlighting something that Marika M says, who at the time of the interview had submitted an application for the allocation of new accommodation (from which she would not have had to travel so far to work) directly to Czechoslovak President Husák, having received no satisfaction from the ONV in Jičín. She even had a plan to "get to him" during a visit to Prague ("during the holidays with the children") and "have a normal conversation with him about how and what". She based her sense of entitlement on the conviction that "these days everyone is building a welfare system, not only the *gadje*, the G*psies are also part of it, maybe even more so, because all of the *gadje* Czechs are escaping to where the work is easier."[291]

It was the inadequate housing, either of poor quality or far from employment opportunities, that was the main factor that led certain families to leave their assigned homes ("premises"). This initial change of residence was reported by all the Roma interviewed by Hübschmannová and Melč. Janeček corroborated matters and said that after two weeks,

---

290 Ibid.
291 Archive of MRK, Brno, f. Pozůstalost Mileny Hübschmannové, kart. 14_ET, sp. Transkripty 70_MH, č. III/7.

none of the relocated families remained in their original location.[292] It is clear from the story of family Š described above that relations between the individual parties involved, be they the Roma or their non-Romani neighbours, also impacted the decision to move. Drawing on what are unusually detailed empirical materials in this context, the example of the resettlement of families from Šemetkovce corroborates the findings of other researchers, to wit, that even in their new abode, the resettled families found themselves in unstable living conditions and a precarious position, often having been allocated housing and employment that other residents had no interest in (see Donert 2017, 167–168; Guy 1977, 319–318). It also shows that the "organised transfer", which was supposed to facilitate greater oversight of the movement of the Roma, not only failed to reduce "arbitrary migration" (see Guy 1977), but actually encouraged it. This involved not only relocation within the same district, but even cross-border movement, with some families returning to Slovakia and others to their relatives in the Jičín district. This movement was alluded to by representatives of the authorities (who deemed it undesirable) in their interviews with Hübschmannová. In his interview, Janeček said that it tended to be individuals rather than families who returned to Slovakia by train, though he added that they were "back within a week".[293] According to him, in "maybe two cases" the movement was in the opposite direction on the part of grandparents who were not from Šemetkovce but from a different village. Their presence in the district was not tolerated by the ONV, which Janeček explained was consistent with the logic of "dispersion", as well as with the broader fear amongst the general public of an increase in the "G*psy population":

> So we had to step in forcibly and tell them that we would not allow an increase in their number, the result being that after a week or two they returned to Slovakia.[294]

Chairman Železniak described a similarly uncompromising approach towards the families returning to Šemetkovce. He cited the case of Peter Š, who returned with his entire family even in advance of the buses which transported the Roma to Jičín, only to find that his shack in

---

292 Archive of MRK, Brno, f. Pozůstalost Mileny Hübschmannové, kart. 14_ET, sp. Transkripty 70_MH, č. III/3.
293 Ibid.
294 Ibid.

Šemetkovce had already been demolished. Železniak recounted that this man had received threats that if he did not leave of his own accord, he would be handed over to the "cops" (the National Security Corps) and would have to pay their costs as well as his own. Peter Š was in such a state that the authorities relented and lent him money, and so "the G*psy left in the morning".[295] Unlike the family that managed to return from Přerov to their house in Kapišová that had not yet been demolished and thus maintain the continuity of the Romani presence in the village (see the Introduction), in Šemetkovce, thanks to an unwillingness to compromise on the part of the authorities, such a return was not possible, and it would appear that no Roma have lived in the village since then. In an interview from 1979, Železniak added that the resettled Roma continued to return to Slovakia, mainly to their relatives in Kapišová, but also to the village where they had originally lived. He added that, while previously "everyone was afraid of them, now they are popular".[296] As I will discuss below, this ongoing movement points to the maintenance of broader cross-border social networks that included not only Romani relatives, but in a sense also their non-Romani neighbours in Slovakia, for well nigh fifteen years after the resettlement.

4.5.7 Nostalgia for Slovakia and cross-border socio-economic networks

When probing into the story of Vasiľ and Helena Š, who had their children taken into care by the authorities following the former's imprisonment, Hübschmannová suggests that the implementation of the central resettlement programme played an important role in their turbulent fortunes. In the questions she asks, as well as the notes she made in the margins of the interview transcripts, she sheds light on the uprooting involved, namely, the disruption of both established networks of socio-economic relations and the transmission of cultural values within the Romani community itself. I do not want to take issue with criticism of the central policy, which is in line with what Hübschmannová wrote about it. However, with the benefit of hindsight and an awareness that Hübschmannová was interested in a broader-based critique of the

---

295 Archive of MRK, Brno, f. Pozůstalost Mileny Hübschmannové, kart. 11_ET, sp. Transkripty 77-83_MH, č. 28.
296 Ibid.

communist regime, I have been able to track stories told by the Roma that necessitate a more complex view of the content and implementation of the programme. At the same time I am aware that unlike Hübschmannová, I have not met these people in person and lack a knowledge of the circumstances surrounding the interviews.

The interviews with the Roma undoubtedly include testimony that supports the criticism earlier formulated by Hübschmannová. Marika M regretted the loss of contact with her parents and siblings.[297] Mária Š spoke of the insecurity of the new environment and the loss of day-to-day bonds: she had been "used to everyone being Roma and suddenly she lived amongst the *gadje*".[298] At the same time, the testimony contained in the interviews threw doubt upon the vision of Czechia as the promised land for the Roma. In answer to a direct question from Hübschmannová regarding what life had been like in Slovakia and whether "there were better *gadje*" there, Helena Š was unequivocal:

> There were better *gadje* there! In Slovakia they go and bring back milk and potatoes, and in this way they offer assistance.[299]

While this testimony supports the idea that the Roma were lower down the pecking order within the hierarchy of socio-economic relations in the rural areas of eastern Slovakia, it also indicates that a degree of socio-economic security was associated with village life in this region. Michal Š also spoke of relations with the non-Romani villagers in Šemetkovce, and said that when he returns to Slovakia (at the time of the interview), the non-Romani villagers invite him into their homes "one by one" (*kher kherestar*), and that on his last visit "they got him so drunk that he had no idea what was going on".[300] Hübschmannová herself noted in the margin of the transcript that this contrasts with Marika M's testimony regarding the humiliation of the Roma in Šemetkovce. Taking into account the assessment of similar visits by the former chairman of the MNV, who said that "everyone was afraid of them, now they are popular", these statements do not have

---

297 Archive of MRK, Brno, f. Pozůstalost Mileny Hübschmannové, kart. 14_ET, sp. Transkripty 70_MH, č. III/7.
298 Archive of MRK, Brno, f. PozůstalostMileny Hübschmannové, kart. 14_ET, sp. Transkripty 70_MH, č. III/4.
299 Archive of MRK, Brno, f. PozůstalostMileny Hübschmannové, kart. 9_ET, sp. Transkripty_ MH, č. 110.
300 Archive of MRK, Brno, f. Pozůstalost Mileny Hübschmannové, kart. 14_ET, sp. Transkripty 70_MH, č. III/4.

to be interpreted as exposing an inconsistency, but rather as two deeply rooted, albeit contradictory, ideologies that are manifest situationally (see Gal 1993, 1995). In this particular situation they can also be interpreted in terms of the evolving context of the actualisation of the relationships described, i.e. from everyday interactions to one-off, time-limited visits to former neighbours. Even if there is an element of nostalgia to what Michal Š says, it is clear that within the context of resettlement one must not overlook the disruption and transformation of relationships not only between the resettled Roma themselves (including those Roma who remained in Slovakia in other villages), but also between the Roma and their non-Romani neighbours, employers, etc. Thus, when Hübschmannová speaks of an external intervention in established socio-cultural systems, one must look behind said systems at the complex network of actors, agency and relations. Such an approach to the situation as a whole allows for a shift in perspective, and now, accompanying the resettlement programme, we see not only the disruption of socio-economic networks of solidarity, but also a certain emancipatory potential, an opportunity for the Roma to break out of their subordinate position in these locally formed systems, as implied by Marika M in her testimony cited above.

4.5.8 The transformation of relationships from a gender perspective

In addition to the gendered contingency of the migratory experience and the severing of family ties in the case of the women who married into Šemetkovce, the testimony of those who underwent resettlement also suggests the need for a new understanding of the division of labour in terms of care for children and the household. Though not stated explicitly by the interviewees, it is evident that having families live in one place, namely, the village settlement, allowed for an intergenerational and broader-based communal distribution of care duties. In the new environment, with each family living separately and in locations often far from the place of work to which both parents commuted, childcare and household duties represented a new challenge and the possible reframing of entrenched gender roles.[301] In their interview with Hübschmannová, this

---

301 For a broader contextualisation of the position of women and the distribution of care in socialist Czechoslovakia, see, for example, Hamplová (2006) and Wagnerová (2017).

is articulated to a degree by Helena and Vasiľ Š, as they speak of the threat of their children being taken into care. The two parents observed that the need to commute to work meant they could not be with their children most of the day and were thus unable to supervise their school attendance.[302] Furthermore, next to the claim made by the director of the company Velveta, where Helena and Vasiľ both worked, that their adult son Ján Š often failed to turn up for work, Hübschmannová noted in the margin that Ján had to remain at home with his younger siblings.[303]

Marika M describes another situation in which she had to remain at home, because her husband was on compulsory national service at the time of the resettlement:

> To begin with [after arriving in Jičín] we lived in Libuň for about two months. I had to work for the JZD [Unified Agricultural Collective]. I really wanted to give it a good go, but I couldn't carry on working because my husband was in the army and I was receiving money for him. So I had to leave the job and remain at home for a while.[304]

She also describes the demands made upon her by life in a remote village. Her children were attending two different schools, she and her husband were commuting to work, and in order to do the shopping they had to travel to Jičín, returning home at eight o'clock in the evening, since by the time they returned home from work, the village store was already closed. Marika also complained of a lack of free time and the fact that, despite she and her husband "still being quite young", they could not go out socially ("to Jičín for a bit of fun"), because she had no one to look after the children.[305]

One might argue, albeit cautiously, that the division of labour as regards childcare and employment in their new home may have possessed a degree of emancipatory potential, since it led to a reshaping of entrenched gender roles. Marika M herself describes how, no longer living with her husband's parents (or in close proximity to his extended family), her husband "had to start listening to her" (she in fact states that

---

302 Archive of MRK, Brno, f. Pozůstalost Mileny Hübschmannové, kart. 11_ET, sp. Transkripty 77-83_MH, č. 38.
303 Archive of MRK, Brno, f. Pozůstalost Mileny Hübschmannové, kart. 11_ET, sp. Transkripty 77-83_MH, č. 37.
304 Archive of MRK, Brno, f. Pozůstalost Mileny Hübschmannové, kart. 14_ET, sp. Transkripty 70_MH, č. III/7.
305 Ibid..

he stopped drinking and beating her), and the full-time employment of both parents necessitated both becoming involved, to some extent at least, in household chores: "[I]f I have to go to work, then he has to look after things and cook."[306]

4.5.9 Resettlement and the logic of "dispersion"

Even though within the context of the precarious conditions of the new environment the interviewees express nostalgia for life in Slovakia, there is no fundamental criticism of the resettlement programme from the Romani side. Insofar as the Roma did not question the need to be relocated from the Šemetkovce settlement and, notwithstanding the diversity of positions (including gendered) involved, saw it as inevitable, they did not in principle contest the logic of dispersion. The interviews certainly reveal Hübschmannová's own sentiments, who criticised the programme for the way it disrupted intra-Romani relationships. In several places she reminds her readers of the saying "the family follows the family" (*fameľija pal e fameľija džal*, see Hübschmannová 1993, 31; 1999b, 127). This was echoed by Janeček, who in direct response noted that "for them [the resettled families] it was a terribly important to know [...] where their relatives lived, how they were to get there and how far away they lived, and the very next day they usually looked up all possible connections, whether by foot or by bus".[307] He added that "overcoming their habits [those of the Roma] was a really complex business and in many cases they even left their assigned house and crowded together, up to three families, in one building... This is what took place in Mlázovice, where we were assigned quite a large building somewhat remote from the village in what had been a spa but was now closed."[308] In interviews, however, the Roma themselves pointed more to the "remoteness" of the accommodation, or its distance from their jobs, than to the mutual separation of individual families. Similarly, when dealing with her own unsuitable housing, Marika M did not criticise the principle of the central policy, but how it was implemented in practice:

---

306 Ibid.
307 Archive of MRK, Brno, f. Pozůstalost Mileny Hübschmannové, kart. 14_ET, sp. Transkripty 70_MH, č. III/3.
308 Ibid.

Because I learned that the G*psies who moved here had huge opportunities /rumour has it/ [note by Hübschmannová]. The district of Jičín received a lot of money for them, except most of these G*psies couldn't read or write, so they didn't understand the papers and did their best to circumvent them, so things settled down and it's quiet and nobody knows anything of it. But I said to myself that I'm not having it, that I'll travel there [to Prague], I'll go there and talk about the situation with him [President Husák].[309]

When asked directly by Hübschmannová about the possibility of returning to Slovakia, Marika M replied that she did not want to go back, that she had "already got used to things here", and denied that she pined for the company of other Romani families:

Not at all, we have learned that we are best when we are alone like this.[310]

Mária Š expressed similar feelings. To begin with she said that "it bothered them [the Roma] that everyone ended up on their own" and that she was not used to living "among the *gadje*" (see above). But like Marika M, Mária subsequently admitted that she no longer wanted to change things (i.e. at the time the interview was conducted), and that she had "got used to it".[311] The preference for living away from other Roma that Marika M expressed was echoed by Vasiľ Š in his interview, in which he spoke of the poor relations he had with other Romani people, including his siblings (see above). His brother, the husband of Mária Š, felt similarly. He reflected upon the explanation offered to the Roma by the ONV in Jičín for the need for "dispersion", and with hindsight assessed it as justified:

We were told in the village that the way they had lived before, when they were G*psies together, that it didn't work, that it would be bad for the children and they wouldn't learn properly like other children. [...] But it's true, Janeček was right. The kids are in year five, they travel to school with me, each one of them

---

309 Archive of MRK, Brno, f. Pozůstalost Mileny Hübschmannové, kart. 14_ET, sp. Transkripty 70_MH, č. III/7. At the same time, the reference to the alleged misappropriation of funds by the district authorities illustrates the overall lack of access of information available to the resettled Roma.
310 Ibid.
311 Ibid.

can read and write, the girls can work machines [...] so it's different to when they were all G*psies together.[312]

I believe that such expressions of agreement with the content of the central policy on the part of Romani people whose lives were directly impacted by it cannot be simply brushed aside. In particular, Michal Š's testimony is fully in line with the official discourse on the "G*psy way of life" as a barrier to their full integration into socialist society. From this perspective it can perhaps be viewed as the acceptance of the dominant narrative ensuing from a regionally implemented awareness campaign. On the other hand, in this particular case one cannot underestimate the experience of the education on offer and the opportunities for the social participation of children, factors that may have been in stark contrast with the position of the Roma in the socio-economic hierarchy of the Slovak village and the segregated education on offer there, an education Marika M claimed was actually non-existent.[313] The preference for living independently of other Romani families can be interpreted in different ways. Vasiľ Š states that he sees other Roma and that "they visit him and chat with him, but he doesn't get along with them", and then adds that this has been the state of affairs since they have been in Czechia.[314] He adds that in Slovakia the older Roma were "kind of calmer", while in Czechia, the young especially, are "schemers who fight amongst themselves and spend time in jail", which is why he prefers to keep them at arm's length.[315] On the one hand, such an assessment supports Hübschmannová's claims regarding the disruption of relationships as a consequence of social engineering on the part of the state. At the same time, however, it chimes with broader migration narratives in which the new environment is associated not only with upward socio-economic mobility, but also with the loss of certain shared cultural values that are ascribed to the place of origin (see Gardner 1993), in this case the countryside of eastern Slovakia (see Guy 1977, 486; Ort and Dobruská

---

312 Archive of MRK, Brno, f. Pozůstalost Mileny Hübschmannové, kart. 14_ET, sp. Transkripty 70_MH, č. III/4.
313 Archive of MRK, Brno, f. Pozůstalost Mileny Hübschmannové, kart. 14_ET, sp. Transkripty 70_MH, č. III/7.
314 Archive of MRK, Brno, f. Pozůstalost Mileny Hübschmannové, kart. 11_ET, sp. Transkripty 77-83_MH, č. 38.
315 Ibid.

2023).[316] Reading Vasiľ Š's testimony through the lens of these migration narratives, it is clear that this is not a simple comparison of pre- and post-migration relationships. Yet his testimony cannot be discounted as merely misty-eyed nostalgic memories. Instead, it must be seen as bearing witness to the speaker's situation and his dissatisfaction at the time the interview was conducted (see Berdahl 1999).

However, the strategy of distancing oneself from other Roma must not be understood merely as the outcome of deteriorating inter-Roma relations, as Vasiľ Š suggests, but as part of a more general effort to break out of a homogenising and stigmatising view of G*psies (see Chapters Two and Three). As Michal Š continues, he highlights the possibility of speaking up for oneself or one's family:

> The *gadje* in Slovakia were good people, but here in Czechia or wherever, it's always "G*psy enclave", "G*psies together", "nothing but G*psies" all the time. But now they don't say such things and the children mix with the *gadje*. Things are different and everyone appreciates how we live.[317]

Moreover, in Michal Š's case the strategy of breaking free from the stigma of G*psyness does not conflict with the maintenance of relationships with other (related) Roma, just as the more general effort of the Roma to leave the settlement described earlier did not necessarily mean severing wider inter-Romani ties (see Chapter Three). Michal Š states this explicitly in response to a question posed by Hübschmannová that reflects her own implicit bias:

> **MH: Do you not miss your brothers and your relatives?**
> But we have families here, all of them. I have my mum, brother-in-law and a brother here.[318]

Janeček's statement that Romani people were first and foremost interested in connecting with other families (see above) need not be in conflict with a preference for a certain autonomy for individual

---

316 I have looked at the deterioration of relations and the disappearance of the values of the "old Roma" within the context of the construction of municipal housing on the site of the original Romani settlement in another village in north-eastern Slovakia (Ort 2021, 2022b).

317 Archive of MRK, Brno, f. Pozůstalost Mileny Hübschmannové, kart. 14_ET, sp. Transkripty 70_MH, č. III/4.

318 Ibid.

families. At the same time, inasmuch as Janeček spoke of a complex process of "overcoming habits" and the "clustering" of certain families,[319] this points both to his stereotypical ideas of the "G*psy way of life" and to the possible diverse preferences of individual families and their development over time. The strategy of individual families may have been different in a period of general uncertainty immediately after the (improvised) resettlement and almost fifteen years later, when the interviews were being conducted. At the same time, such developments may have been related to a gradual integration into local socio-economic structures rather than "overcoming the habits", as Janeček suggests, and converged upon more broadly described Romani strategies of sociability (see Chapters Two and Three).

Finally, the testimony of the Roma of Šemetkovce shows that their resettlement cannot be separated from the broader migratory movement of the Roma from other places in Slovakia. Just as the socio-economic networks of the Roma in Slovakia transcended the borders of individual municipalities, so post-war migration expanded them into a wider "transnational" social field (see the situation in the borderlands, section three of this chapter). This is well illustrated in the testimony of Anna C, who lists her kinship ties not only in Slovakia but also within a relatively wide area of Czechia. She refers to a son in Slovakia, another son in Úpice near Trutnov (north Bohemia), a daughter near Budějovice (south Bohemia), and daughters in Most and Nová Paka (west and north Bohemia). In addition, her maternal cousins lived in Prague.

4.6 Conclusion

The chapters on the removal of the Romani settlements and the relocation of their inhabitants make clear that the position and agency of the Roma are characterised by a state of constant ambiguity. I have shown that, though it was the idea of "dispersing the G*psies" in order to assimilate them and facilitate their supervision that was the target of criticism in post-revolutionary historical publications especially, the vocal critics of dispersion at the time were not so much the Roma themselves, but the non-Romani population of both Slovakia and Czechia. Through

---

319 Archive of MRK, Brno, f. Pozůstalost Mileny Hübschmannové, kart. 14_ET, sp. Transkripty 70_MH, č. III/3.

their representation in the local authorities (National Committees), this segment of the population eventually became the main obstacle to the implementation of "transfer" and "dispersion" according to the set time-table. In an effort to develop these positions more comprehensively in the light of the practice of the policy in specific regions and munici-palities, I have shown that the resettlement of Roma according to the logic of dispersion cannot be satisfactorily separated from the broader phenomenon of their post-war migration as an agentive strategy of socio-economic mobility. There are several reasons why this is the case. First-ly, the ongoing two-way migration of the Roma between Slovakia and Czechia was part of the broader motivation of the central authorities to agree on a "comprehensive solution to the G*psy question", since the government resolution under consideration represented an ongoing attempt to control the movement of the Roma. Secondly, inasmuch as this "arbitrary" migration was to be replaced by an "organised transfer", the implementation of the government resolution had in this respect fai-led. Moreover, the implementation of an organised transfer, like earlier efforts to restrict movement, led to the generation of greater movement. Thirdly, in terms of the position of the Roma in locally formed hierar-chies of socio-economic relations, migration and resettlement were based on similar structural contingencies. Thus if the level claimed of voluntary participation on the part of the Roma in the resettlement programme has been rightly questioned, it is likewise necessary to recall the broader structural pressures and marginalisation of the Roma as pivotal when examining their other migratory movements. From this perspective, even taking into account the role of earlier labour recruitment drives, the boundaries between different forms of cross-border Romani move-ment become blurred. The factor that most sharply distinguishes cont-rolled resettlement from migration is that, in addition to the anticipated removal of the settlements, the implementation of the resettlement pro-gramme was intended to bring the two-way cross-border movement of the Roma to a complete halt. When all was said and done, this target, too, was not achieved. Finally, as I have shown in this chapter, resettle-ment and migration cannot be separated from each other even in respect of the continued maintenance of Romani relationships within a certain "transnational" social field across Czechia and Slovakia, including rela-tions between the Roma in different regions in Czechia.

Understanding the resettlement of the Roma within the context of a broader transnational social field (see for example Basch et al. 1994; Glick-Schiller 1995; Szaló 2007; and for the given context also

Ort and Dobruská 2023), which included various non-Romani actors, allowed me to develop and reshape the critique of the resettlement policy, according to which it was an intervention akin to social engineering in the socio-economic strategies and established socio-cultural systems of the Roma themselves. When analysing the materials that Hübschmannová herself acquired in her capacity as the main (and basically only) public supporter of the criticism thus articulated, I have shown that the Roma found themselves in the position of "evictable" citizens (see van Baar 2016), dehumanised objects to be resettled. However, if one is pointing to the social engineering of established systems, one must also note – and the examples presented in this book demonstrate this quite clearly – that in these systems the Roma have historically been continuously relegated to a subordinate position in local racialised hierarchies of relations. From this perspective, external intervention now acquires a certain emancipatory potential, or, like migration, the potential for upward socio-economic mobility. The situation can also be viewed from the perspective of gender. While the resettlement of the Roma, but also more broadly the migratory context, may have disrupted established gender roles, the challenge raised vis-à-vis the division of labour in the sphere of childcare and household duties in the new environment also embodied a degree of emancipatory potential and the possibility of a more egalitarian reframing of entrenched roles within Romani families (see for example George 2005, 78–118).

In the case of the Romani people originally from Šemetkovce, one can discern a certain ambivalence in their formulated attitudes and experiences, a kind of vacillation between the social security of the eastern Slovak countryside (which, however, was at the expense of the naturally subordinate position of the Roma) on the one hand, and the relative socio-economic mobility and greater room for manoeuvre in negotiating one's own social position (albeit in a new, unfamiliar environment) on the other. I have shown that, in addition to a certain nostalgia for the familiar environment of the eastern Slovak countryside and clearly defined relationships, the Roma also formulated their own strategy for exiting the homogenised image of G*psyness in the new environment, specifically by emphasising their independence from other Roma. This emphasis, though it converged with the objectives of the resettlement programme and its logic of dispersion, did not necessarily come into conflict with the continued maintenance of ties between individual Romani families, which I observed not only in the Jičín district but also in the border region.

Even in the new environment of the borderlands, this strategy had its limits, since the Roma arriving from Slovakia after the war continued to be associated with the category of G*psyness, now supplemented with a locally contingent history of its understanding. While the Roma in the rural environment of eastern Slovakia had an unequal but historically anchored position in locally formed socio-economic structures, in Czechia they acquired the image of orientalised immigrants and (latent) nomads. From this perspective the Roma became a dual object of central policy, both as inhabitants of "G*psy settlements" and as "fluctuants", whose movements were to be subject to restriction and control. In contrast to this exclusionary image, the Roma were able to quickly establish themselves in local relations, in many cases as a much sought-after workforce (see Sadílková 2018). In addition to local employers (see Hübschmannová's interview with the director of Velveta, see also Ort 2022a), this aspect was highlighted by the Roma themselves (see the narrative of the sisters Monika H and Marcela S in this chapter).

Conclusion

When the Czech journalist Saša Uhlová described the historical roots of the marginalisation of the Romani people in the Czech Republic in 2023, she devoted a large part of her text to the impact of the assimilationist policies of the communist regime, specifically the resettlement policy of the 1960s. Uhlová recapitulates the theses regarding the fatal erosion of Romani identity and cultural values. And inasmuch as she grants that the Roma themselves, including the main protagonist of her text, "Grandmatriarch Jolana" (*bába Jolana*), feel rather positively about this period, she explains this as the effect of nostalgia triggered by socio- -economic decline and the racist attacks suffered by the Roma in the 1990s (Uhlová 2023).

I mention Uhlová's text here because it sheds light on the broader way in which the history of the Roma during the communist period in particular, as well as Romani history in general, is still approached in Czechia. Uhlová's text was published in the cultural bi-weekly journal A2, which generally publishes studies that approach the situation before 1989 and the way it is perceived by different layers of society with caution and avoids one-sided judgements of the violence of the totalitarian regime. However, even here, the Roma are potrayed primarily as victims of the assimilationist policies, whose positive relationship to the period is largely downplayed by the author, who believes that such a relationship could only have been achieved by virtue of the "wild nineties drowning out memories" (ibid.). Similarly, although revisionist historians no longer view the population of Czechoslovakia as merely passive victims of the totalitarian regime, but grant them agency in the formation and mainte- nance of its legitimacy (Pullmann 2011), the Roma seem to have remained trapped in the position of a silent group of "eternal outsiders" (see, for example, Sadílková's polemic with Spurný, Sadílková 2013; Spurný 2011).

In the case of Uhlová, another factor may have been the author's long-standing endeavour to name anti-Roma racism and to place it in its proper historical context. This is understandable in a situation in which anti-Roma racism continues to be downplayed in public. However, as I have shown in this book, the narrative presented by Uhlová represents a more widespread interpretation of the situation of the Roma in communist Czechoslovakia that has been repeated somewhat uncriticially in various texts about Romani history, both scholarly or popular, since the 1990s at the latest. In the case of Uhlová, this is no coincidence – she herself was a student of Milena Hübschmannová at Prague school of Romani studies (Charles University). It is Hübschmannová who has repeatedly articulated this story in her capacity as an authority in the field.

Although Hübschmannová herself can hardly be accused of a simplistic and homogenising view of Romani culture, her criticism of the assimilationist policy comes up against certain limits that perhaps stem from her positionality, in which the role of a researcher with a profound interest in the Roma, as well as an activist and defender of the rights of a particular group of people, intersected. This book relies on Hübschmannová's texts in many respects. Indeed, without her input it would have lacked a great deal of ethnographic detail (this is especially true of Chapter Four). This is rare in a historical study and is in sharp contrast with the work of those historians who have focused more on the "history of anti-G*psyism" rather than a "history of the Roma" (see Baloun 2022, 15–24), and who, when examining policies targeting the Roma, left their actual interests and opinions to one side. This book seeks to revise the prevailing view of resettlement policy in particular, and the assimilationist policy of the communist regime in general, by attempting to step outside a strongly evaluative interpretative framework, while at the same time presenting the perspectives of the Roma more faithfully and precisely.

In order to capture the diverse agentive positions, experiences and attitudes of the Roma, they must be removed from the position of an *a priori* homogenised group situated on the outside, and perceived as integral parts of society, including of state structures. Such an approach must at the same time not ignore the fact that, though representatives of such a defined group of the population may have been marginalised and excluded at various times, they may have also actively formed their own ideas about the world and their place in society (see Ort 2022b).

I believe it would be useful to apply such an approach in further research into the position of the Roma in (central) Europe, here, specifically, in order to understand the position of the Roma in the society of communist Czechoslovakia. As regards the implementation of the resettlement programme, using this perspective it is possible to consider not only its impact on the socio-cultural systems of the Roma, but also on the sometimes unexpected practices negotiated within broader, locally rooted networks of actors and relations. I have shown that these relations, in the case of eastern Slovakia, were strongly interwoven with historically embedded racial hierarchies. If, therefore, we extend the theory of the disruption of established socio-economic structures postulated by criticism up till now to encompass the whole of the racialised hierarchies of relations thus conceived of, a policy accentuating the "dispersion of the G*psy population" may be seen as possessing emancipatory potential for the Roma themselves. Such a strategy, however, also led me to attempt a vague delineation of who was ultimately affected by the central policy. The officially defined and locally reinterpreted category of G*psyness did not only determine (non-)inclusion in the primary target group of the resettlement programme, but also participated in the structuring of local relations, not only between the Roma and non-Roma, but also between the Roma themselves (see Chapter Two). Looked at from this perspective, the resettlement policy did not "only" affect the lives of individual families, but had the potential to transform the shape of socio-economic relations in specific places. On the basis of the material presented, we can note the marked heterogeneity of the positions of individual actors within the defined social field, which pulls the rug from under the notion of the state on the one hand, and the Roma on the other, each seen as clearly homogenous agents. Indeed, the boundary of the relationship between the state and its inhabitants becomes blurred at this point. It was not only their non-Romani neighbours that shaped regional political structures, but in many places the Roma themselves, who might be members not only of local councils, but also officials at the district level, such as Mr Goroľ, originally from Podskalka, and Mr Oláh of Stakčín. The adventitious implementation of the centrally defined resettlement policy also depended on these different positions and complex relations in locally anchored socio-economic structures.

With its application of anthropological strategies to historical research, this book can also be seen as a contribution to the debate surrounding methods of researching Romani histories. As much as I have attempted to meet the challenge to examine marginal spaces (see

Chapter One) and to reveal the positions of individual actors during the implementation of the policy under consideration, I have come up against clear limitations as regards the available sources. I have often had to settle for tentative stabs at possible interpretations and directions for further research, without the opportunity to verify them in detail. I was only partially able to supplement archival research with oral history interviews, and in many cases these were mediated recollections of the period under review. Nonetheless, I believe that however much historical research will always be fragmented in nature, it is important to keep in mind its connection to the discipline of anthropology as a kind of internal imperative that, inter alia, can help disrupt dominant concepts and categories and here, for example, broaden the way the diversity of Romani agency is understood.

In addition to examining the implications of the resettlement policy within broader socio-economic systems, I also contextualised individual case studies historically, which permitted me to name the (dis)continuities of certain historical processes. Crucially in respect of this book, the implementation of the resettlement programme was inextricably intertwined with the life strategies of the Roma. Relocating from Slovakia to Czechia cannot be separated from migration as a distinct agentive strategy, even though both had their deeper structural causes, namely, racial exclusion in the already marginalised region of eastern Slovakia. The attempt to remove the settlements cannot be separated from the longer-term phenomenon of the mobility of individual families from these distinctive places. The latter type of mobility included not only migration to Czechia, but also movement from the settlements as stigmatised and often unsatisfactory places in terms of standards of living within the framework of the villages themselves (see Chapter Three). In light of these efforts, the "dispersional" logic of the resettlement policy cannot be separated from the yearnings of individual families for a certain spatial and socio-economic autonomy, which may have also been related to the migratory context (see Chapter Four). After all, the logic of the officially promulgated category of G*psyness also encountered certain ways of defining relations deployed by the Roma themselves, who drew on the postulated category of "civilised/decent G*psies" in their understanding of their own social status, which was based not only on their relationship to the dominant category of G*psyness, but also to specific Roma (groups of Roma) as its alleged embodiment.

On the other hand it must be emphasised that the contents of the central policy were not always fully in line with the interests of the

Roma, however diverse these interests may have been. While the emphasis placed on the removal of settlements may have been an opportunity for individual spatial and ensuing social mobility for specific Romani people, the officially imposed restrictions on movement may instead have been a tool using which local authorities were able to maintain the territorialisation of the Roma. Similarly, the emphasis on relocation to Czechia may have been an opportunity to evict the Roma definitively from specific villages (see Chapter Three). Above all, however, it is clear that the Roma themselves were not necessarily subject to assimilationist pressures when, even accepting aspects of the logic of the central policy, they sought to maintain their distinctive cultural values, just as "dispersion" did not necessarily mean breaking ties with other Romani families. At the same time, as I have shown in the example of Podskalka, not even the way the settlements were looked at by the Roma was necessarily fully subservient to the dominant logic, which framed them as spaces of social deviance and "cultural backwardness".

However, even given the criticism of the resettlement policy in Romani studies literature, it is striking that the Roma themselves rarely criticised the principles of the programme, but instead spoke of how it had failed in practice or been applied inconsistently by the local authorities. Like the resettled farmers in Laos, the Roma in Czechoslovakia projected their desires and expectations onto state policy, and their diverse agency in relation to its implementation in practice can be understood in terms of "experimental consent" (High 2005, 2008). The ambivalence of the Romani attitudes and actions presented here can thus be read not only in terms of the diversity of their experiences and social positions, but also as the negotiation of their relationship with the state and their perception of its different faces (see Das and Poole 2004). At the same time, Romani agency should not only be seen in terms of the assertion of their own interests, but as a way of adapting to existing conditions and accepting seemingly irreversible processes. This is clear in what Elemír T said regarding the inevitability of his house being demolished (Chapter Three) and in the testimony of the Roma of Šemetkovce about having to leave the life-threatening conditions in the local settlement (Chapter Four).

Even in light of the points of intersection with existing processes and the continuity of specific emphases in the policy toward the G*psies, it would be wrong to think of the resettlement programme as a temporally delineated, unnatural and violent intervention in the lives of the Roma, which began with Government Resolution 502/1965 and ended with the declared failure and abolition of the Government Committee on Gypsy Population Issues. Given the material presented, it is questionable just how great this intervention was, especially in view of the significant failure to implement what had originally been its grandiose plans. In my conversations with Romani people who witnessed the events of that time, I often had to explain what the policy had been, since it was clear that it had not left much of an imprint on the wider local memory. As regards the district of Humenné, the "organised transfer" affected only a few individual families: far larger numbers were involved in the ongoing migration. In addition to the fact that the policy under scrutiny may have aligned in multiple ways with the interests of the Roma themselves, another question relates to the extent to which it ultimately affected their lives in Czechoslovakia.

When studying Romani agency in its various historical and social contexts, a dilemma arises as to the extent to which it is appropriate to shine a spotlight on said agency given the often high level of historically rooted, structural anti-Roma racism. In other words, one has to ask whether the study of Romani agency does not involve an element of tokenism if it ignores the extent to which Romani lives are predetermined by the normativity of the non-Romani world. In this regard I agree with the editors of the anthology *Gypsy Economy*, who have expressed their belief that an appropriate response to anti-Roma racism is not to view the Roma as passive victims, but to examine ethnographically their creativity in response to it (Brazzabeni et al. 2015). I believe that the history of the Roma cannot be simply separated from the history of anti-Roma racism, however necessary it is not to view the former as being in thrall to the latter (see Olivera and Poueyto 2018). On the other hand, I am convinced that even a basic attempt to study anti-Roma racism cannot be achieved without taking into account the agency of the Roma, who are not an isolated group of the population standing outside society, but an integral part of the structures being examined. If I apply the above dilemma retrospectively to the material presented in this book, I am obliged to point out that what defined the room for manoeuvre for Romani agency and the realisation of their life strategies were the deeper structural conditions and historically rooted racialised hierarchies of the eastern Slovak countryside, rather than any intervention resulting directly from the implementation of the resettlement programme (see Guy 1977, 1998). Again, I am not saying one should ignore the discriminatory aspects of the central policy, which was suffused with structural racism by its very nature while remaining in thrall to the logic of G*psyness as a naturally inferior mode of being from which it was necessary to break free. In this context, however, it is striking that in the post-war history of the Roma in Czechoslovakia (and by extension in central and eastern Europe), two relatively homogenised epochs are distinguished, with the period of the communist regime being characterised by paternalistic, social engineering and violent policies (at least on the level of symbolic violence), and the post-1989 period featuring a sharp rise in overt racism that accompanied official proclamations of the minority rights of the Roma as a distinctive ethnic and cultural group of people. This book disrupts such a demarcation both by analysing anti-Roma racism as a deep-rooted phenomenon and a key factor in the social exclusion and marginalisation of the Roma prior to 1989 (in this respect one is entitled to speak of a certain historical continuity, see Sokolová 2008), but also through the form of the central policies themselves. A long-term concern for the "G*psy population" was replaced in the wake of the Velvet Revolution of 1989 by a long-absent policy that would relate to the Roma as a group (see also Donert 2017). This was in a situation in which the Roma faced a significant increase in socio-economic exclusion accompanied by anti-Roma attacks and racially motivated murders following the collapse of the previous socio-economic structures. Moreover, even during this period, laws were passed that could be viewed as driven by racial discrimination, thus officially challenging the equal status of the Roma as a group (see the 1993 Citizenship Act, e.g. Miklušáková 1999). Even in respect of developments after 1989, contrary to the prevailing narrative, the resettlement policy can be seen as a state policy that in a hitherto unprecedented way articulated centrifugally the necessity of eliminating racist attitudes in society as a condition for improving the living conditions of the Roma. This was not an abstract struggle against prejudice, but a targeting of concrete institutions, above all local authorities as key actors in the implementation of the policies under scrutiny. And so even in light of the experiences and beliefs of the Roma themselves, the greatest failure of the resettlement programme can ultimately be seen as residing not in the way it intervened aggressively in existing Romani socio-cultural structures, but in the sheer toothlessness of the instruments created to eliminate anti-Roma attitudes. This was all the more evident by virtue of the fact that the assimilationist logic of the central policy reproduced G*psyness as a category of social deviation, while at the same time being unable to free it from ethno-racial characteristics.

References

Published documents

Jurová, A. 2008. Rómska menšina na Slovensku v dokumentoch, 1945–1975. Košice: Spoločenskovedný ústav SAV.

Archives

Archive of MRK (Museum of Romani Culture), Brno
Archive of RTVS (Radio and Television of Slovakia), Bratislava
NA (National Archives), Prague
SOkA (State Archives), Děčín
ŠOkA (State Archives), Bardejov
ŠOkA (State Archives), Humenné
ŠAPO (State Archives), Nižná Šebastová
ŠOkA (State Archives), Svidník
ŠAKE (State Archives), Košice
ZAO (Regional Archives), Opava

Chronicles

Kronika obce Brekov (Chronicle of Brekov municipality)
Kronika obce Nové Lublice (Chronicle of Nové Lublice municipality)

Interviews

Ján Š (b. 1933), Ľubiša, Slovak language, April 2015 (unrecorded).
Koloman Gunár (b. 1948), Brekov, Slovak language, May 2019 (recording in the possession of the author).
Štefan K (b. 1960) and Jolana K. (b. 1961), Podskalka, Romani language, May 2019 and July 2021 (recordings in possesion of the author).
Elemír T. (b. 1940), Podskalka, Romani language, May 2019 (recording in the possession of the author).
Mária K. (b. 1950), Stakčín, Romani language, May 2019 (recording in the possession of the author).
Dušan K (b. 1965), Snina, Slovak language, May 2019 (recording in the possession of the author).

Mayor of the municipality of Hostovice, Hostovice, Slovak language, August 2020 (recording in the possession of the author).

Ján Ž (b. 1946), Papín, Slovak language, July 2021 (recording in the possession of the author).

Monika H (b. 1971) and Marcela S (b. 1977), Dolní Podluží, Czech language, September 2021 and February 2022 (recordings in the possession of the author).

Pavlína B (b. 1948), Březno, Romani and Czech language, September 2021 (recording in the possession of the author).

Aladár D (b. 1950), online, Czech language, September 2021 (recording in the possession of the author).

Koloman S (b. 1946) and Cyril D (b. 1956), Brekov, Slovak language, June 2022 (recording in the possession of the author).

Olga G (b. 1938), Brekov, Slovak language, June 2022 (recording in the possession of the author).

Internet sources

Berkyová, R. 2018. 1. díl: Koncentrační tábor v Letech byl spálen. Písečtí úředníci chtěli po válce postavit pro Romy nový tábor. Online: https://romea.cz/cz/zaostreno/1-dil-koncentracni-tabor-v-letech-byl-spalen-pisecti-urednici-chteli-po-valce-postavit-pro-romy-novy-tabor/ [Accessed 22 July 2023]

Paměť Romů (n.d.). Online: https://www.pametromu.cz/ [Accessed 24 July 2023]

Prague Forum for Romani Histories (n.d.) Online: http://www.romanihistories.usd.cas.cz/home/ [Accessed 24 July 2023]

Súpis Židov (1942), Zoznam obcí okresu Vyšný Svidník (n.d.). Online: https://www.upn.gov.sk/projekty/supis-zidov/zoznam-obci/?okres=448 [Accessed 19 October 2019]

Synková, H. 2006. In the Czech Republic they call you 'Mister': The migration of Slovak Roma as a tactic to overcome exlusion. *migraceonline.cz*. 10. 4. 2006. Online: https://migrationonline.cz/en/e-library/in-the-czech-republic-they-call-you. [Accessed 17 October 2023]

Uhlová, S. 2023. Co bude s potomky báby Jolany? Příběh českých Romů. *A2* (11). [online] Online: https://www.advojka.cz/archiv/2023/11/co-bude-s-potomky-baby-jolany [Acessed 31 July 2023].

Vápenka Brekov (n.d.). Online: http://www.brekov.eu/30-vapenka.htm [Accessed 17 July 2023]

Literature

Abu Ghosh, Y. 2008. Escaping Gypsyness: Work, Power and Identity in the Marginalization of Roma. PhD thesis. Charles University, Prague.

Abu-Lughod, L. 1990. The Romance of Resistance: Tracing Transformation of Power Though Bedouin Women. *American Ethnologist* 17 (1): 41–55.

Agocs, A. 2003. Sociálna identifikácia Bajášov na Slovensku. *Etnologické rozpravy* 2: 41–53.

Ahmed, S. 2014. *The Cultural Politics of Emotion*. Edinburgh: Edinburgh University Press.

Anderson, B. 1983. *Imagined Communities: Reflections on the Origins and Spread of Nationalism*. London: New Left Book.

van Baar, H. 2016. Evictability and the Biopolitical Bordering of Europe. *Antipode: A Radical Journal of Geography* 49 (1): 212–230.

Baloun, P. 2022. *Metla našeho venkova! Kriminalizace Romů od první republiky až po prvotní fázi protektorátu (1918–1941)*. Praha: Scriptorium.

Basch, L., Glick-Schiller, N., Szanton-Blanc, C. 1994. *Nations Unbound: Transnational Projects, Postcolonial Predicaments, and Deterritorialized Nation-States*. London: George Allen.

bell hooks 1984. *Feminist Theory: From Margin to Center.* Boston: South End Press.

Berdahl, D. 1999. '(N)Ostalgie' for the Present: Memory, Longing, and East German Things. *Journal of Anthropology* 64 (2): 192–211.

Bourdieu, P. 1990. *The Logic of Practice.* Redwood City: Stanford University Press.

Bourdieu, P. 1977. *Outline of a Theory of Practice.* Cambridge: Cambridge University Press.

Braid, I., et al. 2009. Reading Too Much into Aspirations: More Explorations of the Space Between Coerced and Voluntary Resettlement in Laos. *Critical Asian Studies* 41 (1): 605–614.

Brazzabeni, M., Cunha, M. I., Fotta, M. 2015. Introduction. In *Gypsy Economy: Romani Livelihoods and Notions of Worth in the 21st Century*, ed. M. Brazzabeni et al., 1–30. New York, Oxford: Berghahn.

Burke, P. 1997. *Varieties of Cultural History.* New York: Cornell University Press.

Cichý, M. 2003. Historie rodu Cichých a Bánomových. Master's thesis. Charles University, Prague.

Cinová, E., Gunár, K., Ort, J. 2024. Romové v Brekově. Rodinné fotografie a historicko-etnografický text Kolomana Gunára. *Romano džaniben* 31 (1): 129–143.

Crenshaw, K. 1991. Mapping the Margins: Intersectionality, Identity Politics, and Violence against Women of Color. *Standford Law Review* 43 (6): 1241–1299.

Das, V., Poole, D. 2004. State and its Margins. Comparative Ethnographies. In *Anthropology in the Margins: Comparative Ethnographies*, ed. V. Das and D. Poole, 3–33. Santa Fe: SAR Press.

Davidová, E. 2000. Poválečný vývoj a osudy Romů v letech 1945–1989. In *Černobílý život*, M. Černá et al., 67–76. Prague: Gallery.

Davidová, E. 1965. *Bez kolíb a šiatrov.* Košice: Východoslovenské vydavateľstvo.

Dirks, N. B. 2002. Annals of the Archive: Ethnographic Notes on the Sources of History. In *From the Margins. Historical Anthropology and Its Futures*, ed. B. K. Axel, 47–65. Durham: Duke University Press.

Dobruská, P. 2018. The Mobility of Roma from a Slovak Village and its Influence on Local Communities. In *Remigration to Post-socialist Europe: Hopes and Realities of Return.* ed. C. Hornstein-Tomic et al., 285–318. Berlin: LIT Verlag.

Donert, C. 2017. *The Rights of the Roma. The Struggle for Citizenship in Postwar Czechoslovakia.* Cambridge: Cambridge University Press.

Donert, C. 2008. "The Struggle for the Soul of the Gypsy": Marginality and Mass Mobilization in Stalinist Czechoslovakia. *Social History* 33 (2): 123–144.

van Dülmen, R. 2000. *Historische Anthropologie. Entwicklung – Probleme – Aufgaben.* Köln: Böhlau.

Elšík, V. 2003. Interdialect contact of Czech (and Slovak) Romani varieties. *International Journal of the Sociology of Language* 162: 41–62.

Facuna, A. 1969. Zväz Cigánov-Rómov na Slovensku. *Demografie* 11 (3): 214–215.

Fečová, O. 2022. *Den byl pro mě krátkej. Paměti hrdé Romky.* Praha: Paseka, Kher.

Fedič, V. (ed.) 2001. *Východoslovenskí Rómovia a 2. svetová vojna.* Humenné: REDOS.

Foucault, M. 1982. Afteword: The Subject and Power. In *Beyond Structuralism and Hermeneutics.* H. Dreyfus and P. Rabinow, 208–226, Chicago: University of Chicago Press.

Foucault, M. 1978. *The History of Sexuality.* Vol. 1: An Introduction. New York: Random House.

Gal, S. 1995. Review: Language and the "Arts of Resistance". Reviewed Work: Domination and the Arts of Resistance: Hidden Transcripts by James Scott. *Cultural Anthropology* 10 (3): 407–424.

Gal, S. 1993. Diversity and Contestation in Linguistic Ideologies: German Speakers in Hungary. *Language in Society* 22 (3): 337–359.

Gardner, K. 1993. Desh-Bidesh: Silhety Images of Home and Away. *Man* 28 (1): 1–15.

Gay Y Blasco, P. 2001. 'We don't know our descent': How the Gitanos of Jarana Manage the Past. *Journal of The Royal Anthropological Institute* 7 (4): 631–647.

Gay Y Blasco, P. 1999. *Gypsies in Madrid: Sex, Gender and the Performances of Identity*. New York: Berg.

Geertz, C. 1973. *The Interpretation of Cultures*. New York: Basic Books.

George, S. 2005. *When Women Come First: Gender and Class in Transnational Migration*. Oakland: University of California Press.

Gerlach, D. 2010. Beyond Expulsion: The Emergence of "Unwanted Elements" in the Postwar Czech Borderlands, 1945-1950. *East European Politics and Societies* 14 (2): 269–93.

Giddens, A. 1979. *Central Problems in Social Theory: Action, Structure and Contradiction in Social Analysis*. London: Red Globe Press.

Ginzburg, C. 1983. *The Night Battles: Witchcraft and Agrarian Cults in the Sixteenth and Seventeenth Centuries*. New York: Routledge.

Ginzburg, C. 1980. *The Cheese and the Worms: The Cosmos of a Sicteenth Century Miller.* New York: Routledge.

Glick-Schiller, N., Basch, L., Szanton-Blanc, C. 1995. From Immigrant to Transmigrant: Theorizing Transnational Migration. *Anthropological Quarterly* 68 (1): 48–63.

Grill, J. 2015a. 'Endured Labour' and 'Fixing Up' Money: The Economic Strategies of Roma Migrants in Slovakia and the UK. In *Gypsy Economy: Romani Livelihoods and Notions of Worth in the 21st Century*, ed. M. Brazzabeni et al., 88–106. New York, Oxford: Berghahn.

Grill, J. 2015b. Historické premeny štruktúry medzikultúrnych vzťahov. Formy spolužitia v prípade Tarkoviec na východnom Slovensku. In *Čierno-biele svety. Rómovia v majoritnej spoločnosti na Slovensku*, ed. T. Podolinská and T. Hrustič, 146–171. Bratislava: Veda.

Grill, J. 2012. 'Going up to England': Exploring Mobilities among Roma from Eastern Slovakia. *Journal of Ethnic and Migration Studies* 38 (8): 1269–1287.

Gunár, K. 2020. Roztvárali sme nožnice, chceli sme o sebe dať vedieť celému Slovensku. *Rómovia 30 rokov po...*, ed. K. Mojžíšová, 109–129. Košice: Rozhlas a televízia Slovenska (RTVS).

Gunár, K. 2010. *História osídľovania obce Brekov Rómami*. [self-published]

Gupta, A., Ferguson, J. 1992. Beyond 'Culture': Space, Identity, and the Politics of Difference. *Cultural Anthropology* 7 (1): 6–23.

Guy, W. 2001. Roma in Czechoslovakia: Another False Dawn? In *Between Past and Future: The Roma of central and Eastern Europe*, ed. W. Guy, 285–332. Hatfield: University of Hertforshire Press.

Guy, W. 1998. Ways of Looking at Roma: The Case of Czechoslovakia. In *Gypsies: An Interdisciplinary Reader,* ed. D. Tong, 13–68. New York: Garland Publishing.

Guy, W. 1977. *The Attempt of Socialist Czechoslovakia to Assimilate Its Gypsy Population.* Unpublished PhD thesis. University of Bristol.

Haišman, T. 1999. Romové v Československu v letech 1945–1967. Vývoj institucionálního zájmu a jeho dopady. In *Romové v ČR (1945–1998)*, 137–183. Prague: Socioklub.

Hajská, M. 2024. *The Stojka Family: Spatial Mobility and Territorial Anchoredness of Lovara Vlax Roma in the Former Czechoslovakia.* Prague: Karolinum Press.

Hajská, M. 2022. "We Had to Run Away": The Lovára's Departure from the Protectorate of Bohemia and Moravia to Slovakia in 1939. *Romani studies* 32 (1): 51–83.

Hajská, M. 2020. Forced Settlement of Vlach Roma in Žatec and Louny in the Late 1950s. *Slovenský národopis / Slovak Ethnology* 68 (4): 340–364.

Hajská, M. 2017. Economic Strategies and Migratory Trajectories of Vlax Roma from Eastern Slovakia to Leicester, UK *Slovenský národopis / Slovak Ethnology* 65 (4): 357–382.

Hajská, M. 2015. Gadžikanes vaj romanes? Jazykové postoje olašských Romů jedné východoslovenské komunity ke třem místně užívaným jazykům. In *Čierno-biele svety. Rómovia v majoritnej spoločnosti na Slovensku,* ed. T. Podolinská and T. Hrustič, 346–373. Bratislava: Veda.

Hajská, M. 2012. "Ame sam Vlašika, haj vorbinas vlašika!" (My jsme Olaši a mluvíme olašsky!). Nástin jazykové situace olašských Romů z východního Slovenska v etnicky smíšené komunitě. *Romano džaniben* 19 (2): 35–53.

Hajská, M. et al. 2013. *Situační analýza Rumburk a Staré Křečany: ASZ.* Praha: Multikulturní centrum Praha.

Halbmayr, B. 2009. The Ethics of Oral History? Expectations, Responsibilities, and Dissociations. In *Oral History: The Challenges of Dialogue,* ed. M. Kurkowska-Budzan and K. Zamorski, 195–203. Amsterdam: John Benjamins.

Hamplová, D. 2006. Women and the Labor Market in the Czech Republic: Transition from a Socialist to a Social-Democratic Regime? In *Globalization, Uncertainty and Women's Careers,* ed. H. Blossfeld and H. Hofmeister, 224–246.

Higgs, E. 2004. *The Information State in England: The Central Collection of Information on Citizens Since 1500.* London: Macmillan Education UK.

High, H. 2009. Complicities and Complexities: Provocations from the Study of Resettlement in Laos. *Critical Asian Studies* 41 (4): 615–620.

High, H. 2008. The Implications of Aspirations: Reconsidering Resettlement in Laos. *Critical Asian Studies* 40 (4): 531–550.

High, H. 2005. Village in Laos: An Ethnographic Account of Poverty and Policy among the Mekong's Flows. PhD thesis. Australian National University, Canberra.

Hlaváčová, V. 2016. Migrace slovenských Romů do Karlových Varů po roce 1945 (případová studie – usídlování rodu Bílých a Sivákových v Karlových Varech v letech 1945–1952). Bachelor's thesis. Charles University, Prague.

Holomek, M. 1969. Současné problémy Cikánů v ČSSR a jejich řešení. *Demografie* 11 (3): 203–209.

Holomek, T. 1969. Problematika Cikánů ve světle zákonné úpravy. *Demografie* 11 (3): 210–213.

Holubec, S. 2014. 'We Bring Order, Discipline, Western European democracy, and Culture to this Land of Former Oriental Chaos and Disorder: Czech Perceptions of Sub-Carpathian Rus and its Modernization on the 1920'. In *Mastery and Lost Illusions: Space and Time in the Modernization of Eastern and Central Europe,* ed. W. Borodziej et al., 223–250. München: Oldenbourg Wissenschaftverlag.

Horváth, K. 2012. Silencing and Naming the Difference. In *The Gypsy "Menace". Populism and the New Anti-Gypsy Politics,* ed. M. Stewart, 117–136. London: C. Hurst & Co.

Horváth, K. 2005. Gypsy Work – Gadjo work. *Romani Studies* 15 (1): 31–49.

Horský, J. 2014. Historický aktér. In *Koncepty a dějiny. Proměny pojmů v současné historické vědě,* ed. L. Storchová, 95–101. Praha: Scriptorium.

Horváthová, J. 2005. Meziválečné zastavení mezi Romy v českých zemích (aneb tušení souvislostí). *Romano džaniben* 12 (3): 63–84.

Horváthová, J. 1994. Možnosti integrace na příkladu moravských Romů. *Romano džaniben.* 1 (1): 8–19.

Horváthová, E. 1964. *Cigáni na Slovensku: historicko-etnografický náčrt.* Bratislava: Vydavateľstvo Slovenskej akadémie vied.

Houdek, L. 2008. *Romové ve Stříbře. Případová studie – historie a sociolingvistická situace rodu Absolonů.* Bachelor's thesis. Charles University, Prague.

Howe, L. 1998. Scrounger, Worker, Beggarman, Cheat: The Dynamics of Unemployment and The Politics of Resistance in Belfast. *The Journal of the Royal AnthropologicL Institute* 4 (3): 531–550.

Hrustič, T. 2015a. Emické vnímanie úžery v segregovaných rómskych osadách na východním Slovensku. In *Čierno-biele svety. Rómovia v majoritnej spoločnosti na Slovensku*, ed. T. Podolinská and T. Hrustič, 208–223. Bratislava: Veda.

Hrustič, T. 2015b. Usury among the Slovak Roma: Notes on Relations between Lenders and Borrowers in a Segregated Taboris. In *Gypsy Economy: Romani Livelihoods and Notions of Worth in the 21st Century*, ed. M. Brazzabeni et al., 31–48. New York, Oxford: Berghahn.

Hudousková, R., Ort, J., Sadílková, H. [unpublished]. Romové v Praze. (Texty k historii Romů v Praze po roce 1945).

Humphrey, C. 1994. Remembering an 'Enemy': The Bogd Khann in Twentieth-Century Mongolia. In *Memory, History, and Opposition under State Socialism*. ed. R. S. Watson, 21–44. Santa Fe: School of American Research Press.

Hübschmannová, M. [forthcoming]. *Po Židoch cigáni*. Vol II. Prague: Triáda.

Hübschmannová, M. 2005. *Po Židoch cigáni. (1939–srpen 1944): svědectví Romů ze Slovenska 1939–1945*. Vol I. Prague: Triáda.

Hübschmannová, M. 2000a. Slovesnost a literatura v romské kultuře. In *Černobílý život*, 123–148. Prague: Gallery.

Hübschmannová, M. 2000b. Vztahy mezi Romy a Židy na východním Slovensku před druhou světovou válkou. *Romano džaniben* 7 (1): 17–23.

Hübschmannová, M. 1999a. Několik poznámek k hodnotám Romů. In *Romové v České republice 1945-89*, 16–66. Praha: Socioklub.

Hübschmannová, M. 1999b. Od etnické kasty ke strukturovanému společenství. In *Romové v České republice 1945–1998*, 115–136. Praha: Socioklub.

Hübschmannová, M. 1998. Economic Stratification and Interaction (Roma, an Ethnic Jati in East Slovakia). In *Gypsies: An Interdisciplinary Reader*, ed. D. Tong, 233–270. New York: Garland Publishing.

Hübschmannová, M. 1995. Historeo znamená pátrám. *Romano džaniben* 2 (1-2): 61–66.

Hübschmannová, M. 1993. *Šaj pes dovakeras – Můžeme se domluvit*. Olomouc: Vydavatelství Univerzity Palackého.

Hübschmannová, M. 1970. Co je tzv. cikánská otázka? *Sociologický Časopis / Czech Sociological Review* 6 (2): 105–120.

Hübschmannová, M. 1968. cikáni = Cikáni? *Reportérova ročenka 1968*

Hübschmannová, M. 1967. Veľká Ida. *Literární noviny*, 8 July 1967, 2–3.

Hübschmannová, M.; Lacková, E. 2010. *Narodila jsem se pod šťastnou hvězdou*. Prague: Triáda.

Jamnická-Šmerglová, Z. 1955. *Dějiny našich cikánů*. Praha: Orbis.

Jandáková, L.; Habrovcová, J. 2022. Tak jak to bylo. In *Den byl pro mě krátkej. Paměti hrdé Romky*, O. Fečová, 177–183. Prague: Paseka, Kher.

Jurová, A. 2002. Historický vývoj rómskych osád na Slovensku a problematika vlastníckych vzťahov k pôde ("nelegálne osady"). *Člověk a spoločnosť* 5 (4): 13–43.

Jurová, A. 1993. *Vývoj rómskej problematiky na Slovensku po roku 1945*. Bratislava: Společenskovedný ústav Slovenskej akadémie vied v Košiciach, Goldpress.

Kandert, J. 2004. *Každodenní život vesničanů středního Slovenska v šedesátých až osmdesýtých letech 20. století*. Prague: Karolinum Press.

Kobes, T. 2012. "Naši Romové" – difrakční vzorce odlišnosti východoslovenského venkova. *Romano džaniben* 19 (2): 9–34.

Kobes, T. 2009. *Tu zme šicke jedna rodzina, tu zme šicke jedna fajta: příbuzenství východoslovenského venkova*. Prešov: Centrum antropologických výskumov.

Kovai, C. 2012. Hidden Potentials in "Naming the Gypsy": The Transformation of the Gypsy-Hungarian Distinction. In *The Gypsy "Menace": Populism and the New Anti-Gypsy Politics*, ed. M. Stewart, 281–294. London: C. Hurst & Co.

Kramářová, J. et al. 2005. *(Ne)bolí: vzpomínky Romů na válku a život po válce.* Prague: Člověk v tísni.

Kurej, A. 1996. Čar, veša, phuv – oda miri bacht / Tráva, lesy, země – to je moje štěstí. *Romano džaniben* 3 (1): 109–113.

Levi, G. 2001. On Microhistory. In *New Perspectives on Historical Writing*, ed. P. Burke, 96–119. University Park: Pennsylvania State University Press.

Lhotka, P., Schuster, M., Závodská, M. 2009. *Svaz Cikánů–Romů (1969–1973). Doprovodná publikace k výstavě Muzea romské kultury "Svaz Cikánů–Romů (1969–1973). Z historie první romské organizace v českých zemích."* Brno: Muzeum romské kultury.

Lucassen, L. 2008. Between Hobbes and Locke. Gypsies and the Limits of the Modernization Paradigm. *Social History* 33 (4): 423–441.

Lužica, R. 2021. *Zväz Cigánov/Rómov a štátna moc na Slovensku v rokoch 1968–1989.* Nitra: Univerzita Konštantína Filozofa v Nitre, Fakulta sociálnych vied a zdravotníctva.

Lüdtke, A. (ed.) 1995. *The History of Everyday Life: Reconstructing Historical Experiences and Ways of Life.* Princeton: Princeton University Press.

Magnússon, S. G. 2020. *Emotional Experience and Microhistory: A Life Story of a Destitute Pauper Poet in the 19th Century.* London: Routledge.

Mann, A. B. 2018. *Rómski kováči na Slovensku.* Bratislava: Úľuv.

Marushiakova, E.; Popov, V. (ed.). 2022. *Roma Portraits in History: Roma Civic Emancipation Elite in Central, South-Eastern and Eastern Europe from the 19th Century until Wold War II.* Paderborn: Brill.

Marushiakova, E.; Popov V. 2021. Introduction. In *Roma Voices in History: A Sourcebook*, ed. E. Marushiakova and V. Popov, xviii–xxxvi. Paderborn: Brill.

Marushiakova, E.; Popov, V. 2020. Roma Identities in Eastern Europe: Ethnicity vs. Nationality. In *Ciganos. Olhares e perspectivas,* ed. M. P. L. Goldfarb et al., 39–64. João Pessoa: Editura UFPB.

Medick, H. 1987. "Missionaries in the Row Boat"? Ethnological Ways of Knowing as a Challenge to Social History. *Comparative Studies in Society and History* 29 (1): 76–98.

Memorandum SCR k základním otázkám cikánské problematiky a vymezení společenského postavení Cikánů-Romů. 1970. *Románo ľil,* 2: 11–12.

Miklušáková, M. 1999. Stručný nástin důsledků zákona č. 40/1993 Sb., O nabývání a pozbývání státního občanství ČR. In *Romové v České republice (1945–1998),* 267–270. Prague: Socioklub.

Mišková, M. 2016. *Miznúci svet V.* Humenné: Retrospektíva.

Mižigár, M. 2016. *Romové v Písku: případová studie poválečného osídlení.* Bachelor's thesis. Charles University, Prague.

Molnár, M (ed.) 2017. *Brekov.* Michaľovce: Jaroslav Mihaľko, Polygrafické práce.

Mücke, P. 2013. Deset krátkých zastavení nad možnostmi a mezemi české orální historie. *Dějiny – teorie – kritika* 2: 296–301.

Nečas, N. 1999. *The Holocaust of Czech Roma.* Prague: Prostor.

Nováček, K. 1968. *Cikáni včera, dnes a zítra.* Prague: Socialistická akademie.

Olivera, M. 2012. The Gypsies as Indigenous Groups: the Gabori Roma Case in Romania. *Romani studies* 5 (1): 19–33.

Olivera, M., Poueyto, J. 2018. Gypsies and Anthropology: Legacies, Challenges, and Perspectives. *Ethnologie Francaise* 172 (4): 581–600.

Ort, J. 2022a. Belonging, mobility, and the socialist policies in Kapišová, Slovakia. *Romani studies* 32 (1): 23–50.

Ort, J. 2022b. *Facets of a Harmony. Roma and Their Locatedness in Eastern Slovakia.* Prague: Karolinum Press.

Ort, J. 2021. Romové jako místní obyvatelé? Přináležení, cikánství a politika prostoru ve vesnici na východním Slovensku. *Sociologický časopis / Czech Sociological Review,* 57 (5): 581–608.

Ort, J., Dobruská, P. 2023. Continuities and Discontinuities in a Transnational Social Field. The Case of the Margovany Roma. *Český lid* 110 (2): 211–242.

Pavelčíková, N. 2010. Několik poznámek k proměnám identity spojeným s příběhy českých a slovenských Romů ve 20. století. *Romano džaniben* 17 (2): 71–95.

Pavelčíková, N. 2006. Milena Hübschmannová a historie Romů po 2. světové válce. *Romano džaniben* 13 (1): 191–207.

Pavelčíková, N. 2004. *Romové v českých zemích v letech 1945–1989.* Prague: Úřad dokumentace a vyšetřování zločinů komunismu PČR.

Pavelčíková, N. 1999. *Romské obyvatelstvo na Ostravsku (1945–1975).* Ostrava: Ostravská univerzita.

Prins, G. 2001. Oral History. In *New Perspectives on Historical Writing,* ed. P. Burke, 120–156. University Park: Pennsylvania State University Press.

Portelli, A. 1991. *The Death of Luigi Trastulli: Form and Meaning in Oral History.* New York: State University of New York Press.

Prečan, V. 1990. *Charta 77 1977–1980. Od morální k demokratické revoluci. Dokumentace.* Bratislava: Schenfield.

Pullmann, M. 2009. Diktatura, konsensus a společenská změna: K výkladu komunistické diktatury v českých akademických diskusích po roce 1989, In *Paralely, průsečíky, mimoběžky: Teorie, koncepty a pojmy v české a světové historiografii 20. století,* ed. L. Storchová and J. Horský, 231–246. Ústí nad Labem: Albis International.

Pullmann, M. 2012. Writing History in the Czech and Slovak Republics: An Interview with Michal Pullmann. *Social History* 37 (4): 384–401.

Pullmann, M. 2011. *Konec experimentu. Přestavba a pád komunismu v Československu.* Praha: Scriptorium.

Roman, R. B., Zahova, S., Marinov, A. (ed.). 2021. *Roma Writings: Romani Literature and Press in Central, South-Eastern and Eastern Europe from the 19th Century until World War II.* Paderborn: Brill.

Charta 77 – 3. část. *Romano džaniben* 6 (3–4): 4–7.

Rabinach, A. 2006. Moments of Totalitarianism. Review Article. *History and Theory,* 45 (1): 72–100.

Růžičková, A. 2012. *Romská komunita ve Vsetíně.* Bachelor's thesis. Charles University, Prague.

Sadílková, H. 2020. The Postwar Migration of Romani Families from Slovakia to the Bohemian Lands: a Complex Legacy of War and Genocide in Czechoslovakia. In *Jewish and Romani Families in the Holocauts and Its Aftermath,* ed. E. R. Adler and K. Čapková, 190–217. New Jersey, London: Rutgers University Press.

Sadílková. H. 2019. Historie a historiografie nucených sterilizací romských žen v Československu a jejich přesahu do současnosti. Úvod k tematickému číslu Romano džaniben. *Romano džaniben* 26 (2): 5–18.

Sadílková, H. 2018. (Ne)chtění spoluobčané? Romové v poválečném Československu. In *"Nechtění" spoluobčané: Skupiny obyvatel perzekvovaných či marginalizovaných z politických, národnostních, náboženských i jiných důvodů v letech 1945–1989,* ed. J. Pažout and K. Portmann, 98–115. Prague: ÚSTR.

Sadílková, H. 2017. Resettling the Settlement: From Recent History of a Romani Settlement in South-Eastern Slovakia. In *Festschrift for Lev Cherenkov,* ed. K. Kozhanov and D. Halwachs, 339–351. Graz: Grazer Romani Publikationen.

Sadílková, H. 2016. *Poválečná historie Romů ve vzpomínkách pamětníků: Možnosti rekonstrukce poválečné migrace vybrané skupiny Romů ze Slovenska do českých zemí*. PhD thesis. Charles University, Prague.

Sadílková, H. 2013. Čí jsou to dějiny? Dosavadní přístupy k interpretaci poválečných dějin Romů v ČS(S)R. *Romano džaniben* 20 (2): 69–86.

Sadílková H. et al. 2024. *Equality and Representation: Social and Political Engagement of Roma in Communist Czechoslovakia 1948–1968*. Paderborn: Brill.

Sadílková, H. et al. 2018. *Aby bylo i s námi počítáno: Společensko-politická angažovanost Romů a snahy o založení romské organizace v poválečném Československu*. Brno: Muzeum romské kultury.

Sadílková, H., Závodská, M. 2021. Asserting a Presence in the Public Sphere: Autobiographies by two Romani Holocaust Survivors in Communist Czechoslovakia. In *The Legacies of the Romani Genocide in Europe since 1945*, ed. C. Donert, 183–213. Oxford, New York: Routledge.

Scott, J. C. 2010. *The Art of Not Being Governed: An Anarchist History of Upland Southeast Asia*. New Haven: Yale University Press.

Scott, J. C. 1998. *Seeing Like a State: How Certain Schemes to Improve the Human Condition Have Failed*. New Haven: Yale University Press.

Scott, J. C. 1990. *Domination and the Arts of Resistance*. New Haven: Yale University Press.

Scott, J. C. 1985. *Weapons of the Weak: Everyday Forms of Resistance*. New Haven: Yale University Press.

Serinek, J., Tesař, J., Ondra, J. 2016. *Česká cikánská rapsodie*. Prague: Triáda.

Shmidt, V. 2022. The Rights of the Roma: The Struggle for Citizenship in Postwar Czechoslovakia by Celia Donert (review). *Romani studies* 32 (1): 140–144.

Shmidt, V., and Jaworsky, B. N. 2020. *Historicizing Roma in Central Europe: Between critical whitness and epistemic injustice*. London: Routledge.

Sidiropolu Janků, K. 2015. *Nikdy jsem nebyl podceňovanej. Ze slovenských osad do českých měst za prací. Poválečné vzpomínky*. Brno: Munipress.

Skupnik, J. 2007. Světy se zrcadlem. Marginalizace a integrace z hlediska sociopsychologické dynamiky společnosti. *Sociologický časopis /Czech Sociological Review* 43 (1), 133–148.

Slačálek, O. 2023. Toto není český Floyd. Romové a cesta postkoloniální teorie do střední Evropy. *Romano džaniben* 30 (1): 119–131.

Slačka, D. 2015. *"Cikánská otázka" na Hodonínsku v letech 1945–1973*. Diplomová práce. Historický ústav, Filozofická fakulta, Masarykova univerzita v Brně.

Sokolová, V. 2008. *Cultural Politics of Ethnicity: Discourses on Roma in Communist Czechoslovakia*. Soviet and Post-Soviet Politics and Society, Vol. 82. Stuttgart: Ibidem-Verlag.

Sommer, V. et al. 2019. *Řídit socialismus jako firmu: Technokratické vládnutí v Československu 1956–1989*. Prague: Nakladatelství Lidové noviny.

Spurný, M. 2016. *Most do budoucnosti. Laboratoř socialistické modernity na severu Čech*. Prague: Karolinum Press.

Spurný, M. 2011. *Nejsou jako my: česká společnost a menšiny v pohraničí (1945-1960)*. Prague: Antikomplex.

Stewart, K. 1996. *A Space on the Side of the Road: Cultural Poetics in an "Other" America*. Princeton, NJ: Princeton University Press.

Stewart, M. 2013. Roma and Gypsy 'Ethnicity' as a Subject of Anthropological Inquiry. *Annual Review of Anthropology* 42 (1): 415–432.

Stewart, M. 1997. *The Time of the Gypsies*. Boulder: Westview Press.

Sus, J. 1961. *Cikánská otázka v ČSSR*. Praha: SNPL.

Sutre, A. 2014. They Give a History of Wandering over the World. A Romani Clan's Transnational Movement in the early 20th Century. *Quaderny storici* 49, 146 (2): 471–498.

Szaló, C. 2007. *Transnacioníální migrace. Proměny identit, hranic a vědění o nich.* Brno: Centrum pro studium demokracie a kultury.

Šebová, B. 2006. Migrace slovenských Romů do českých zemí po roce 1945 (případová studie – usídlování Romů v Rokycanech mezi lety 1945–1952). Bachelor's thesis. Charles University, Prague.

Tauber, E., Trevisan, P. 2019. Archive and Ethnography – the Case of Europe's Roma and Sinti (19th-20st Centuries): An Introduction. *La Ricera Folklorica* 74: 3–12.

Theodosiou, A. 2004. 'Be-longing' in a 'Doubly Occupied Place': The Parakalamos Gypsy Musicians. *Romani studies* 14 (2): 25–58.

Tilly, Ch. 1999. Power – Top Down and Bottom Up. *Journal of Political Philosophy,* 7 (3): 330–352.

Tsing, A. L. 1994. From the Margins. *Cultural Anthropology* 9 (3): 279–297.

Ulč, O. 1969. Communist National Minority Policy: The Case of the Gypsies in Czechoslovakia. *Soviet Studies* 20 (4): 421–443.

Ústav pro veřejné mínění 1971. *Mínění o Cikánech a o řešení cikánské otázky.* Prague: Ústav pro výzkum veřejné mínění.

Yow, V. 1995. Ethics and Interpersonal Relationships in Oral History Research. *The Oral History Review.* 22 (1): 51–66.

Vansina, J. 1985. *Oral Tradition as History.* Melton: James Currey Publishers.

Vaněk, M. 2022. Twenty Years in Shades of Grey? Everyday Life During Normalisation Based on Oral History Research. In *Czechoslovakia and Eastern Europe in the Era of Normalisation, 1969–1989,* ed. K. McDermott and M. Stibbe, 145–169. London: Palgrave Macmillan.

Vaněk, M. 2019. *Sto studentských evolucí: vysokoškolští studenti roku 1989: životopisná vyprávění v časosběrné perspektivě. [One Hundred Student Evolutions: University Students of 1989. Life-stories in a Longitudinal Perspective.]* Prague: Academia.

Vaněk, M., Mücke, P. (ed.) 2016. Velvet Revolutions: An Oral History of the Czech Society. New York–Oxford: Oxford University Press.

Wacquant, L. 2007. Territorial stigmatization in the age of advanced marginality. *Thesis Eleven* 91: 66–77.

Wagnerová, A. 2017. *Žena za socialismu: Československo 1945–1974 a reflexe vývoje před rokem 1989 a po něm.* Prague: SLON.

Zahra, T. 2016. *The Great Departure: Mass Migration from Eastern Europe and the Making of the Free World.* New York: W. W. Norton & Company.

Zapletal, T. 2012. Přístup totalitního státu a jeho bezpečnostních složek k romské menšině v Československu (1945-1989). In *Sborník archivu bezpečnostních složek.* Vol. 10/2012, 13–83. Prague: Archiv bezpečnostních složek.

List of abbrevations

JRD   –   Jednotné roľnícke družstvo (United Agricultural Cooperative, Slovakia)

JZD   –   Jednotné zemědělské družstvo (United Agricultural Cooperative, Czechia)

KNV   –   Krajský národní výbor / krajský národný výbor (Regional National Committee)

MNV   –   Místní národní výbor / miestny národný výbor (Municipal National Committee)

MsNV –   Mestský národný výbor (Town National Committee)

ONV   –   Okresní národní výbor / okresný národný výbor (District National Commitee)

USSR –   Union of Soviet Socialist Republics

VŽKG –   Vítkovické železárny Klementa Gottwalda (Klement Gottwald Vítkovice Ironworks)

Register

Abu Lughod, Lila – 48, 55

Act no. 74/1958 (*Zákon o trvalém usazení kočujících osob*) – 14, 19, 21, 29, 35, 76, 81, 83, 102, 111, 163, 184–6, 192–3, 206–10, 218

Alltagsgeschichte (history of everyday life) – 38, 56

anti-G*psyism (*see also* anti-Roma racism) – 42, 48, 194, 246

anti-Roma racism (*see also* anti-G*psyism) – 12, 17–20, 22, 26–30, 41, 97, 119, 121, 137, 140, 144, 149–54, 174, 177–8, 181, 186, 212–3, 246, 250–1

assimilation – 17, 19–20, 22–6, 29–32, 39–40, 48–9, 69, 75–6, 79–85, 89–90, 92–3, 95, 103, 107, 125, 128, 135, 138–40, 162–3, 174–5, 181, 184–5, 193, 197, 199, 207, 241, 245–6, 249, 251

autonomy – 40–1, 55–57, 165, 169, 178, 203–4, 240, 248

'backwardness' (a dominant concept) – 18–9, 32, 34, 39–40, 51–2, 74–5, 79–84, 89, 92, 95–100, 104–6, 112, 116, 118, 127–8, 135–8, 140, 146, 165, 170, 176, 183–4, 187–9, 192, 223, 249

Bardejov – 34, 58–59, 180, 182, 197, 212, 219, 223–4, 228

belonging – 13, 16, 18, 32, 51–4, 75, 79, 97–102, 106, 109–10, 127, 132, 135, 139, 141–2, 170, 176, 198, 200, 228

Bohemian Roma (sub-ethnic group) – 17, 98

borderland – 13, 18, 33–4, 47, 91, 182, 184, 197–8, 201–11, 222, 224, 228, 241–4

Bruntál – 144, 167, 194, 211, 221

capital
– economic – 18, 46, 93, 100, 149, 173, 178
– educational – 18, 93, 99–100
– social – 18, 46, 93, 99–100, 132, 139, 149, 173, 178

capitalism – 54, 106, 203, 206

categorisation (of the Roma; *see also* classification) – 23, 39, 75, 94, 126, 128, 174, 221

classification (of the Roma/populace, *see also* categorisation) – 16, 22, 76–8, 81, 87, 95, 111, 125–7, 184, 206, 223

collaborative research – 65

Communist Party – 21, 24–6, 86, 93, 96, 103, 105–6, 108, 122, 127, 129, 134, 153, 159–160, 173, 184–5, 189, 194

complaints (archival source) – 31, 36, 44, 76–7, 89, 108, 120–1, 123, 132

conflict (inter-ethnic, intra-ethnic) – 81, 112, 116–125, 128, 177, 217, 146–7, 158, 175, 188–90, 210, 219, 227

continuity (*see also* discontinuity) – 14–6, 18, 28, 41, 49, 62, 78, 99, 101, 139, 140–4, 148–149, 155, 178, 181–6, 190, 198, 200, 203, 205, 208–9, 211, 233, 248–9, 251

culture – 45, 56, 78–9, 83, 138, 142
– culturality – 103–6
– housing – 103–4, 107

marginalisation – 12–4, 18, 21, 34, 37–8, 43, 46–7, 50, 52, 54, 56–7, 60–1, 99–100, 108, 128, 130, 133–4, 139, 141, 147, 156, 163–5, 186, 198, 200, 208, 211–2, 223, 242, 245–8, 251

margins (a concept in anthropology) – 38, 45–7, 70, 182, 247

media – 22, 25, 54, 84–88, 93, 95–6, 173, 191

Medick, Hans – 56–7

memory – 67–70, 240, 245

microhistory – 16, 33, 38, 56–8, 60–1, 69, 140

Moravian Roma (sub-ethnic group) – 17, 34, 98, 191, 193

nomadism – 35, 40, 53, 76, 81, 83, 102, 111, 184–6, 192–3, 206–9, 218, 224, 244

Nováček, Karel – 79–83, 92–3, 96, 98, 104, 184–5, 207

oral history – 16, 38, 61–71, 142, 178–9, 248

outsiders
– eternal 16, 33, 246
– social 54, 69, 114, 204

Opava – 144, 167, 171, 194–7, 211, 221

participation (of the Roma)
– political – 19, 46, 95–6, 107, 151, 154, 156–8, 160, 163, 173–4, 193, 247
– social – 32, 40, 43, 46, 48, 53–54, 78, 95, 118, 149, 165, 239, 247

photographs (archival sources) – 64–5, 68–9, 134, 167

Poole, Deborah – 38, 46–7, 50, 55, 249

public opinion research – 88, 91–3, 99

race
– racial segregation – 14, 18, 21, 32, 40, 91, 139
– racialisation – 12–3, 18, 30, 34, 41, 43, 46, 50, 78–81, 94–5, 119, 128, 142, 185, 198, 243, 247, 250

racism (see also anti-Roma racism) – 18, 44, 66, 78–9, 84, 87, 90–3, 95, 98–9, 108, 119, 121, 135, 137, 140, 150, 156, 245–6, 250–1

re-education – 19, 22, 35, 75, 79–80, 84, 86, 89, 91, 94–5, 98, 155, 187, 191–2, 206–7, 209, 215

representativeness – 38, 58

resistance – 37, 43–4, 47–50, 54, 56, 75, 101, 158, 195, 211, 221, 223

Romani history/histories (a historical approach) – 12, 28, 31, 33, 37, 52, 59, 62, 245–7

Sadílková, Helena – 12, 17–8, 26–9, 32, 43, 49, 57, 62–3, 65, 69–70, 86, 91, 93, 95, 140, 151, 170, 176, 181, 189–91, 193, 198, 200, 203, 212, 244–6

scale of research – 38, 56–7, 196

Scott, James C. – 37, 42–4, 46–50, 60, 134, 183

Second World War (World War II) – 11, 13, 17–8, 34–5, 62–3, 67–8, 97, 110, 130, 185, 198, 216

securitisation – 21, 31, 39, 86, 119, 121, 134, 205, 210

security (social) – 70, 139, 234, 243

segregation (see also race – racial segregation) – 14, 18, 21, 32, 40, 91, 108, 132–3, 139, 141, 176, 178, 199, 239

smithery – 109, 111, 203, 216

sociability – 16, 33, 44, 53–4, 127, 141, 182–3, 241

status (social) – 12, 15, 46–7, 50–2, 54, 55, 61, 82–3, 99–100, 110, 113, 116–9, 125, 127–8, 132–3, 139–40, 157, 162, 164, 177, 188, 193, 199–200, 204–5, 217, 220, 248, 251

Sokolová, Věra – 47, 51, 62, 75, 78–9, 185–6, 208, 251

solidarity – 91, 197, 203, 235

sources (methodology) – 16, 29, 34, 60–70, 88, 123, 157–8, 165–6, 178, 181–2, 195–6, 205, 215, 248
– oral – 61–3
– written – 60–5
– Romani provenance – 65, 120

Soviet Union – 91, 185

state (anthropological approaches) – 16, 29, 32–3, 37–8, 42–3, 46–50, 60, 70

sterilisation – 32, 43, 86–7, 91, 96–7

stickiness (a concept in anthropology) – 128

stigmatisation (see also territorial stigmatisation) – 107, 139–41, 203, 240, 248

sub-ethnic groups – 33–5, 98, 192

Svidník – 11, 34, 58, 197, 212, 216, 219, 228

symbolic violence – 12, 141, 251